that Job never loses faith in God, and that finally Job is brought by Yahweh himself to see that his own relationship with God must be based entirely on trust and faith: "It is not so much that Job has passed the test but that he comes to recognize that the retribution principle has failed. . . . Job moves from the debate about God's justice to the recognition that God transcends justice as being understood in human terms" (180, 187). Such insight is relevant in all contexts, not only in Thailand, but also around the world. Well done, indeed!

Rev James W. Voelz, PhD
Dr Jack Dean Kingsbury Professor of New Testament Theology,
Concordia Seminary, St Louis, MO, USA

In what the author originally wrote as her doctoral dissertation submitted and approved ten years ago at Concordia Seminary, MO, USA, she struggled with one of the hardest and most important issues of biblical theology, the question of our moral accountability, and one of the toughest and longest books of the Hebrew Old Testament – Job. Right in Job 1 God himself testifies to Job's impeccable moral quality. Why did God allow Job to suffer so terribly? Satan is introduced as God's agent here. Hence some modern scholars have sought to account for this moral dilemma by invoking the dualistic mythological ideas prevalent in the ancient Near East. Dr Churnai competently combats this modern trend, advising us not to read the book of Job in terms of the too narrowly focused theology of divine retribution. She argues that the other face of God, his grace, is not to be lost sight of. An engaging, important Asian contribution to Old Testament scholarship.

Takamitsu Muraoka, PhD
Professor Emeritus, Biblical Philology, Leiden University, Netherlands
British Academy, 2017 Burkitt Medal for Hebrew Bible Studies

The book of Job is the masterpiece of Scripture, whether one speaks of its profundity, its poetic and literary beauty, its boldness and intensity of struggle, or its resilience of faith. There may be similar outbursts in the psalms or glimpses in the prophets, but not the depth and the passion of the book of Job.

At issue are attempts by Job's friends and by Job to make sense of Job's crisis of life and faith. By inherited wisdom the friends appeal to divine justice, which imputes guilt to Job. Rejecting any guilt, Job paints divine governance as arbitrary and unjust. The impasse lies between the bankruptcy of retribution, and Job's terrifying vulnerability before a capricious God. Only God's self-revelation moves beyond the impasse.

Dr Churnai has presented an insightful, masterful study of a book that both tantalizes and defies platitudes. By extension, she gives also a word of hope to all who wrestle with similar issues.

Henry Rowold, DTh
International Research Emeritus Professor,
Concordia Seminary, St Louis, MO, USA

Questions of theodicy have haunted every people and tribe: how do we explain and master the injustice and inexplicability that all experience in one or another facet of life, especially in death? Therefore, Job has attracted and fascinated readers around the world throughout the centuries. With attention directed to the role of death in Job's anguished struggle for justification, Churnai uses a literary approach that concentrates on the structure of the book to explore its meaning. With penetrating insight and sensitivity to the book's literary structures, she shifts the focus away from the principles of retributive justice that hold Job's friends' reality together and perceives that Job concludes that trust in the Creator's person must ground personal interpretation of reality. Churnai explains how this dialogue over retribution versus trust shapes the dialogues between Job and his friends, and Job and God. This excellent study is a must read not only for exegetes but also for systematicians and those dedicated to pastoral care.

Rev Robert A. Kolb, PhD
Professor of Systematic Theology,
Concordia Seminary, St Louis, MO, USA

Many interpreters, and most casual readers, treat Job as if it were discussing "suffering" in a very generic sense. What makes Dr Churnai's treatment of Job distinctive is that she situates the book firmly within the tradition of Israelite wisdom literature and properly understands it as a reflection on the problems created by an overly simplistic application of the retribution principle. Dr Churnai's insightful reading not only helps to explain why the book unfolds as it does but provides an important insight into the theological debates that shaped ancient Israel's wisdom theology.

David L. Adams, PhD
Associate Professor of Exegetical Theology,
Concordia Seminary, St Louis, MO, USA

In her close, literary reading of Job, Varunaj Churnai grapples with deep theology (e.g. the nature of God) and seemingly contradictory passages (e.g. Job's several views of death), which she does by privileging the progress of the narrative over Ancient Near East mythology and even more general, OT views of retribution. Using the problem of death as entre to a consideration of theodicy – specifically, the "retribution principle" – she argues persuasively

Beyond Justice

Death and the Retribution Principle
in the Book of Job

Varunaj Churnai

MONOGRAPHS

© 2018 Varunaj Churnai

Published 2018 by Langham Monographs
An imprint of Langham Publishing
www.langhampublishing.org

Langham Publishing and its imprints are a ministry of Langham Partnership

Langham Partnership
PO Box 296, Carlisle, Cumbria CA3 9WZ, UK
www.langham.org

ISBNs:
978-1-78368-455-7 Print
978-1-78368-456-4 ePub
978-1-78368-457-1 Mobi
978-1-78368-458-8 PDF

Varunaj Churani has asserted her right under the Copyright, Designs and Patents Act, 1988 to be identified as the Author of this work.

All rights reserved. No part of this publication may be reproduced, stored in a retrieval system or transmitted, in any form or by any means, electronic, mechanical, photocopying, recording or otherwise, without the prior written permission of the publisher or the Copyright Licensing Agency.

Scripture quotations are from The Holy Bible, English Standard Version® (ESV®), copyright © 2001 by Crossway, a publishing ministry of Good News Publishers. Used by permission. All rights reserved.

British Library Cataloguing-in-Publication Data
A catalogue record for this book is available from the British Library

ISBN: 978-1-78368-455-7

Cover & Book Design: projectluz.com

Langham Partnership actively supports theological dialogue and an author's right to publish but does not necessarily endorse the views and opinions set forth here or in works referenced within this publication, nor can we guarantee technical and grammatical correctness. Langham Partnership does not accept any responsibility or liability to persons or property as a consequence of the reading, use or interpretation of its published content.

To the memory of my father,
Kasem R. Prapaporn,
whose death drew me near to God,
and to my beloved husband,
Kitsanapong Churnai,
and our cherished children,
Sky and Micah

לְשֵׁמַע־אֹזֶן שְׁמַעְתִּיךָ וְעַתָּה עֵינִי רָאָתְךָ׃

איוב 42:5

Contents

Abstract xi
Acknowledgements xiii
Abbreviations xv

Chapter 1 1
Introduction
    The Thesis 1
    Current Scholarship Pertaining to the Thesis 2
        Mythological and Literary Readings of the Text 2
        The Retribution Principle 17
    The Research in the Context of Current Scholarship 29
    The Methodological Procedure to Be Employed 34

Chapter 2 41
Views of Death and the Retribution Principle in the Prologue and in Job's First Lament
    The Prologue (Job 1–2) 41
        Scene 1 42
        Scene 2 45
        Scene 3 46
        Scenes 4, 5 and 6 48
        Summary of the Prologue 52
    Job's First Lament (Job 3) 59

Chapter 3 69
Views of Death and the Retribution Principle in the Dialogues and in Elihu Speeches of the Book of Job
    The Dialogues: The Three Friends and Job 71
        The First Cycle of the Dialogues 72
        The Second Cycle of the Dialogues 100
        The Third Cycle of the Dialogues (Summarized) 120
    Elihu Speeches: Elihu 127
        Elihu's Views of Death: Chapters 33:15–18, 19–22,
            23–30; 34:11 128
        Summary of the Friends' (and Elihu's) Ideas of Death
            and the Retribution Principle 135

Summary of Job's Views of Death and the
  Retribution Principle..138

Chapter 4 143
Views of Death and the Retribution Principle in the Two Speeches of YHWH and in the Epilogue
  The Two Speeches of YHWH and Job's Responses 145
    The First Speech of YHWH (38:1–39:30) 146
    Job's First Response (40:4–5) 156
    The Second Speech of YHWH (40:6–41:26 [41:34]) 160
    Job's Second Response (42:2–6) 171
    Summary of Two Divine Speeches and Job's Responses...........177
  The Epilogue..180

Chapter 5 187
Conclusion
  Job 1 187
  Job 2 188
  Job 3 189
  The Friends and Their Views of Death and the
    Two Faces of YHWH 190
  Job, Death Wishes, and His View of the Two Faces of YHWH 192
  The YHWH Speeches – The Resolution of the Book 195
  Job's Restoration from Death to Life 200
  Some Theological Reflections...204
    Job's Wife..204
    Job and the Afterlife...205
    Job and Christian Theology 205
    Death in the Mythological and Literary Readings of Job..........207
    Job in the Canon 210
    Job and the Reference in James 5:10–11 211

Epilogue 213
The Application in Thai Context

Bibliography... 215

Abstract

In recent decades, scholars have tended to interpret what Job says about death either as part of the broader reading of the Old Testament about death, or by imposing ancient Near Eastern mythological concepts upon the text of Job, read apart from the Old Testament's wisdom tradition. This book attempts to redress the latter trend of interpretation by articulating that what Job says about death is related to Job's struggle to understand his relationship to God in relation to a theology that asserts that an individual's relationship to God is rooted in his own personal righteousness. It provides also a theological explanation of how the concept of death in Job relates to Job's broader understanding of the relationship of the individual to God. The book proposes that what the book says about death must be understood in the light of the relationship between God and man that emerges from the book's re-evaluation and ultimate rejection of the theology of retribution.

The book begins by examining the prologue (Job 1–2) and Job's first lament (Job 3). It demonstrates that while the prologue functions literarily as the controlling background of the book as a whole, the assumption at the nature of divine justice inherent in the retribution principle serves as the principle conceptual problem of the story. The prologue also serves as a microcosm of the position of the entire book. It lays out the right position (1:21) which Job will return at the conclusion of the struggle at the end of the book.

Next is the examination of how the problem of death and the influence of the retribution principle are presented in the dialogues between Job and the three friends. This examination includes Elihu's idea of death as he has the same basic view of death and the retribution principle as the three friends. The reader will see in particular the connection between the two faces of YHWH and the understanding of death in the book of Job. Then the perspective of death in the two speeches of YHWH will be analyzed including Job's two responses and the idea of death in the epilogue of the book. The resolution of Job's problem, including his view of death, is profoundly met in these two divine speeches, which invite both Job and the reader to move beyond the retribution principle and to simply trust in the gracious, but hidden, God.

The final chapter of the book summarizes through the narrative flow of the book findings and implications of the study. The conclusions are: (1) Job's reflection on the subject of life and death are part of the broader issue within the book, namely, the relationship between God and man, and not as sometimes suggested, between God and Satan, (2) the problem of death in Job, therefore, involves not only moving beyond the theology of God's justice, which seeks to constrain God within the limits of human reason, but also replacing this principle with trust in the graciousness of God, who is free and not constrained by human logic, (3) the mythological reading of the text of Job is not only a false approach to understanding the concept of death in the book of Job, but leads to a mistaken conclusion that death is a competing power or god (i.e. Mot, the god of death, in the Canaanite culture), and (4) the literary reading of Job is a competent reading that brings out the main message of the story and is able to lead the reader to see the development of the argument and the resolution of the argument at the end of the book.

Acknowledgements

I wish to express my appreciation first and foremost to the direction and enthusiastic support of my *Doktorvater*, Dr David L. Adams. For his acute suggestions and thorough responses throughout the work with this dissertation, I am deeply grateful. I wish to thank also Dr Henry L. Rowold who brought the topic of death in Job to my attention when I was in his Job class in Fall 2002. His meaningful insight and enthusiasm in Job benefitted my writing during the process. I also highly appreciate the other two readers on my dissertation committee, Dr Christopher W. Mitchell and Dr Paul R. Raabe (the latter served on the committee only during the proposal stage) for their useful suggestions and keen observations on the relevant issues in Job. I greatly appreciate Dr Mitchell whose passionate interest and insight in the book of Job are highly contagious. He granted me not only his time but also his expertise and wisdom.

I owe personal gratitude to all my excellent exegetical professors of Concordia Seminary who have equipped me with a profound study in biblical languages. They have made Hebrew, Aramaic, and Greek philology a delight to learn. Special mention goes also to the Deans and the Director of the Graduate School: the former dean, Dr James Voelz, the present dean, Dr Bruce Schuchard, and the present director, Dr Reed Lessing. They and their staffs have been very supportive, attempting in every effort to aid and smooth all the matters during the stay here in the foreign country. It has been an honor to be an international student at the Graduate School of Concordia Seminary.

I am also indebted to many people who assisted and supported me in various ways. The Arthur Vining Davis Foundation granted me fellowship awards for four consecutive years. The Foundations' grants to the Seminary helped me pursue doctoral studies at Concordia. I was honored to receive their grants. My big extended family (the R. Prapaporns): my mom, brothers, sisters, and those in-laws, particularly Mr Somchart Wiwatviriya. I would have never expressed my gratitude enough for their love and support in every aspect of my needs during the stay in Saint Louis. They never cease to believe in me. In addition, I greatly appreciate the faculty colleagues of Bangkok Institute of Theology who trust in me and pray for me faithfully. I wish to thank in particular Rev Dr Pongsak Limthongviratn and the Thai Community Church in Chicago for their support and encouragement. I am grateful also for the friendship and encouragement of my many friends in the States who always aid me and my family during the time in need. They are the source of my strength. They thus share with me the success of this dissertation.

My greatest debt is to my husband, Kitsanapong Churnai. I owe him his love and patience during the many years that I had to pursue my advanced studies. He is the better half of my life. Our two sons, Sky and Micah, join their dad and truly are the source of my comfort during the stay in St. Louis. These three men are indeed my faithful comforters.

הללוּ־יה
St Louis, MO
2010

Abbreviations[1]

AB	Anchor Bible
ABD	*Anchor Bible Dictionary*
AcT	*Acta Theological*
BDB	*A Hebrew and English Lexicon of the Old Testament* (Brown, Driver and Briggs)
BibInt	*Biblical Interpretation*
CAT	Commentaire de l'Ancien Testament
CBQ	*Catholic Biblical Quarterly*
CBQMS	Catholic Biblical Quarterly Monograph Series
CurBS	*Currents in Research: Biblical Studies*
CurTM	*Currents in Theology and Mission*
DCH	*Dictionary of Classical Hebrew*
Di	*Dialogue*
diss.	dissertation
ed(s).	editor(s), edited by
e.g.	*exempli gratia*, for example
et al.	*et alii*, and others
etc.	*et cetera*, and the rest
HALOT	*The Hebrew and Aramaic Lexicon of the Old Testament*
HTR	*Harvard Theological Review*
HUCA	*Hebrew Union College Annual*

---

1. Abbreviations not listed here may be found in Patrick H. Alexander et al., eds., *The SBL Handbook of Style: For Ancient Near Eastern, Biblical and Early Christian Studies* (Peabody, MA: Hendrickson, 1999), §8.

ICC	International Critical Commentary
IDB	*The Interpreter's Dictionary of the Bible*
i.e.	*id est*, that is
Int	*Interpretation*
JBQ	*Jewish Bible Quarterly*
JSOTSup	Journal for the Study of the Old Testament: Supplement Series
JSS	*Journal of Semitic Studies*
MT	Masoretic Text
NIB	*The New Interpreter's Bible*
NIV	New International Version
OBT	Overtures to Biblical Theology
PEGLMBS	Proceedings Eastern Great Lakes and Midwest Biblical Societies
RevExp	*Review and Expositor*
SJT	*Scottish Journal of Theology*
SVT	Supplements to Vetus Testamentum
TDOT	*Theological Dictionary of the Old Testament*
TEV	Today's English Version
ThTo	*Theology Today*
TLOT	Theological Lexicon of the Old Testament
VT	*Vetus Testamentum*
WBC	Word Biblical Commentary
WTJ	*Westminster Theological Journal*
ZAW	*Zeitschrift für die alttestamentliche Wissenschaft*

CHAPTER 1

Introduction

The book of Job contains many references to death. Some scholars see these statements (more than 180 expressions) as referring to the underworld and its realm.[1] "More than 100 different verbs are used to speak about the process of dying, going to the underworld, death, and the stay in the grave."[2] Thus, death is one of the major themes of the book of Job. This book will investigate the role that the concept of death plays in the Wisdom book that speaks of it most, the book of Job, and demonstrate that what Job says about death is related to Job's struggle to understand his relationship to God in relation to a theology that asserts that Job's relationship to God is rooted in his own personal righteousness, as that struggle is reflected in the narrative flow of the book itself. In addition, this book will attempt to provide a theological explanation of how the concept of death in Job relates to Job's broader understanding of the relationship of the individual to God.

The Thesis

Scholars have tended to interpret what Job says about death either as part of the broader reading of the Old Testament about death, or by imposing ancient Near Eastern mythological concepts upon the text of Job, read apart from the Old Testament's wisdom tradition. However, by reading Job as literature on its own terms it becomes clear that Job's complex and sometimes apparently conflicting statements about death and the tension inherent in

---

1. Walter L. Michel, "Death in Job," *Di* 11 (1972): 184.
2. Michel, 184.

Job's encounter with the "two faces of God"[3] are seen as connected to the theology of the retribution principle and to the claim that its view of divine justice allows humans to know the hidden God, and are resolved for Job by moving beyond this theology with trust in the graciousness of God.

Current Scholarship Pertaining to the Thesis

This book will address two main matters emerging from the secondary literature on the book of Job which are necessary for understanding the concept of death in the book. The first matter is the debate between two alternative approaches to understanding the concept of death in Job: the mythological reading and the literary reading. Second is the theme of the retribution principle: how this theological position has been used by scholars in understanding the message of the book, especially the relationship between Job's understanding of this view of divine justice and his understanding of death. The strengths and weaknesses, voids, and ongoing needs of these studies will be considered.

Mythological and Literary Readings of the Text

A survey of approaches to the concept of death in the book of Job reveals that those approaches have emphasized two issues: (1) death is understood within the character of God and of creation in relation to the status of evil or chaos, even to "Satan";[4] (2) death is considered as being under the relationship between God and Job, and by implication of all humanity. For the former issue the interpretation of Behemoth and Leviathan is crucial. These two main issues read the same texts differently depending on whether

---

3. For a fuller discussion on the meaning of the "two faces of God," see pages 31–33 of this book. Cf. Norman C. Habel, "In Defense of God the Sage," in *The Voice from the Whirlwind: Interpreting the Book of Job*, eds. Leo G. Perdue and W. Clark Gilpin (Nashville: Abingdon, 1992), 21–38.

4. In the book of Job the word הַשָּׂטָן is appropriately rendered as "the satan" (i.e. "the accuser"), who is a legitimate member of the celestial council. However, the term "Satan" also appears in this book with an attached wider biblical view. Hereafter, while "the satan" connotes the idea of an angel in heavenly court, performing certain functions within the parameter that God has set for him, the term "the Satan" or "Satan" will intend to mean God's competing force or power or god as understood by those proponents of mythological reading.

a combat myth or sapiential tradition is used as the primary hermeneutical lens.[5]

Mythologically Oriented Reading of Job. Those who view death as being controlled by the power of evil depend heavily upon the Ugaritic materials. Interestingly, the biblical Hebrew of the book of Job shows a remarkable similarity with the Ugaritic texts both in vocabulary and style. In addition, because terms and expressions that occur in Ugaritic literature appear throughout the whole book of Job, many scholars have concluded that the author of the book of Job has appropriated not only a body of terminology but also the theological perspective of the Canaanite mythological literature.

Nicholas J. Tromp. In his 1969 *Primitive Conceptions of Death and the Nether World in the Old Testament,* Nicholas J. Tromp argues that the biblical motifs of death and the nether world originated from myth.[6] Tromp makes use of the Ugaritic materials, especially the Baal-cycle, and points to it whenever applicable. He points out that the number of biblical names for the nether world reflects both Israelite thought and her nature.[7] He reinterprets a large number of Hebrew terms and texts in the underworld sense. Tromp, agreeing with Dahood, interprets, for instance, the term אֶרֶץ in Job 12:7–8 as "underworld," taking the view that the four terms – animals, bird, אֶרֶץ, and fish represent a quadripartite division of the universe: earth, heavens, underworld, and sea respectively. This interpretation sees their meaning as a parallel to the Ugaritic text ('nt III 19–22):[8]

rgm 'ṣ wlḫšt abn	Speech of wood, whisper of stone
tant šmm 'm arṣ	converse of heavens with the nether world
thmt 'mn kbkbm	the deeps with the stars

---

5. See Carol A. Newsom, "Considering Job," *CurBS* 1 (1993): 87–118, who includes many examples of this kind of mythologically oriented interpretation in her quick survey of commentaries and articles concerning the book of Job.

6. Nicholas J. Tromp, *Primitive Conceptions of Death and the Nether World in the Old Testament* (Rome: Pontifical Biblical Institute, 1969). Note that from his index references on pages 225–227, Tromp makes 126 specific references to the book of Job.

7. Tromp, 4.

8. Tromp, 42; M. Dahood, "Northwest Semitic Philology and Job," in *The Bible in Current Catholic Thought,* ed. J. L. McKenzie (New York: Herder and Herder, 1962), 58; M. Pope, *Job,* AB 15 (Garden City, NY: Doubleday, 1965), 88, 91.

Other examples of Tromp's reinterpretation of terms and phrases that appear in Job are: הַמְּרוֹתָם as "miry depths" (Job 17:2), another netherworld phenomenon (instead of "their provocation"); לַמְמִתִים as "to the waters of Death" (Job 33:22), a chaotic connotation of nether world (instead of "to those who bring death"); and רַחֲבֵי־אָרֶץ as "the vast expanse of the nether world" (Job 38:18) (instead of "the expanse of the earth"); etc. In addition, Tromp believes that there are traces of dualism in the Old Testament.[9] He prefers to divinize death as "a threatening demon" or "Sir Death," the enemy *par excellence.* He concludes that

> death was experienced, not as an abstract power or an inexplicable fate, but as a personal reality, the Arch-enemy, . . . a threatening demon . . . No doubt there exists some connection between mythological Death and the biblical figure of Sir Death, who, despite some traces of dualism in the Old Testament, is generally subject to Yahweh. The pedigree then continues with the devil, personification of moral evil. The use of the same symbols in these three cases (e.g. the devouring lion) suggests an intimate relation between them. As these realities remained outside Yahwism for a considerable time, popular custom must have kept up the ancient mythological traditions, although the OT shows that already in an early period Mot was subdued to the God of Israel.[10]

It is true that "some" biblical names connote the idea of the nether world. However, merely depending upon names and phrases with the assumption that the Joban author using these words with a certain idea of mythology in the book of Job not only fails at "getting at the essence of things,"[11] but also misses certain features in context which appear to pose for the monotheistic

---

9. Tromp, *Primitive*, 197, n. 102. Those biblical traces are, for example, Pss 94; 34:23, 24; 71:20, 23; 115:17.

10. Tromp, 213.

11. Robert Alter, *The Art of Biblical Narrative* (New York: Basic Books, 1981), proposes a competent reading of the biblical dialogue with a serious concern of the role of language both in effecting and in disclosing the intentions of wills, human and divine. He states (70) that spoken language is the substratum of everything human and divine that transpires in the Bible, and the Hebrew tendency to transpose what is preverbal or nonverbal into speech is finally a technique for getting at the essence of things.

outlook of the Joban author. For example, the Ugaritic text cited by Dahood above is different in context and content. It does not use animals for the other three elements. "It simply mentions the heavens groaning to the earth (אֶרֶץ) and does not propose any consultation of nature."[12] Therefore אֶרֶץ, "earth," in Job 12:8 refers to obvious and accessible sources of knowledge, not the underworld.

Tromp's contribution may be that his book gives an impression that there was a greater Israelite interest in the underworld than had previously been thought. But his methodological assumption does not fairly treat Job, for it fails to deal with the question of the book contextually. Because the character of his studies is heavily influenced by Canaanite mythology, the terms death and the nether world are understood from the Baal-cycle background. Significantly, it does not regard the problem of death in the narrative development of the book of Job itself. His study, therefore, illustrates instead the lack of treatment of the question within a framework of the development of the book.

Walter L. Michel. In a similar vein, Walter L. Michel, who follows M. Dahood and M. Pope (his teacher), attempts to offer a new concept of death in the book of Job.[13] Michel also suggests that "many expressions [in the book of Job] can be interpreted as mythological or mythopoetics."[14] Michel strongly believes that about 150 expressions were interpreted as referring to Yahweh and his realm and about 180 expressions to the underworld and the realm of the forces of death. Many of these names and epithets were found to be the same or similar to expressions in the Ugaritic texts.[15] His new translation of the book of Job proposes a variety of "forces of death"

---

12. See Philip S. Johnston, *Shades of Sheol* (Downers Grove: InterVarsity, 2002), 101. Johnston argues against Tromp (and Dahood) that the four sources of knowledge are not given in a typical cosmological order (e.g. heaven, earth, sea, underworld). Besides, the other three, namely animals, bird, and fish, are animate, while "earth" alone is inanimate.

13. See Walter L. Michel, "The Ugaritic Texts and the Mythological Expressions in the Book of Job: Including a New Translation of Philological Notes on the Book of Job," PhD diss. (The University of Wisconsin, 1970); Mitchell Dahood, *Psalms*, 3 vols. AB 16–17A (Garden City, NY: Doubleday, 1965–1970); Pope, *Job*.

14. Michel, "Death," 184.

15. Michel, "The Ugaritic Texts," 17–143.

epithets.[16] These epithets are personal and mythological. They refer to the king of the underworld, Mot himself, the god of death in the Canaanite culture. Moreover, Michel, in his dissertation, tries to link a relationship between Satan, Death, Leviathan, Behemoth and all the other deadly creatures mentioned in Job. He concludes that "The one unifying characteristic of them all is that they are used by the poet of Job to symbolize various kind and degrees of misery and death among nature and men."[17]

Michel's translation interprets Job on the basis of the assumption that it is not only employing mythological literary motifs but is operating within a conceptual framework provided by Canaanite and other Near Eastern ideas. Both Michel and Tromp, for instance, do not treat Job's understanding of death contextually. They do not treat it within the framework of the book itself or within the genre of Old Testament wisdom. Rather they understand it in terms of ideas brought into the book from outside the tradition of biblical wisdom, especially from ancient Near Eastern mythological contexts.

---

16. Walter Michel, *Job: In the Light of Northwest Semitic: Prologue and First Cycle of Speeches, Job 1:1–14:22*, vol. 1 (Rome: Biblical Institute Press, 1987). Note that this book is dedicated to Mitchell J. Dahood with the purpose "to collect in convenient form Dahood's many contributions to the study of the text of Job and to add his voice to the symphony praising this ancient classic" (1). Both Michel and Dahood have a methodological assumption that Eblaite, Ugaritic and Phoenician-Punic are greater value for the understanding of Job than Aramaic, Arabic or post-biblical and rabbinic Hebrew. By using the Ugaritic-based approach, Michel is able to find many names and epithets for Mot, Sir Death, or the Underworld. Among these are: "Agitation" (*rgz*, Job 3:17), "Crusher, Splitter, Breaker, Destroyer" (*rgʻ*, Job 7:5), "Behemoth" (*bhmh*, Job 12:7, 40:15), "Death" (*mwt*, Job 3:21; 5:20), "Dread" (*phd*, Job 3:25; 4:14; 13:11), "Emptiness, Hunger" (*šwʼ*, Job7:3), "Enemy, Archenemy-Tyrant" (*ṣr*, Job 6:23), "Evil One" (*rʻ, rāʼ*, Job 1:1 [cf. 1:8] 5:19, 27:7, 30:26), "Firstborn-Death" (*bkwr mwt*, Job 18:13), "King of Terror" (*melek ballāhôt*, Job 18:14), "Leviathan" (*lwytn*, [= *ltn*], Job 3:8; 7:12; 40:25), "Strangler" (*mḥnq*, Job7:15), "Sword" (*ḥrb*, Job 5:15, 20), "Terror" (*sʻt*, Job 13:11; *ḥtt*, Job 6:21), "Thirsty One" (*ṣmym*, Job 5:5), "Violence" (*šd*, Job 5:21, 22), "Wicked One" (*ršʻ*, Job 9:24; 27:7), "Wicked" (*ʼwn*, Job 5:6), "Worm" (*rmh*, Job 7:5), etc. In addition, Michel also remarks those forces of Mot and Underworld through the following names, for example: "Assemblies of Footmen" (*mwʻ dy rgl*, Job 12;5), "Council of the Wicked" (*ʻṣt ršʻ ym*, Job 10:3), "Creatures of the Land" (*ḥyt hʼrṣ*, Job 5:22), "Darkeners of Day" (*mryry ywm*, Job 3:5), "Devastators, Demons" (*šddym*, Job 12:6), "Packs" (*pḥdym*, Job 15:21), "Rahab, Helpers of Rahab, Anger, Strong Ones, Warriors, Vassals" (*rhb*, Job9:13; *ʻzry rhb* 26:12; *ʼpk*, Job14:13), "Resheph, Sons of Resheph" (*Rešep, Rešeph, bny ršp*, Job 5:7), "Sons of the Field" (*ʼbny hśdh*, Job 5:23), "Vexation" (*kʻś*, Job 5:2), "Zeal" (*qnʼh*, Job 5:2), etc. Michel regards as many as 180 phrases as names or epithets in the book of Job. His translation is a good example of a heavy reading Job in the light of Ugaritic (since 1929), and other Northwest Semitics languages, especially Phoenician and Punic, and Eblaite (since 1974).

17. Michel, "The Ugaritic Texts," 106–107.

Philip S. Johnston. In *Shades of Sheol*, Philip S. Johnston attempts to analyze the concept of the Hebrew word *Sheol*.[18] He argues that "Sheol cannot be identified simply as the Hebrew term for the underworld which awaits all. It is exclusively reserved for those under divine judgment, whether the wicked, the afflicted righteous, or all sinners."[19] The righteous, specifically Jacob, Hezekiah, Job, and a psalmist (Gen 37:35 etc.; Isa 38:10; Job 17:13–16; Ps 88:4) only envisage descent to Sheol. All speak in the context of extreme trial, whether loss, illness, affliction or abandonment, which they interpret as divine punishment. Johnston's conclusion is convincing and is helpful in understanding this complex Hebrew term. However, *Shades of Sheol* mainly provides the meaning of the term Sheol from the perspective of the whole Hebrew Bible. In dealing with Job, most of his studies analyze those key words which may carry the meaning relating to Sheol (e.g. אֶרֶץ in Job 10:21–22; 12:7–8; 15:29; 38:18; מְרָה in Job 17:2; רְפָאִים in Job 26:5; etc.).[20] Johnston does give some lengthy study on the text of Job 19 (about five pages), arguing that the text, especially 19:25–27, is not the assertion of Job's thought of after death; it is instead presenting the idea of vindication in this life.[21] To summarize, Johnston's conclusion is too general in dealing with the concept of death from Job's perspective. Johnston's book does not treat Job's concept contextually (i.e. within the literary framework of the book itself). Specifically, it does not give a sense of how Job's view of death develops within the book.

Robert S. Fyall. An interesting book which has come out recently is *Now My Eyes Have Seen You: Images of Creation and Evil in the Book of Job*, written by Robert S. Fyall.[22] This book aims at giving "a holistic reading of Job particularly in terms of its depiction of creation and evil."[23] One of Fyall's arguments is that there is a tension between the incomparability of Yahweh and the existence of other gods whose power is real and menacing.

---

18. Johnston, *Shades of Sheol*.
19. Johnston, 83.
20. Johnston, 98–114, 123, 128–149, etc.
21. Johnston, 209–214.
22. Robert S. Fyall, *Now My Eyes Have Seen You: Images of Creation and Evil in the Book of Job* (Downers Grove: InterVarsity, 2002).
23. Fyall, *My Eyes*, 17.

This tension is captured in the basic image of the heavenly court. Fyall tries to prove that God, instead of Job, is Satan's adversary.[24] Fyall concludes that the Behemoth is a figure like the Canaanite Mot, the god of death, who is not simply a rhetorical figure but a real actor in the drama. Behemoth is related both to the world of the dead and to that of Leviathan. Behemoth is identified with Mot, god of death. He is "the king of terrors" (Job 18:14), presiding over the netherworld. Leviathan is the power of evil, the so-called "Satan."

In Fyall's point of view, the whole book of Job is not about explaining the suffering of a righteous individual, but about the conflict between Yahweh and Satan interpreted in the light of mythological motifs from the Mot-Baal Canaanite cycle. His interpretation, namely the conflict between two divine beings (as with Baal and Mot in the Ugarit), implies that the book of Job presents a conflict between Yahweh and Mot. This imposes a framework for interpreting the book that does not emerge from the book itself or from within the genre of Old Testament wisdom, but comes from outside. While Fyall does something different in his book, his interpretation has much in common with the others: that is, there is the notion of bringing in something from the outside and trying to impose it upon Job, rather than developing the idea from the book itself.[25]

Reflection on Mythologically Oriented Reading of Job. The above approaches raise some questions concerning the use of Ugaritic texts as background for their interpretations. It is true that the above examples, except *Shades of Sheol*, attempt to take advantage of the results obtained by philological research of the Ugaritic texts and their application to biblical

---

24. Fyall, 36.

25. The notion about the tendency to impose an interpretation drawn from the mythological world upon the Old Testament text is a modern version of the same kind of interpretation that was done in the latter half of the nineteenth century in Germany, the so-called "Babel-Bibel" controversy. This controversy surrounded exactly this issue, the extent to which it was appropriate to interpret the entire Old Testament in the light of literature that at that time just came to be known from Babylon. The main scholars in the Babel-Bibel controversy were basically doing for the entire Old Testament what some of these people do for the book of Job; namely, they are taking the external framework as their basis of reading the Old Testament as if the Old Testament were simply an ancient Near Eastern mythological record. Thus, in the case of Job, it seems that we are revisiting some of these issues. For an overview of the controversy, see, for example: Friedrich Delitzsch, *Babel und Bibel* (Leipzig: J. C. Hinrichs, 1902), and Friedrich Delitzsch, *Babel and Bible: Two Lectures* (New York: G. P. Putnam's Sons, 1903).

literature. However, their heavy dependence on external sources creates some problems. There are many issues that we need to consider. These interpretations, which reveal a tendency of contemporary scholarship to impose a mythological thought world upon biblical texts, assume that the use of mythological literary motifs implies adoption of mythological religious conceptions. In addition, the contents of the texts that deal with mythologies are ambiguous, even controversial. Their numbers are few and the corpus of text is not as long and detailed as the biblical texts. Thus these shortcomings of the texts cause their interpretations to be problematic.

In interpreting the biblical text on the basis of materials from the ancient Near East, we have to keep in mind that most of those extra-biblical materials were written from the perspective of a different theological framework than that of the Old Testament. That means that all cognate words and ideas have to be viewed through a different conceptual framework and that makes a tremendous difference in many cases. For example, the conclusion of Fyall's work is doubtful and may lead the reader to the mistaken conclusion that there is a kind of dualism in the biblical text.[26] The proponents of this mythical reading fail to read Job within the genre of Old Testament wisdom. Thus, in relation to the concept of death, this approach views death as under the dark power in all its ferocity. The whole book of Job is perceived as being about a relationship between a transcendent God and his battle with evil at both a cosmic and an earthly level.[27] Indeed, the entire concept

---

26. This is also an example of a repeated mistake of the nineteenth-century Babel-Bibel controversy. In *My Eyes*, Fyall states, 192, "these sagas [Baal's battle with Yam the sea god and Baal's struggle with Mot the god of death] speak of the great discords in creation and of people's fear of the powers of chaos and death. The Job poet uses these well-known materials in a way consistent with his own worldview." Fyall misapplies the ancient Near East context upon the context of the book of Job.

27. Cf. Fyall, *My Eyes*, 137. It is true that there are some cosmic battle materials in the Hebrew Bible (e.g. Ps 74:13–14, telling of Yahweh's victory over "Sea" (*yam*) and the crushing of the heads of the "Sea Monster" (*tannînîm*) and of Leviathan; Ps 89:10–11, referring to Yahweh's reign on the back of the "Sea" (*yam*) after defeating the dragon Rahab; Isa 27, where Leviathan is seen as a "Sea Monster" (*tannîn*), and perhaps too as a fleeing, wriggling snake, if the mythological monsters in this verse are all various epithets for the same cosmic foe; etc.). It seems also that this combat motif is reflected in the book of Job (e.g. Job 3:8, referring to Leviathan; 7:12, mentioning to the "Sea Monster" (*tannîn*) as cosmic foes of the created order; 26:12, where God is credited with smiting Rahab; 40–41, where the poet contrasting God's power over Behemoth and Leviathan with the powerlessness of one such as Job; etc). This combat motif is not necessarily part of mythological matter, but it is echoed as part of the rhetoric of the book of Job. See Robert A. Oden, Jr., "Cosmogony, Cosmology," *ABD*

of a "cosmic conflict" or dualistic perspective on reality assumes the kind of polytheistic theological framework that the Old Testament in general and the book of Job in particular explicitly reject.

Literary-Oriented Reading of Job. Concerning the relationship between God and man, this approach offers the result of recent studies of the structural and literary dimensions. Some scholars such as Norman C. Habel, J. Gerald Janzen, Robert Alter, Terence E. Frietheim, Samuel E. Balentine, etc. approach Job from a literary perspective.[28] Through their efforts, literary features like plot development, characters, setting, keywords, motifs, signals of continuity, etc. have come under consideration. The following are some examples which illustrate how these studies demonstrate that death is viewed as being under the relationship between God and man.

The Two Speeches of Yahweh. Generally speaking, it has been accepted that the two speeches of Yahweh (38:1–41:26 [Eng 41:34]) are the climax of the book of Job.[29] One of the few things about which commentators agree in Joban interpretation is that these divine speeches are beautiful in their literary structures and their imagery. The grand descriptions fo בְּהֵמוֹת (Job 40:15–24) and לִוְיָתָן (Job 40:25–41:26 [Eng 41:1–34]) receive great attention. Contemporary scholars are divided as to whether these two creatures were understood by the Joban author as mythical monsters or as the natural animals, namely the hippopotamus and the crocodile respectively.[30] How

---

1:1162–1171; Elmer B. Smick, "Mythology and the Book of Job," in *Sitting with Job: Selected Studies on the Book of Job*, ed. Roy B. Zuck (Grand Rapids: Baker, 1992), 221–229; Smick, "Another Look at the Mythological Elements in the Book of Job," 231–244.

28. Norman C. Habel, *The Book of Job: A Commentary* (Philadelphia: Westminster, 1985); J. Gerald Janzen, *Job* (Atlanta: John Knox, 1985); Robert Alter, "Truth and Poetry in the Book of Job," in *The Art of Biblical Poetry* (New York: Basic Books, 1985), 85–110; Terence E. Frietheim, *God and World in the Old Testament: A Relational Theology of Creation* (Nashville: Abingdon, 2005); Samuel E. Balentine, *Job* (Macon, GA: Smyth & Helwys, 2006).

29. This is because the two speeches of Yahweh, particularly the second discourse of God, deal specifically with the central issues of the book: the relationship between God and man. One of the supportive interpretations of this understanding is that in the first discourse the Joban author presents five pairs of animals, the sixth and last pair is portrayed in the second discourse, recalling the creation of human being on the sixth day as the crown of creation. See Samuel E. Balentine, "What Are Human Beings, That You Make So Much of Them?" in *God in the Fray: A Tribute to Walter Brueggemann*, eds. Tod Linafelt and Timothy K. Beal (Minneapolis: Fortress, 1998), 259–278.

30. For mythical interpretation, see, for example, Pope, *Job*, 265–287; Samuel Terrien, *Job*, CAT 13 (Neuchâtel: Delauchaux et, 1963), 258–267; N. H. Tur-Sinai, *The Book of Job: A New Commentary* (Jerusalem: Kiryath Sepher, 1957), 556–557; Fyall, *My Eyes*. For

one interprets these two creatures does affect the understanding of death in the book of Job. The proponents of the "mythical" interpretation see that Yahweh has created the wonders of nature: They are heavenly, mythic beings with which Yahweh alone is able to cope.[31] The proponents of a "natural" reading see Behemoth and Leviathan as two magnificent creatures which, like the natural phenomena and creatures described in Job 38 and 39, accentuate the divine power.[32] However the hermeneutically crucial question, as asked by Carol Newsom, is how the relationship between God and these creatures is represented in this second divine speech.[33] There is considerable variety in the interpretation of these two beasts. Some scholars, for example Richard Clifford, argue that Behemoth and Leviathan are "mere playthings" in the powerful divine hands.[34] Others find more explicit violence in the texts. For example, Tryggve Mettinger sees an "antagonistic theology" in Job;[35] Jon D. Levenson states, "While Behemoth is declared to be a creature of God, Leviathan is not so described in the longer section devoted to him . . . We hear only of God's heroic capture and conquest of the great sea beast."[36] But "do we really [hear that]?"[37] It is true that these two animals, especially

---

naturalistic interpretation, see, for instance, S. R. Driver and G. B. Gray, *A Critical and Exegetical Commentary on the Book of Job*, ICC (Edinburgh: Clark, 1921), 351–371; Edward J. Kissane, *The Book of Job* (Dublin: Browne & Nolan, 1939), 280–292; G. Fohrer, *Das Buch Hiob* (Gütersloh: Mohn, 1964), 521–531; Robert Gordis, *The Book of God and Man: A Study of Job* (Chicago: University of Chicago, 1965); Edouard Dhorme, *Commentary on the Book of Job* (Leiden: Brill, 1967), 618–625; Francis I. Andersen, *Job: An Introduction and Commentary* (Downers Grove: InterVarsity, 1974), 288–291.

31. See a brief summary of various interpretations in Habel, *The Book of Job*, 557–558.

32. They are magnificent because Behemoth is viewed as the fiercest land animal, and Leviathan as the most terrifying sea creature.

33. Carol A. Newsom, *The Book of Job: A Contest of Moral Imaginations* (New York: Oxford University Press, 2003), 248.

34. Richard Clifford, *Creation Accounts in the Ancient Near East and in the Bible*, CBQMS 26 (Washington, DC: Catholic Biblical Association, 1994), 196.

35. Tryggve Mettinger, "The God of Job: Avenger, Tyrant, or Victor?" in *The Voice from the Whirlwind: Interpreting the Book of Job*, eds. Leo G. Perdue and W. Clark Gilpin (Nashville: Abingdon, 1992), 39–49.

36. Jon D. Levenson, *Creation and the Persistence of Evil: The Jewish Drama of Divine Omnipotence* (San Francisco: Harper & Row, 1988), 49.

37. Kathleen M. O'Connor, "Wild, Raging Creativity: The Scene in the Whirlwind," in *A God So Near: Essays on Old Testament Theology in Honor of Patrick D. Miller*, eds. Brent A. Strawn and Nancy R. Bowen (Winona Lake, IN: Eisenbrauns, 2003), 171–179, especially 176. She correctly comments (177) that the two speeches of Yahweh are "not about battle,

Leviathan, carry some mythic overtones; but what was the focus of the poet?[38] A closer look on the form, setting, and content of the speeches draws an alternative interpretation. For example, while Fyall understands Behemoth as a figure of death and Leviathan as Satan himself, who is "now fighting it [the battle] again and using Job as the scene of that [the primeval] battle,"[39] John G. Gammie views both Behemoth and Leviathan as a didactic image for Job himself.[40] Gammie views these two beasts figuratively.[41] He proposes that both animals become exemplars of divine pride, both are mirrors of Job's self: his own beauty and fearlessness.

Gammie, following the lead of Samuel Terrien,[42] approaches the text (specifically the second speech of YHWH, Job 40:6–41:26 [Eng 41:34]) by examining it on a grammatical and syntactical basis. Gammie points out that there are linguistic clues within the Behemoth pericope (e.g. 40:15, inviting Job to make a comparison between himself and Behemoth; 40:16–18, a regenerative power to restart his life and family again, etc.), as well as clues found elsewhere in the book (e.g. 12:7–12, בְּהֵמוֹת as one(s) who will instruct man, etc.), supporting the notion that animals can provide instruction for

---

nor conflict, nor hostility with God, nor primarily about Job's inability to conquer these creatures. It is about God's pleasure in their beautiful wildness."

38. Newsom rightly observes that "the old dispute about whether Behemoth and Leviathan are animals or mythical monsters engages in a false dichotomy." Carol Newsom, *The Book of Job*, NIB 4 (Nashville: Abingdon, 1994), 165. She also suggests that the characteristics of these two monsters place themselves somewhere between "mere" animals and extraordinary, supernatural creatures (615).

39. Fyall, *My Eyes*, 143.

40. John G. Gammie, "Behemoth and Leviathan: On the Didactic and Theological Significance of Job 40:15–41:26," in *Israelite Wisdom: Theological and Literary Essays in Honor of Samuel Terrien*, eds. John G. Gammie, Walter A. Brueggemann, W. Lee Humphreys, and James M. Ward (New York: Scholars Press, 1978), 217–231.

41. Cf. Alter, *Biblical Poetry*, 107, comments on the presentation of Behemoth and Leviathan that "the poetic logic" of the divine speeches arrives at the climax of the "movement from literal to figurative, from verisimilar to hyperbolic, from general assertion to focused concrete image."

42. Samuel Terrien, *Job: Poet of Existence* (Indianapolis: Bobbs-Merrill, 1957). Although Terrien adheres to the "mythic" view of Behemoth and Leviathan as the "forces of evil" and as directly related to the subject matter of the book as a whole (237–238), he also has another perspective on these two beasts when he says: "These brutish creatures are not only caricatures in themselves, they are also caricatures of human endeavor" (237). This view raises a question, asked by Gammie, "Behemoth and Leviathan," 218, that "is it possible that the author of the pericopes on Behemoth and Leviathan is holding these two creatures up as mirrors through which Job may view his own existence of suffering and protest?"

man. Gammie also suggests that the reader considers the original meaning of the poet. Likewise, Leviathan should not be viewed as a "crocodile" or "a mythic being," but as "a caricature of his [Job's] verbal defenses and yet an affirmation of his [Job's] very protests (Job 41:17–21, 22–26 [Eng 41:25–29, 30–34])."[43] Gammie concludes that

> the second discourse of God must be viewed as a passage replete with an irony of divine comfort and affirmation: seeming to portray exemplars of the divine defeat of proudful man (Job 40:12–14), it portrays instead the divine pride in human triumph over oppression (Job 40:19a; 41:26 [Eng 41:34]); seeming to portray Job's inability to conquer such marvelously wrought beasts as Behemoth and Leviathan, the beasts themselves celebrate instead Job's triumph.[44]

In a similar vein, Samuel E. Balentine regards these two animals as "models that invite exploration of what it means for human beings [i.e. Job] to be created 'in the image of God,' i.e. as mortal creatures who are nevertheless 'a little lower than God' (Ps 8:5 [MT 6])."[45] In his view, the revelation that Job receives from the whirlwind is not considered a rebuke or a denial of Job, but rather as a radical summons to a new understanding of what it means for humankind that God is committed to nurture and sustain.[46] His conclusion comes from consulting the inter-biblical materials by exploring Psalm 8 (cf. Job 7:18) and the image of the firstborn that Job and Eliphaz have mentioned (Job 4:17–19; 15:7–16; 22:1–11) and which reappears in God's speech about Behemoth and Leviathan.[47] In short, Behemoth and Leviathan represent the sixth and final pair of animals, recalling the creation

---

43. Terrien, *Job: Poet*, 225.
44. Terrien, 226.
45. Balentine, "What Are Human Beings," 270, n. 37.
46. Balentine, 260; see Janzen, *Job*, 229, also Gammie, "Behemoth and Laviathan," 231. Note that both Balentine and Gammie interpret Behemoth and Leviathan as positive models for Job. However, while both of them agree that both creatures serve to instruct and console Job, Balentine is not persuaded about the element of rebuke as assumed by Gammie.
47. On the rhetorical links and differences between Job 7 and Psalm 8, see especially Michael A. Fishbane, *Biblical Interpretation in Ancient Israel* (Oxford: Clarendon, 1985), 285–286; Fishbane, "The Book of Job and Inner-Biblical Discourse," in *The Voice from the Whirlwind: Interpreting the Book of Job*, eds. Leo G. Perdue and W. C. Gilpin (Nashville: Abingdon, 1992), 87–90.

of humankind on the sixth day as the crown of God's cosmic design.[48] From this perspective, God provides through Behemoth and Leviathan a particular model for Job (and humanity) of what it means to occupy this privileged position within creation. Therefore, the climax of the book of Job does not represent the combat between God and the competing powers or gods as understood by those proponents of a mythical reading but rather the intimate relationship between God and man. By implication, the expression of death and life at the end of the book, for example, "Job died, old and full of days" (Job 42:17), "becomes an invitation to a larger understanding of what it means to live in relation with God."[49]

The theophanies at the end of the book mark a special revelation that brings God into an intimate relationship with human beings. Kathleen M. O'Connor rightly observes that "If the ancient combat myth of creation lurks here [the second speech of Yahweh], it has been seriously defanged."[50] Thus, from this literary approach, the issue of life and death is considered entirely from within the Hebrew theology of creation and within the context of the message of the book of Job. In other words, life and death can appropriately be seen as connected to the understanding of the images of God and the world.

A variation of this literary approach may be a concern about the divine speeches, whether they are a rebuke to Job and his friends or a summons to a new understanding of the nature of human existence in the image of God, or both. In either case while the interpretation of images of world and God is different, death is viewed as under the control of God. It is an element and a part of life before God. In addition, the satan in the book of Job plays no significant role. He is not the "controlling reality" behind the entire book.[51] The book of Job does not present dualism and the satan is

---

48. This also explains the lack of human beings in the divine speeches.

49. Balentine, *Job*, 718.

50. O'Connor, "Wild, Raging Creativity," 176. O'Connor is in line with Gammie's interpretation of these two beasts. She concludes (177) that "God invites Job to step beyond his constricted view of himself, of God, and of the world. God challenges Job to recognize his participation in the beauty and wild freedom of creation and its Creator."

51. Therefore we must not presume that the satan's activities continue after the prologue. There is no connection between the satan in the prologue and Leviathan in the epilogue as assumed by Fyall et al.

not a competing god, but one of those ministerial angles, serving Yahweh in the heavenly court.[52]

Conclusion. This book argues that the proper approach to understanding the theological meaning that the book of Job communicates is through careful attention to the text in its literary character, especially an appreciation of Job as Old Testament wisdom. This literary approach opens a possible reading to understand the issue of death from within the context of Israel's wisdom tradition, namely from its literary point of view that flows consistently through the entire book.

Through the literary lens of reading the reader sees that while the image of God and the world play an important role at the end of the book, the image of the human being receives its climax in the divine speeches as well. Janzen, for instance, heads the idea that the rhetorical questions of God, appearing prominently in the two speeches of Yahweh, are qualified by an irony that enables them to be heard either as simple rhetorical questions or as genuine existential questions: Who are you? Where were you? Are you able? The function of the divine speeches, hence, is not only to construct the divine image but also the human image.[53] Thus, a peaceful death at the end of the book comes to be understood after the reconstruction of Job's understanding of the nature of human existence in the image of God.

Literary Reading and the Theme of Retribution Principle. The book of Job is a complex mixture of several literary genres.[54] Certain themes (e.g. the retribution principle, creation motif, legal metaphor, lament, etc.) are employed by the Joban author to present the problem and answer of the

---

52. Andersen, *Job*, 83, rightly comments that, "The contribution of the satan to the action of the book is minor. His place in its theology is even less. In the subsequent discussions the misfortunes of men are never traced to a diabolical foe, and it is impossible to believe that the purpose of this tremendous book is to teach us an explanation of evil that Job and his friends never think of, namely that human suffering is caused by the Devil. The satan does not appear again after Job 2:7." Fyall, *My Eyes*, 183, argues against Andersen's statement by stating, "Job and his friends are trapped in their mechanical world. Though they [the friends] believe that God is supreme, they fail to see the sheer power and personality of evil."

53. Janzen, *Job*, 229, states, "To be a human being is to be a creature who is yet God's addressee and whom God confronts with the rest of creation vocationally."

54. Andersen, *Job*, 33, comments that the book of Job is "an astonishing mixture of almost every kind of literature which is found in the Old Testament." In addition to the main genres – the lawsuits, the lament, the dispute; many proverbs, riddles, hymns, curses, and lyrical nature poems can be isolated and identified within the various speeches of the book.

book, which is the relationship between God and man. For the images of God and the world, some scholars may miss the point of these themes in their interpretations. For example, Habel concludes that this world is "a world in balance, with polarities and play, with patterns and paradoxes, with yin and yang."[55] Correspondingly, the Creator God who speaks to Job is not "a God who intervenes or reacts, but one who modulates and constrains."[56] Habel summarizes that

> the God of the prologue is too arbitrary and selfish, intervening at will in human lives . . . the God of the friends is too mechanical, reacting according to a rigid code of reward and retribution . . . the God of Job in his anguish is too violent, harassing humans and creating anarchy . . . the God of the poet's commentary in Job 28 is too remote and inaccessible.[57]

Habel's "world in balance" indirectly connotes the implicit idea of dualism. In his comments on the several images of God, Habel places an undue emphasis on thinking that the Job story is to make a point about God rather than the limits of human understanding of God. Habel is right in seeing that the forces of chaos and death are present in this world but constrained. Furthermore, Behemoth and Leviathan, though representative of chaotic forces, are also evocative of Job himself and hint at his place vis-à-vis God in the "delicate ecology of life."[58] However, his view of God and the world is too systematic. There are many mysterious things in this world which are not "in balance." The book emphasizes instead the limits of human understanding of world and God. These limits of human knowledge are conveyed under the dogma of the retribution principle, which is the most important theme in the book of Job.

---

55. Habel, "In Defense of God the Sage," 35.

56. Habel, 35. To the contrary, Mettinger, "The God of Job," 45–47, understands the God of the theophany as a God who intervenes, God the Victor who battles against the forces of chaos, represented in chapters 40–41 by Behemoth and Leviathan. Mettinger (48) finds an explicit violence in the texts of Job, and sees an "antagonistic theology" in Job.

57. Habel, "In Defense of God the Sage," 33.

58. Habel, 37.

For the images of the world, Scripture does affirm that God's creation is good.[59] In a more specific fashion than Habel, Fretheim properly states that "in being what it was created to be (and become), the world has the potential of adversely affecting human beings, quite apart from the state of their relationship with God."[60] He adds that, "God's good world is not a risk-free world, but has the potential of bringing great harm to even the most righteous of individuals."[61] The theology of divine justice offered by the retribution principle purports to explain both blessing and suffering in terms that man may easily comprehend. But as the book of Job makes clear, we cannot fully understand God's "not-a-risk-free" world. In other words, the images of the world reflect not only the character of God, but also the limitations of Job's understanding of God. At the end of the book Job comes to understand that his own worldview cannot be used to explain everything in God's good world. The worldview with which Job and his friends operate in the dialogue of the book, namely the concept of the retribution principle, exercises influence over his understanding of suffering and death and his struggle with the two faces of God.

The Retribution Principle[62]

The problem of divine justice and retribution is an issue throughout the Old Testament, including legal, prophetic, and wisdom tradition.[63] While

---

59. Genesis 1.

60. Fretheim, *God and World*, 244. Fretheim, 237, comments further that "to say that the creation is good . . . is not to say that it is perfect; at the same time, to say that creation is not perfect is not to say that evil makes it so. For Job to understand his suffering, then, would be to recognize that God neither created a risk-free world nor provided danger-free zones for the pious to be kept free from any harm . . . And so God will sustain such an ordered and open-ended creation even in the face of the suffering ones who wish that God would have created a world wherein human beings could be free from suffering."

61. Fretheim, 244. Note that Fretheim emphasizes the theology of creation as an overarching theme for interpreting the whole Bible. However, in the book of Job specifically concerning the concept of death, the primary point of the divine speeches, as well as the rest of the book, is not only about creation, but about God and the limitation of Job's understanding of him and his way. To be more specific, it is about God's lordship and his mystery which transcend human's knowledge. Implicitly, it is an invitation to resume Job's proper relationship with God.

62. The word "retribution" is from the Latin "*re*" ("back") + "*tribuere*" ("to pay"). The idea is that God "repays" virtue with reward and vice with punishment.

63. This idea can be found in each section of the Hebrew canon – Torah (e.g. Deut 30:15–18), Prophets (e.g. Hos 4:1–3; Amos 4:1–3, 6–13; Mic 3:9–12), and Writings (e.g. Ps 1).

the traditional theory of retribution is reflected in the book of Proverbs,[64] it is only in the book of Job and Ecclesiastes that it is seriously controverted.[65] The theory is biblical, namely there is a connection between sin and suffering: prosperity is attained by the wise and virtuous, but destruction is the fate of the foolish and wicked. Significantly, the blessing or punishment is attributed to the direct intervention of God. But "the book of Job is a vehement attack on this view."[66]

The Old Testament Context of the Retribution Principle. In fact, the retribution principle has its root in the Old Testament as an attempt to understand God's justice. The traditional law of retribution is basically that of the book of Deuteronomy, where it is applied to the nation. In the deuteronomistic history (the book of Joshua to Kings), the doctrine is portrayed by the history of the nation: when Israel was faithful to Yahweh, it prospered; when it was unfaithful, it suffered.[67] Sometimes, however, the doctrine was pressed harder such as when the wrongdoer was punished in his descendants. Rebellion against this perspective is marked in Ezekiel 18:2, "The fathers have eaten sour grapes, and the children's teeth are set on edge?" (cf. Jer 31:29). This proverb was being advanced against the sweeping application of the traditional doctrine, namely the children pay for the sins of their fathers.

In the book of Job, the three friends apply this theology of divine justice to Job's personal situation: Job must have sinned; no other explanation is possible. They commit what later generations of logicians would call the logic

---

64. For instance, Prov 3:12, 35; 6:23; 10:17; 11:18; 13:14; 22:8; 24:16; etc.

65. Roland E. Murphy, *The Book of Job: A Short Reading* (New York: Paulist Press, 1999), 7. Cf. Brevard S. Child, *Introduction to the Old Testament as Scripture* (Philadelphia: Fortress, 1979), 544, comments that "it [the book of Job] supplies a critical corrective to the reading of the other wisdom books, especially Proverbs and Ecclesiastes."

66. Murphy, *The Book of Job*, 7. He suggests further that "it would be a mistake to regard these latter works [Job and Ecclesiastes] as 'anti-wisdom.' Rather, they open wide the windows of wisdom and purify it by criticizing foolhardy conclusions." To be more specific, the book of Job does attack the wisdom view from another deeper wisdom. That is, the book of Job uses wisdom to refine and deepen wisdom.

67. The Bible does teach that both obedience and sin have appropriate consequences. The covenant provides the framework for that idea by setting forth laws that if they are obeyed, they are met by blessings; but if disobeyed, by curses. Examples of these passages may be found in deuteronomistic theology of retribution (e.g. Deut 4:25–31; 11:26–28; 28:1–2; 30:15–20; etc.).

or "fallacy of affirming the consequence:" If x then y; if y exists, therefore x must exist.[68] As applied to Job: If x (Job sins) then y (he will suffer); since y (he suffers), therefore x (he must have sinned). Their point of view, the theology of divine justice that we call the retribution principle, is a human attempt to understand God and to explain divine justice in human terms.[69] Moreover, this notion is governed by a limited perspective, that is, retribution had to take place in this life. At the same time, the Bible does affirm that divine retribution has an extended reach. But both the Old Testament in general and the book of Job in particular also affirm that God's justice stands in relation to God's mercy. Yahweh is understood to be compassionate and gracious, slow to anger, and abounding in steadfast love and faithfulness, "keeping steadfast love to the thousandth generation, forgiving iniquity and transgression and sin, but who will by no means clear the guilty, visiting the iniquity of the fathers on the children and the children's children, to the third and the fourth generation" (Exod 34:7). Hence, while the theology of retribution may explain the judgmental face of God, it is not sufficient to explain Yahweh's gracious face. Moreover, as expressed by Job's friends, this overly-mechanical understanding of divine justice binds the freedom of God who has declared: "I [Yahweh] will be gracious to whom I [YHWH] will be gracious, and will show mercy on whom I [YHWH] will show mercy" (Exod 33:19). Receiving the Lord's mercy depends upon the gracious nature of God alone, and cannot be explained in terms of human reason. The overly simplistic application of the retribution principle as it appears, for instance, in deuteronomistic texts, to Job's individual situation by Job and his friends' leads to the wrong conclusion about both the cause of and the solution to Job's problem. Job's friends want to reduce man's relationship with God, and especially God's grace, to a kind of moral calculus, which Exodus 33:19 explicitly rules out. This leads to Job's crisis of faith as he faces suffering and death, a crisis that is finally only resolved by God's own intervention.

---

68. In formal logic this is recognized as a fallacy because it misreads "If x, then y," for "If and only if x, then y." Job's friends make the same mistake by assuming that y (Job's suffering) must be explained solely in terms of x (Job's righteousness or sinfulness). The book makes it clear from the outset that there is a completely different explanation for Job's suffering.

69. In a very few passages, Eliphaz does at one point speak of suffering as discipline (Job 5:17). But this is not a dominant theme in the book of Job.

Some other biblical texts (e.g. Gen 18:22–32; Jer 12:1–4; Pss 37; 73; Hab 2:1–4; etc.) have also raised this problem of retribution principle.[70] These texts resolve the problem of divine justice in a different way by affirming that we will only see divine justice revealed in the eschaton. Although the book of Job deals with a similar problem as these texts, it is different and unique in the extent that it emphasizes the problem of justice within the framework of *this* life. The Joban author does not argue that justice will be done in the eschaton. Job's story is an attack on the retribution principle as an explanation of why people suffer in this life. It is in this context that death becomes an important question. The role of death and the understanding of death as the ultimate conclusion of suffering become more significant for Job than any of the other texts, which see the retribution principle from the perspective of eternity. The law of retribution is ultimately shown to be invalid in the case of Job, and by implication, in many other cases. It has been enunciated and even defended with the best arguments by the Joban author, who tried to be even-handed, as well as upholding Job's arguments against those of the three friends at the same time. He obviously presents the three friends' hardheaded view of the retribution principle (and sometimes of Job's) as a *reductio ad absurdum* (cf. Job 42:7).[71] The Joban author precisely gives an alternative answer in the divine speeches that it is not a case of this cause-effect relation; rather, the mystery of divine governance remains.[72]

Retribution in Job on Trial. One of the central questions that shapes the way in which one reads the book of Job is the question of exactly who or what is on trial in the narrative. Some interpreters take the view that

---

70. Example of other texts which raise hard questions about divine judgment that seem inappropriate are: Exod 32:11–12; Jer 15:18; 17:15–18; 20:18; Hab 1:1–4, 12–17; Pss 10:1; 13:1–4; 22:1–2; 44:17–26; 74:1, 10–11; 79:5; 88:13–14; 89:46–49; etc.

71. Roland E. Murphy, *Seven Books of Wisdom* (Milwaukee: The Bruce, 1960), 57. Also Balentine, *Job*, 717, rightly observes that "Appealing to the doctrine of retribution, Bildad assured Job that if he would only confess his guilt, then God would make his 'beginning' seem small in comparison to the prosperity of his 'latter days.' In view of God's declaration that the friends 'have not spoken what is right' about God, Bildad's assurance now sounds ironic at best. The blessing God gives seems to be Job's reward for *not* conforming to his friends' theology." See also J. B. Curtis, "Why Were the Elihu Speeches Added to the Book of Job?" *PEGLMBS* 8 (1988): 93–99, who sees Elihu as "the *reduction ad absurdum* of traditional theology."

72. See D. J. A. Clines, *Job 1–20*, WBC 17 (Dallas: Word Books, 1989), xlvi, who points that the divine speeches suggests that "retribution is not the issue, but whether God can be trusted to run his world."

Job is on trial in the book. Still others suggest that God is on trial.[73] This thesis will contend that neither Job nor God is on trial, but rather it is the theology of divine justice reflected in the retribution principle as a basis for understanding human suffering and the relationship between God and man that is on trial, and is ultimately found lacking, in the book of Job.

Death appears in the book of Job, as in Scriptures generally, as unavoidable. In fact, it is considered not from a physiological, nor biological, nor pathological interest. Rather, death is viewed from the perspective of theological, theocentric categories: "it is part of life with/before/under God (*coram Deo*). To that extent, death is problematic; the true problem lies with God."[74] There is always an inherent tension in the dichotomy of death as divine judgment and death as a gateway to eternal life with God. That is, Job struggles between understanding death either as a surrender of the guilty to the ultimate punishment or as the peaceful end of a life lived with God. Because the issue of life and death is theological, some scholars argue that God is on trial in the book. Christopher R. Seitz, for instance, raises this serious question:

> What theology or the study of God, does the book present? What can we say about a book in which God strips a mortal of home, possessions, family, health, and sanity? The appearance of a satanic accuser in chapters one and two as the agent of God's hand hardly resolves our doubts about God. For what ungodly reasons or by what standards of justice can explain this difficult view of God? No amount of shifting attention to other problems of the book, even passionate questions about the moral order, suffering, and the punishment or reward of good/evil, can remove the difficult view of God we/the reader see in the opening chapters.[75]

---

73. Cf. Shimon Bakon, "God and Man on Trial," *JBQ* 21 (1993): 226–235.

74. Henry Rowold, "Life and Death, Death and Life: Echoes from the Book of Job," (unpublished paper presented at the 17th Symposium of Concordia Seminary, St. Louis, MO, 20 September 2006), 1.

75. Christopher R. Seitz, "Job: Full-Structure, Movement, and Interpretation," *Int* 43 (January 1989): 5–17.

For Seitz, the prologue raises the theological stakes in the dialogue by sharing with the reader one key question: "Can a mortal love and serve God under an extraordinary set of circumstances?"[76] This question hovers over all that follows in the Job story. Thus, the portrayers of God and Job in the prologue imply that both are on trial.

Habel also raises the ethical issue of God's behavior in the book of Job. He writes,

> The way in which God agrees to test Job's integrity raises serious doubts about God's own integrity. He is apparently vulnerable to incitement by the Satan in his heavenly council. He succumbs to a wager – twice . . . he afflicts Job without cause or provocation, and his capacity to rule justly is thrown into question.[77]

Besides, in his article, "In Defense of God the Sage,"[78] as addressed above, Habel proposes the idea that the reply of God from the whirlwind is a theological defense of God as the Sage. He says, "This *apologia* offers a profound alternative to the various characterizations of God offered in the rest of the book."[79] Habel links Job 28 with the purpose of the divine speeches. That is Job 28, which describes God as the first sage who discovers wisdom, anticipates the defense of God the sage, which takes place through the sapiential questioning of Job 38–41. However, the fact that God is portrayed by several images does not mean that God is on trial as Habel's proposal implies. These images of God in the book of Job, except in the two speeches of Yahweh, are viewed through a human's perspective (i.e. through Job's, and the friends') on God. In other words, these are portrayers of God that are forced upon Job because the retribution principle is controlling and functioning behind these human's perceptions on God. The challenges to divine morality to what Seitz and Habel point are resolved by the recognition that it is the retribution principle itself that is on trial, and the narrative's vindication of God is a declaration that the retribution principle is false.

---

76. Seitz, "Job," 9.
77. Habel, *The Book of Job*, 61.
78. Habel, "In Defense of God the Sage," 33.
79. Habel, 21. Italics original.

The book of Job makes it clear at the outset that a man's lot is not simply the consequence of his deeds. The prologue affirms that in the one exemplary case (i.e. Job) with which it is concerned, human suffering is not explained by the theology of divine justice inherent in the theology of retribution. Therefore, it is not so much that the prologue raises a hard question about God but that it raises the question about the retribution principle, for God does reserve his freedom in his will and acts. The two speeches of Yahweh at the end of the book give the answer to the problem of the book (i.e. the relationship between God and man). In both speeches, God neither declares his own innocence, nor is he found to be guilty. Thus, it is a literary irony that gives away the answer to the reader, who sees that neither Job nor God is on trial, but the retribution principle.[80] God's action of accepting the satan's challenge does at least show that God is not bound by the retribution principle. As far as the prologue serves as a controlling background of the entire book, the assumption at the nature of divine justice inherent in the theology of retribution serves as the principle conceptual problem of the book. What Job says about death reflects his struggle to understand his relationship with God in terms of the retribution principle. For example, Job's referring to God as abusive and horrible does not appear anywhere else in the Bible. Job can characterize God in this way because if the retribution principle is correct God must be unjust since he allows the righteous Job to suffer as unrighteous. In reality this is a false picture of God that reveals the failure or the bankruptcy of the retribution principle, which has led him to view God as arbitrary, capricious, and evil during the discourse with the friends.[81]

The description of Job as the one who fears God, and shuns evil (1:1, 8), as well as his confessions of faith (1:21; 2:10), affirm that Job believes in the one and only God who omnipotently governs all things according to his own will.[82] In other words, for Job there are no "accidents" in the ultimate

---

80. Contra to Bakon, "God and Man on Trial." Though Bakon, 226–235, recognizes the retribution principle in the book of Job, he emphasizes the insignificance of man and the justice of God which is challenged by man (i.e. by Job; cf. by Abraham, by Moses, by Jonah, by Jeremiah).

81. Examples of Job's referring to God as arbitrary, capricious, and evil may be seen in Job 6:4; 9:17; 12:9; 13:21; 16:12–14; 19:6–12, 21; 23:15–16; 30:19, 21–22.

82. The whole Bible assumes this, see, for instance, Pss 66:7, 89:9–13, 103:19, 104; Matt 6; Acts 17:24–28; 1 Cor 8:4–6; etc.

sense. God is the only one who is responsible for all things. This is a view of a monotheistic religion. Unlike polytheistic religion, where human suffering may be, at least in part, explained by the conflict between the wills of the various deities, monotheism must explain how human suffering can be reconciled with the idea of a God who loves and cares for his creation.[83] Suffering and death raise the question concerning the issue of "theodicy" (God, "*theos*"; justice, "*dike*"), which defenders of the faith are forced to answer. Traditional theodicy implies that the experience of human suffering demonstrates that God is either (1) not just, (2) not loving, or (3) not omnipotent. The three friends (cf. Abraham, Moses, Jeremiah, Habakkuk, and the Psalters) seek to counter questions that dispute divine justice by pronouncing God "Not guilty."[84] Their defense may be justified, for God will certainly punish the wicked. However, as the book unfolds, the three friends exemplify how this theology of divine justice may be overstated or misapplied. The doctrine of retribution attempts to fill the gap by striving to explain suffering and death as part of the justice of God: How this one God will lead to both goodness and suffering and death. Since the doctrine is based on a principle of causality, it provides a logical understanding that every action has an appropriate and corresponding result. "The responsibility for maintaining the concept of retribution lies with God, who guarantees the result. God is actively involved in this cause-effect relation."[85]

This theology of retribution reduces the two faces of Yahweh to a moral equation. The wrathful face of Yahweh reflects the negative side of the equation: If a man sins, suffering must be the punishment. Likewise, the suggestion of the friends for Job to repent of his sin(s) reduces the gracious face of Yahweh, who will show mercy to the repentant, as merely the positive side of this equation. Thus, the two faces of Yahweh are predictable in terms of

---

83. In the Zoroastrian dualism of the two cosmic forces – Ahriman, the principle of darkness, and Ahura-Mazda, the principle of light – are engaged in an eternal struggle. Thus, it also provides an explanation of the existence of "evil." However, in the mainstream Buddhism, the law of karma is used instead as an indicator of how a man does suffer in this life.

84. J. Crenshaw, *Theodicy in the Old Testament* (Philadelphia: Fortress, 1983), 6; Crenshaw, *Defending God: Biblical Responses to the Problem of Evil* (Oxford: Oxford University Press, 2005).

85. See Matitiahu Tsevat, "The Meaning of the Book of Job," in *The Meaning of the Book of Job and the Biblical Studies: Essays on the Literature and Religion of the Hebrew Bible* (New York: KTAV, 1980), 1–37, especially 36; repr. from *HUCA* 37 (1966): 73–106.

the retribution principle. However, in the case of Job the basic mistake of the three friends is to work the principle backward: suffering, interpreted as punishment, is seen to point back to sinfulness. Job is suffering; therefore he must be experiencing the judgmental face of Yahweh, which is God's punishment. As noted previously, in terms of traditional logic this constitutes the fallacy of affirming the consequence. It is true that God does reward the faithful and does punish the disobedient. However, one cannot reason backward and conclude that in every case suffering is a sign of wrongdoing on the part of the sufferer; prosperity is a sign of virtuous action. This is a fundamental logical mistake of the three friends in their arguments (also in Elihu's, and in Job's sometimes). But the reader is informed at the outset of the narrative that there is another reason for Job's suffering, namely that the satan has called upon God to prove that Job is truly a righteous man, and that he is not merely being righteous because he has been blessed. The reader recognizes at the outset that it is this simple mechanical view of divine justice that is on trial. Job and his friends, including Job's wife and Elihu, view death as part of this principle. Moreover, they try to make it understandable in the "here and now." Thus, their understanding of death is under the influence of the retribution theology.

The Retribution Principle as a Key to Understanding Job. Though many scholars have noticed the doctrine of divine retribution in the book of Job,[86] only a few scholars view it as a device for interpreting the purpose and message of the book of Job. Gregory W. Parsons, for instance, employs three key themes – the dogma of divine retribution, the creation motif, and legal metaphors, as a guide to understand the development of the purpose of the book (i.e. to show the proper relationship between God and man).[87] Parsons proposes that the purpose of Job is "the refutation of the retribution dogma and its corollary that man's relationship to God is a business contract binding in court."[88] For Parsons, the doctrine of divine retribution is the

---

86. For example, Crenshaw, *Theodicy*; Crenshaw, *Defending God*; Murphy, *The Book of Job*, 122–124; Balentine, *Job*, 108–109; Clines, *Job 1–20*, xlvi–xlvii; Leo G. Perdue and W. Clark Gilpin, "Introduction," in *The Voice from the Whirlwind: Interpreting the Book of Job*, eds. Leo G. Perdue and W. Clark Gilpin (Nashville: Abingdon, 1992),11–18, especially 15; etc.

87. Gregory W. Parsons, "The Structure and Purpose of the Book of Job," in *Sitting with Job: Selected Studies on the Book of Job*, ed. Roy B. Zuck (Grand Rapids: Baker, 1992), 17–33.

88. Parsons, "Structure," 23.

most important theme in the book of Job. Likewise, Matitiahu Tsevat uses an equilateral triangle to explain the central idea in the book of Job, which rests on three elements: God (G), Job as the upright man (J), and Retribution (R).[89] Tsevat observes that

> it is the purpose of the book to demonstrate the impossibility of the coexistence of these three ideas and the consequent logical necessity to give up one of them. The friends cancel J, maintaining G and R. God eliminates R, maintaining G and J. Job all but gives up G, as he maintains J and R . . . He [Job] maintained J and R and despaired of, yet did not surrender, G. At times observation of reality led him nonetheless to the conclusion that R was wrong, i.e. that the world is not governed by justice . . . he [Job] could only conceive of the dichotomy justice/injustice.[90]

Tsevat is right in viewing these three ideas (G, J, and R) as explaining the narrative flow of the book.[91] However, his concluding statement that "he [God] who speaks to man in the book of Job is neither a just or an unjust god but God"[92] is not clear. Tsevat proposes that God reveals to Job the dichotomy between justice-injustice and nonjustice, when he states,

> as Job could only conceive of the dichotomy justice/injustice, until God showed him that this dichotomy is not adequate for the structuring of reality, for it lacks the third required element: nonjustice. These three elements should indeed be grouped in a dichotomy, but in the form: justice-injustice/ nonjustice.

According to Tsevat, only by eliminating the traditional dogma of divine retribution was it possible to reconcile Job's innocence with God's permitting

---

89. Matitiahu Tsevat, "The Meaning of the Book of Job," in *Sitting with Job: Selected Studies on the Book of Job*, ed. Roy B. Zuck (Grand Rapids: Baker, 1992), 189–218.

90. Tsevat, "Book of Job," *Sitting*, 217–218.

91. Tsevat aims to present that the problem of the innocent's suffering starts at the beginning (i.e. the prologue) of the book. For the answer of the problem, it is neither in the middle of the book (e.g. in chs. 19 or 28) nor in the speeches of Elihu, as proposed by some scholars; rather it is found at the end of the book (i.e. 38:1–42:6, God's speeches and Job's response). The retribution principle functions as the book's total conceptual content in understanding the problem and the answer the book of Job posed to the reader.

92. Tsevat, 218.

him to suffer.⁹³ However, his idea about God is not complete, for it does not explain the nature of God's "nonjustice" and how it reflects the proper relationship between God and man. Correspondingly, in as much as the ambiguousness of the term "nonjustice" may carry, death may be viewed as under a capricious or arbitrary God. In sum, Tsevat fails to see that it is not "justice" per se that is the issue, but the retribution principle as an adequate way of understanding God's justice. His point, that God transcends the retribution principle, is exactly correct. But beyond that, through Job's struggle the narrative of the book of Job invites us to join God in moving beyond the retribution principle as the basis for understanding both human suffering and death and the relationship between God and man. As the narrative of Job makes clear, the retribution principle fails because (1) man does not know all that God knows, (2) God's מִשְׁפָּט integrates not only the ideas of human jurisprudence, but also divine sovereignty,⁹⁴ and (3) consequently, God remains free to have mercy on whom he would have mercy and to have compassion on whom he would have compassion.

Contrary to Tsevat, S. Fischer provides a more informative evaluation of retributive concepts in the book of Job.⁹⁵ Fischer agrees with Tsevat's viewing that Job gradually abandons the retributive concept during the discourse and finally denies it entirely. Job has come to realize that the time and way of death is not in accordance to a retributive concept (Job 24:1, 12). God executes death in a mysterious way (Job 21:22–26).⁹⁶ Job, therefore, turns to God and doubts retribution. However, Fischer proposes a new equilateral triangle explaining that Job replaces the retribution element with faith; thus the new three elements are: God, Job, and Faith. Therefore, Job is not anymore looking for a retributive reward. What Job gets in the end "is not a

---

93. Cf. the same conclusion in Parsons, "Structure," 18.
94. See the two-dimension meaning of the word מִשְׁפָּט ("justice," e.g. in Job 40:8) in Sylvia Huberman Scholnick, "The Meaning of מִשְׁפָּט (Justice) in the Book of Job," in *Sitting with Job: Selected Studies on the Book of Job*, ed. Roy B. Zuck (Grand Rapids: Baker, 1992), 349–358.
95. S. Fischer, "How God Pays Back: Retributive Concepts in the Book of Job," *AcT* 20 (2000): 26–41. See also W. Edward Glenny, "How Well Do You Know God? The Dangers of "Retribution Principle," *Searching Together* 23 (1995): 13–17.
96. Fischer, "How God Pays Back," 37.

retributive payment but a free gift of God, who is above all system."[97] Thus, God is the Sovereign who is above all principles.

At the end of the book, the two speeches of Yahweh bring hope to Job in his suffering by revealing that God is not subject to human reason, and that God's will and acts cannot be explained on the basis of the retribution principle or any other principle. God's justice transcends our ability to understand his actions in this world. Suffering and death are not merely explained as the natural consequences of the retribution principle, but find their meaning only in Job's encounter with the self-revealing God. The two speeches of Yahweh invite Job to realize his own limited knowledge of things in this world (42:3b). They illustrate not only that man cannot know all of the ways that God works, but also that the full knowledge of God and his ways remain a mystery to human reason (cf. Exod 33:19). There is a limit to man's knowledge. Many things including suffering and death are mysterious in the hand of God. Eventually, Job not only moves beyond the retribution principle but comes to realize that his attitude toward divine retribution is wrong. The revelation from God provides Job a new understanding that God is free and not bound by the retribution principle. While still in the face of what seems to be unmerited, unfair suffering and death Job can nonetheless behold the gracious face of God and hope in God's love, goodness, and mercy. His final appropriate response is to simply trust in Yahweh. Death, which is concerned and threatening at the beginning of the book, now has become a secondary, unimportant thought. Job finally "dies, an old man, and full of days." His death is natural and peaceful in the hand of God, fulfilling his shalomic life.

In summary the shifting perspective on concept of death in the book of Job reflects Job's own struggle to understand his relationship with God in terms of the theory of divine justice offered by the retribution principle. The Joban author employs the dogma of retribution as a device to serve the

---

97. Fischer, 35–39. See also Henry L. Rowold, "The Theology of Creation in the Yahweh Speeches as a Solution to the Problem Posed by the Book of Job" (ThD diss., Concordia Seminary in Exile, 1977), 20, 29. Rowold notes that as the main problem of the book (i.e. the relationship between God and man) is posed before suffering enters the scene and is solved before the suffering is removed, Job's restoration is not a reward or payment in the retribution principle, but "a free gift, accepted freely." This is because "Yahweh's greatest gift had already been given, his fellowship, which had given Job a resolution already while still in the midst of his suffering" (29, n. 22).

purpose of the book and to articulate its argument in the narrative flow of the book. The answer of the problem posed by the Joban author is found in the divine speeches at the end of the book. The divine speeches do not illustrate God's effort to sustain justice in creation, in spite of the presence of chaos and evil; instead, they illustrate that the two faces of God are not merely the natural outcomes of the moral calculus of the retribution principle. By affirming the mystery of God and his ways, they implicitly reject the validity of the theology of God's justice inherent in the theology of retribution. Job's view of death is dramatically and radically changed to what we have at the end of the book. The rejection of the retribution principle allows Job to behold the gracious face of God. Job is called to simply trust in God's mercy, in his graciousness and compassion, even in the face of undeserved suffering and imminent death. From this perspective, though it is mysterious, death has become a secondary subject to God and is in the hand of Yahweh. Trust in the graciousness of God rather than a comprehension of the nature of divine justice becomes the basis on which Job can live in confidence and die in peace before God.

The Research in the Context of Current Scholarship

The purposes of the current book put some limitations on the scope and focus of this study. It is a study of how Job's thinking about death reflects his struggle and his encounter with God in the narrative flow of the book of Job.[98] Therefore, it will not presume to explicate the concept of death

---

98. A discussion of many wider perspectives on life and death in the Old Testament or even in the wisdom literature lies outside the scope of the study. It is generally recognized that life and death in the Old Testament are viewed not from a physiological, nor biological, nor pathological interest. For further study see, for example, Robert Martin-Achard, *From Death to Life* (Edinburgh; London: Oliver & Boyd, 1960); Alexander Heidel, "Death and the after Life," in *The Gilgamesh Epic and Old Testament Parallels* (Chicago: University of Chicago Press, 1963), 137–223; Bruce Vawter, "Intimations of Immortality and the Old Testament," *JBL* 91 (1972): 158–171; John Barclay Burns, "The Mythology of Death and the Old Testament," *SJT* 26 (1973): 327–340; Hans Walter Wolff, *Anthropology of the Old Testament* (London: SCM Press, 1974); John Joseph Collins, "The Root of Immortality: Death in the Context of Jewish Wisdom," *HTR* 71 (1978): 177–192; Hartmut Gese, "Death in the Old Testament," in *Essays on Biblical Theology*, trans. Keith Crim (Minneapolis: Augsburg, 1981), 34–59; Lloyd R. Bailey, *Biblical Perspective on Death*, OBT (Philadelphia: Fortress, 1983); K. Richards, "Death," *ABD* 2:108–110; etc.

throughout the entire Old Testament or to cover all the related texts in the Hebrew Bible where God is viewed as hostile.[99] But the study will relate Job to other Old Testament texts in a limited way to clarify commonalities and distinctiveness where appropriate. Hence, the focus of the study is limited to the Hebrew text of the book of Job.

This book is not a comparative study of Israelite and ancient Near Eastern religious conceptions. As already mentioned, there is a tendency of reading the Old Testament from an ancient Near Eastern mythological perspective; that is, reading for a "dualistic" interpretation (e.g. God and evil, etc.) of the biblical texts. Therefore, the study will deal cautiously with the ancient Near Eastern texts to the extent necessary to demonstrate how Job's understandings of death differ from their ancient Near Eastern context. It is the conviction of the present author that Job must first be read within its own context in the Hebrew Bible. Next is to evaluate its precise meaning in the book of Job – where it belongs. Then, a meaningful comparison will be considered within the intertextual support first, and the extra-biblical evidence last.[100]

The survey of the above scholarship has shown that the issue of the development of Job's understanding of life and death has seldom been treated as a separate subject matter. In particular, little attention has been given contextually to the aspect of death in the book of Job, particularly in treating it according to its own literary nature and as it unfolds through its narrative flow. As a result of his encounter with God at the end of the book, Job's understanding of suffering, his struggle to understand God, his view of God's justice, and his understanding of death have been changed radically. Therefore, the study will fill the gaps left by previous research by examining the following questions: How does Job's reflection on death relate to his concept of God and man's relation to him? How does the concept of death as given in the book of Job relate to the understanding of death that emerges from the literature of the Old Testament read within its own theological

---

99. Cf. Ingvar Floysvik, *When God Becomes My Enemy: The Theology of the Complaint Psalms* (St. Louis: Concordia Academic Press, 1997).

100. There are many books that are helpful for a comparative study. For example: Heidel, *The Gilgamesh Epic and Old Testament Parallels*; Bailey, *Biblical Perspective on Death*; Foster McCurley, *Ancient Myths and Biblical Faith: Scriptural Transformations* (Philadelphia: Fortress, 1983); John Day, *Yahweh and the Gods and Goddesses of Canaan* JSOTSup 265 (Sheffield: Sheffield Academic Press, 2000); etc.

context? What role does death play in the development of the overall theme of the book of Job? How should the reader understand Job's death wishes which appear throughout the story? By exploring these questions, this study will argue for the following interpretation of how Job's views of suffering and death relate to the understanding of his relationship with God that emerges from Job's struggle.

As has been noted above, the purpose of the book of Job is to show the proper relationship between God and man, and not, as is sometimes suggested, between God and Satan. The evaluation of the theology of retribution as a basis for understanding divine justice and human suffering, which permeates the book, is the key concept employed by the Joban author to serve the purpose of the book and to assist in developing its argument. Thus, the book will propose that what the book says about death must be understood in the light of the God-man relation that emerges from the book's re-evaluation of the theology of retribution. In addition, the problem of death in Job involves not only moving beyond the theology of God's justice, which seeks to constrain God within the limits of human reason, but also replacing this principle with trust in the graciousness of God, who is free and not constrained by human logic.

Job's struggles with death reflect how the character Job encounters the two faces of Yahweh.[101] Job's response to the friends is rooted in the theology of retribution. In light of this theology God is encountered as either punishing or rewarding, based on the unrighteousness or righteousness of the person. These faces are a projection of the human expectations of God, predictable based on the understanding of God's justice, rooted in the theology of retribution. This is God as known to the friends (including Elihu) and Job himself during the discourse with them. The friends assert that everyone, Job included, can know how a man encounters God: if a man is good, he is rewarded; if not, he will be punished.[102] While the friends see God's treatment of Job in light of this belief as just, Job knows that as unjust, for Job does not

---

101. For the useful article concerning the two faces of God, see Paul R. Raabe, "The Two 'Faces' of Yahweh: Divine Wrath and Mercy in the Old Testament," in *And Every Tongue Confess: Essays in Honor of Norman Nagel*, eds. Gerald S. Krispin and Jon D. Vieker (Dearborn, MI: Nagel Festschrift Committee, 1990), 283–310.

102. For instance, Eliphaz in 4:7–11; 15; Bildad in 8:4; 18:5; Zophar in 11:20; and Elihu in 36:8–12.

receive what he ought to receive based on the retribution principle;[103] the suffering of a righteous man is not in accord with the principle. Job knows that he is not sinful, and yet he is still experiencing the judgmental face of God. So while the friends affirm the punishing/rewarding faces of God promoted by the theology of retribution, Job rejects them. But in denying the retribution principle, Job is left with an evil, arbitrary, and capricious face of God. Therefore, this face of God that Job is experiencing is different from the one that the friends are seeing.

The second, gracious, face of Yahweh is the revealed face.[104] It is hidden from man's reason. Job cannot figure it out on his own. It is knowable only to the extent that God himself reveals to a man. God reveals about himself that he is gracious, that he has compassion and mercy upon those who do not deserve it. The theology of justice with which the friends are working cannot explain this gracious face of God, for it reduces God's mercy to a reward for good behavior. It regards the positive face of God to be as predictable as his negative face, and by so doing eliminates any notion of these grace or mercy. The true gracious face of God is hidden and is beyond the retribution principle. At the end, it is mercy and not justice that God gives to Job.

Job's encounter with these two faces of Yahweh reflect his struggle to understand the relationship between divine justice (as understood according to the retribution principle), and true divine mercy. The explanation of suffering and death offered by the retribution principle is a fundamental problem. That is the crux in Job's understanding in his relationship with God. Consequently, his understanding about death is tied up with both his understanding of the nature of human suffering and his understanding of God's nature. The retribution principle does explain the problem of suffering, but at the same time, it allows us to be able to control God, or, at least, to predict what God is going to do (i.e. if you do good, God will reward

---

103. For example, in Job 29 Job pictures his previous condition and prosperity. He wishes that "I [Job] were as in the months of old, as in the days when God watched over me" (29:2). Job continues to wish that "I shall die in my nest, and I shall multiply my days as the sand" (29:18). Thus, the concept of death in his understanding here seems to be a happy death, fulfilling his long life, under God's "gracious" face in the theology of God's justice. Cf. also Job 14:13, where Job wishes to take a refuge in Sheol, a hiding place from God "wrathful" face.

104. This revealed face appears not in the prologue, but at the end of the book in the two speeches of Yahweh.

you; if not, God will punish you according to your deed). The retribution principle provides psychological security for the believer at the cost of limiting God's freedom. While the friends strongly affirm this explanation, Job rejects it and struggles against its concept of divine justice. But in rejecting it Job is left facing a God who is both fearful and evil, who causes arbitrary suffering even for the righteous. However, this is a face of God that Job fears, but does not actually encounter.

Eventually, God does reveal himself to Job. God comes to Job with marvelous revelations in the two speeches of Yahweh and yet comes only in the storm. To encounter the hidden, but gracious, face of God, Job must give up the false security offered by the retribution principle and learn to accept suffering and death with a trust in Yahweh that transcends the limits of human understanding, and affirms the justness of God even when he appears unjust, as measured by the retribution principle. Suffering and death are a problem when viewed from the perspective of human reason. The only resolution of this problem is to trust in the love and grace of Yahweh, and consequently to move beyond the retribution principle. As the book unfolds, Job comes to reject the desire to explain God's action, and embraces the fear of Yahweh which is the beginning of wisdom (a central tenet of the Israelite wisdom tradition). Job comes to understand his relationship with God as a creature, and to know that his limitations as a creature prevent him from questioning God. At the end of the book, what Job is called to do is to put trust in God's mercy, in his graciousness and compassion, even while experiencing unfair and unmerited suffering and death. What Job thinks about suffering, death, and about God are all changed in the end. Job comes to accept whatever comes from God.

In summary, by reading Job as literature on its own terms, Job's complex and sometimes apparently conflicting statements about death and the tension inherent in Job's expectation of God are seen as connected to his struggle to understand the nature of divine justice and the character of God that the theology of retribution, promoted by his friends, forces upon him. The bankruptcy of the theology of retribution has led Job to demand the encounter even with an arbitrary and cruel God. In the end Job encounters the hidden/gracious face of God, and moves beyond retribution theology by putting his trust in the grace of God. This literary approach allows us to read Job contextually. Thus, we will see that nowhere in the book does Job view death as an independent competing power or god. Rather he views death as an element of life either directly or indirectly under the control of Yahweh. In addition, the doctrine of the retribution principle, portrayed by the Joban author, is an inadequate way to understand the relationship between God and man. God is the Sovereign who is free and above all human thought. Death, as well as life, is still mysterious in the hand of Yahweh; but in the face of God's graciousness, it is no longer something to be afraid of, but just to be accepted and faced in the peace that comes from faith in a merciful God. With this literary treatment of Job, this book will contribute to the contextual understanding of death in the book of Job, specifically the call to trust in Yahweh's graciousness, even when evidence, according to the theology of retribution, is against it. This will be a new contribution to the scholarly works of the area.

The Methodological Procedure to Be Employed

The focus of the study is the problem of death in the narrative flow of Job as connected to the theology of the retribution principle and the hidden God and resolved by moving beyond the retribution principle with trust in the graciousness of Yahweh. Three main assumptions are necessary for the study of death in the book of Job.

First is the assumption that the fundamental message of the book of Job is the proper relationship between God and man. Many scholars have identified the issue of the book in different ways. This is because the book of Job presents many sub-themes (e.g. the innocent suffering, the right behavior in suffering, the meaning of faith, the theodicy, the refutation of the retribution principle, the legal metaphor, the creation motif, etc.) which are integral to the book. These sub-themes have been identified by various scholars as the main theme of the book. While these various identifications of the book have suggested a meaningful integrality of the book, the present author would understand that the central message of the book is the problem of relationship between God and man. Job's suffering is a sub-theme under this relationship. Others who have recognized this relation as a fundamental problem of the book include Habel, for instance, who states, "Central to the book of Job is the conflict between God and Job, between the integrity of the Creator and the integrity of a particular mortal."[105] There is also John W. Wevers, who thinks "The basic problem of Job . . . is *the relation of finite man to an infinite God.*"[106] Robert W. E. Forrest says, "what, if any, is the nature of the divine-human relationship and how may a man live in this universe."[107] Parsons also views that the purpose of the book is "*to show that the proper relationship between God and man is based on the sovereign grace of God and man's response of faith and submissive trust.*"[108] In addition, Rowold, in his dissertation, provides some examples of scholars who have held to various options as the main theme of the book of Job.[109] He notes that these various sub-themes have hindered the recognition of the real central problem – the relationship between God and man.[110]

Second, the central question of the book is whether the concept of divine justice expressed in the retribution principle is an adequate way to understand the relationship between God and man. It is established implicitly in the prologue of the book. It is developed further by the dialogues and resolved at the end of the book. The question of death in the book is related to a bigger question (i.e. the relationship between God and man). Job's understanding of death grows out of his struggle to understand whether the divine retribution is right or wrong in his case. If it is right, Job must have sinned and is under God's punishment, and therefore, Job must either escape death or see death as a punishment because he has done something wrong that he does not understand. But if the retribution principle is wrong, then despite of the suffering and imminent death Job can look at death and find peace in it, and see in it rest and peace. The fact that he is suffering in this life, and the fact that he will eventually die, is not evidence of God's wrath and judgment upon him. But it is related to the relationship between him

---

105. Habel, *Book of Job*, 60.

106. John W. Wevers, *The Way of the Righteous: Psalms and the Books of Wisdom* (Philadelphia: Westminster, 1961), 75. Italics original.

107. Robert William Edward Forrest, "The Creation Motif in the Book of Job" (PhD diss., McMaster University, 1975), 20.

108. Parsons, "The Structure and Purpose," 22, 33. Italics original.

109. See Rowold, "Theology of Creation," 11, 18–19.

110. Rowold, 11, 18–19. In his dissertation, Rowold argues that the problem raised by the book of Job (i.e. the relationship between God and man) is answered by the theology of creation in the two speeches of Yahweh. Rowold, 2.

and God. The book of Job, viewed as a whole, reflects the question or the reality of the holistic view of life in the retribution principle. Thus, the study will examine how this theology shapes the thinking of the friends and sometimes of Job himself, what is its conclusion, application, and its limitation. This will be used as a background for the understanding of the concept of divine retribution in this life, how this concept has an impact on Job's views of death, and to see how it is misused or misapplied in the book of Job.

The third methodological assumption of the book is that there is a literary coherence to the book, and that recognizing this coherence is necessary to resolve its problems. As the study presumes a world in which Job is a believer in Yahweh, this world behind the text of Job is informed by biblical understandings of God and his relationship to man.[111] Thus, reading Job within its own world is appropriate in interpreting it. This presupposition is in contrast to those who rely heavily on Ugaritic material, with the presuppositions of the Ugaritic/Canaanite world in understanding the text of Job. Moreover, as already mentioned, the main message of the book concerns the relationship between God and man, not, as is sometimes suggested, God and Satan. Therefore, what it says about death must be understood in the light of this relationship between God and man.[112] With these assumptions in mind, it is appropriate for the book to approach the concept of death in the Hebrew text of Job with a literary reading and by following the narrative flow of the book of Job.

The prologue (Job 1–2) and Job's opening lament (Job 3) will be investigated in chapter 2 of this study. This chapter will present the Joban author's intention to present the clash of two truths: the truly divine truth in the

---

111. In Job 1:1, Job is introduced as "a man in the land of Uz." The name Uz signifies that the land is not in Israel. However, it does not mean that Job necessarily is a foreigner. The patriarchs themselves – if that is the time the story is set – were almost as often to be found outside the land as within it. The author of the book simply does not say whether or not Job is an Israelite. Although the author leaves the question of Job's nationality, he does present Job as a model of a righteous wise man who epitomizes the advice of the Israelite sage (Prov 3:7; 14:16; Job 1:1; 28:28; cf. Clines, *Job*, 10; Habel, *Book of Job*, 86–87).

112. Concerning this theological problem, one may see the relationship between the book of Job, some lament psalms in the Psalter, the book of Lamentations, and several complaints in the book of Jeremiah. However, in this book, the study will deal with this problem only within the book of Job. Cf. Claus Westerrmann, *The Structure of the Book of Job: A Form-Critical Analysis* (Philadelphia: Fortress, 1977), 2, who proposes that the lament dominates the book of Job, which treats an existential question fundamentally.

heavenly court and the false truth of divine retribution in the land of Uz. The Joban author masterfully establishes the plot in the very beginning of the story of Job. In order to destroy the false truth of the retribution principle and to establish the truly divine truth in the land of Uz, the Joban author offers some clues for the reader to investigate through the responses of the character Job. The chapter will summarize also how the prologue functions literarily as the vital background of the book as a whole. Structurally, the reader will see how Job's two responses at the end of the book correspond to his first two responses in the prologue.

Chapter 3 of this book will examine how the problem of death and the influence of the retribution principle are presented in the dialogue section of the book. Thus, the three friends' views of death (4:6–11; 5:8, 26–27; 15) and Job's various concepts of death (1–2; 3:17–23; 6:8–10; 7; 10:18–22; 13:13–16; 14:7–15, 18; 16:18–22; 17: 8–9, 11–16; 19:23–27; 29–31; 42:5–6) will receive attention. In addition, as Elihu has the same basic idea of death and the retribution principle as the three friends, Elihu's idea of death (33:15–30; 34:11) will be included in this chapter. This chapter will demonstrate in particular the connection between the two faces of Yahweh and the understanding of death in the book of Job. The treatment of all these passages will focus on what each contributes to the development of Job's view of death and will refrain from treating exegetical issues that are unrelated to this question.

Next, chapter 4 will examine the perspective of death in the two speeches of Yahweh (38:16–18; 39; 40:15–24; 40:25–41:26 [41:1–34]), Job's two responses (40:4–5; 42:4–6), and the idea of death in the epilogue of Job (42:7–17).[113] This chapter will show how the view of death from Yahweh's perspective is absolutely different from that of the human beings in chapter 3. Structurally, the resolution of Job's problem, including his view of death, is profoundly met in the two speeches of Yahweh. Theologically, his view of death is radically changed by Yahweh's speeches to what we have at the end of the book. The reader will see that the truly divine truth is known

---

113. Note that the book will adopt a Standard English translation (i.e. ESV) and use it, except where the study needs to commend on it. The study will deal with these passages and do detailed exegetical treatment of those issues that affect Job's thinking about death and the two faces of Yahweh; otherwise the study will either adopt a standard translation version or treat other issues in a more cursory manner.

only through acceptance of the mystery of God's grace. The two speeches of Yahweh invite both Job and the reader to move beyond the retribution principle and to simply trust in the gracious, but hidden, God.

The last chapter, chapter 5, will demonstrate that Job's own expressions about death are related to his struggle to understand the two faces of Yahweh in terms of the retribution principle and in his recognition of the loving but hidden God in the two speeches of Yahweh. Thus, the study will summarize through the narrative flow of the book that Job does not easily come to understand the fallacy of the friends' theology of God's justice. Job, a normal man but a man of faith, does not come to understand its fallacy through the horrible experience of his suffering, but only by the revelation that comes from Yahweh. Only by trusting in the mercy of God who reveals himself through his speeches does Job come to transcend the retribution principle and learn to be at peace with the possibility of death. Job steps beyond the divine retribution and understands that not all suffering is a result of an encounter with the judgmental face of Yahweh, and death is not always to be understood as the ultimate recompense, nor the ultimate will of God. As the narrative of Job gradually unfolds, the reader will see the shift from the understanding of one's relationship with God in terms of the retribution principle to the understanding of one's relationship with God in terms of faith. Some theological reflections will be offered as well.

The purpose of the book is to show that what Job says about death must be understood within the framework of the book itself and in its context of the Hebrew Scriptures, and must not be imposed upon it from outside.[114] Thus, this approach of the text of Job will provide a better explanation of what the book says about death than a mythological approach, for it provides a more coherent reading of the book. While the mythological approach depends on reading between the lines of the texts and on a different conceptual context, the literary approach will yield an interpretation which flows from what the text itself says. Along with a better explanation, the study will

---

114. It is true that Job uses mythic language. However, the simple fact of using mythic language does not mean that the book has all the same mythological idea associated with that language. The book of Job has its own unique and specific context within the Hebrew Bible, specifically within the Israelite wisdom literature. It is in this context and this kind of literature that the book of Job must be read and understood, not in a broader ancient Near Eastern context, especially in a mythological context.

demonstrate the falseness of those scholars who want to over-emphasize the ancient Near Eastern aspect in the text of Job. The literary reading offers a competent reading allowing the reader to understand death as part of the elements of life and under the lordship of Yahweh. Death, therefore, is not a competing force(s) and must be viewed as being under the relationship between God and man.

CHAPTER 2

Views of Death and the Retribution Principle in the Prologue and in Job's First Lament

The concept of life and death in the case of character Job bracketed in the retribution principle will be explained here (Job 1–2). It will provide also the literary irony that suffering and death is not a punishment from the wrathful God, but God's pride and his will to testify Job's integrity. Next, Job's view of death in his first lament (Job 3), which stands in contrast to those in the prologue, will be examined. This will include the exposition of a transitional stage of Job's view of death from accepting death to questioning it.

The Prologue (Job 1–2)

The book of Job is composed of two main parts, the prose and the poetic sections. The poetic sections are framed with the prosaic prologue and epilogue. The prologue opens the narrative story of Job by introducing the main characters, the conflict, and the setting of the story. The six scenes of the prologue succeed in setting the dramatic story in which themes and motifs will develop and proceed in the following sections of the book.[1]

Scene 1   1:1–5   Job's way of life and his fortune
Scene 2   1:6–12   God's first dialogue with the satan about Job
Scene 3   1:13–22   Job in the first phase of his trial

---

1. A thorough investigation of the text of Job 1–2 can be found in Meir Weiss, *The Story of Job's Beginning: Job 1–2: A Literary Analysis* (Jerusalem: Magnes, 1983).

Scene 4	2:1–7a	God's second dialogue with the satan about Job
Scene 5	2:7b–10	Job in the second phase of his trial
Scene 6	2:11–13	The three friends come to "console and comfort" Job

From the setting of the story there are more scenes taking place on earth than in heaven. Weiss suggests that the concern of the story is to primarily present events here on earth rather than those in heaven.[2] God is the protagonist in heaven and Job is the protagonist on earth. Both God and Job are present in all scenes, even though they may not appear or speak; their presence is assumed through mentioning and reference. It is this relationship between the two protagonists, God and Job, which the prologue concerns and does the rest of the book.[3] The plot is relatively simple: Job, a wealthy and righteous man, becomes a focus of a disagreement between Yahweh and a heavenly subordinate, the accuser (i.e. the satan), over the real basis for Job's loyalty to God. Yahweh, then, agrees to subject Job to a horrendous test to see if Job will curse Yahweh when all the blessings are taken away. Note that the horrendous degree of suffering raises the implicit question or at least causes Job, his wife, and his friends (including the reader) to wonder whether God is cruel. This question is reflected explicitly in the dialogue section of the book. For Job, if he did not sin, then God must be cruel. For the friends, it leads to the accusation that Job has sinned because God could not be cruel according to the divine justice.

Scene 1

The story of Job is located in the land of Uz.[4] The Joban author skillfully and masterfully describes Job's full life within the first five verses of the story (1:1–5):

---

2. Weiss, *Story of Job's Beginning*, 43, also proposes that the juxtaposition of these two worlds (i.e. the land of Uz below, where Job lives, and the heavens above, where God dwells) is intentionally to show the absolutely different truth between these two worlds: the false worldview of wisdom in the land of Uz and divine truth in the heavens.

3. Also Weiss, 16.

4. The Joban author specifically locates the story in אֶרֶץ עוּץ ("the land of Uz"). Weiss insightfully points out that the sound of this place name עוּץ resembles the word עֵצָה

There was a man in the land of Uz whose name was Job. That man was blameless and upright, one who feared God and turned away from evil.	1:1	אִישׁ הָיָה בְאֶרֶץ־עוּץ אִיּוֹב שְׁמוֹ וְהָיָה הָאִישׁ הַהוּא תָּם וְיָשָׁר וִירֵא אֱלֹהִים וְסָר מֵרָע:
There were born to him seven sons and three daughters.	1:2	וַיִּוָּלְדוּ לוֹ שִׁבְעָה בָנִים וְשָׁלוֹשׁ בָּנוֹת:
He possessed 7,000 sheep, 3,000 camels, 500 yoke of oxen, and 500 female donkeys, and very many servants, so that this man was the greatest of all the people of the east.	1:3	וַיְהִי מִקְנֵהוּ שִׁבְעַת אַלְפֵי־צֹאן וּשְׁלֹשֶׁת אַלְפֵי גְמַלִּים וַחֲמֵשׁ מֵאוֹת צֶמֶד־בָּקָר וַחֲמֵשׁ מֵאוֹת אֲתוֹנוֹת וַעֲבֻדָּה רַבָּה מְאֹד וַיְהִי הָאִישׁ הַהוּא גָּדוֹל מִכָּל־בְּנֵי־קֶדֶם:
His sons used to go and hold a feast in the house of each one on his day, and they would send and invite their three sisters to eat and drink with them.	1:4	וְהָלְכוּ בָנָיו וְעָשׂוּ מִשְׁתֶּה בֵּית אִישׁ יוֹמוֹ וְשָׁלְחוּ וְקָרְאוּ לִשְׁלֹשֶׁת אַחְיֹתֵיהֶם לֶאֱכֹל וְלִשְׁתּוֹת עִמָּהֶם:
And when the days of the feast had run their course, Job would send and consecrate them, and he would rise early in the morning and offer burnt offerings according to the number of them all; For Job said, "It may be that my children have sinned, and curse[5] God in their hearts." Thus Job did continually.	1:5	וַיְהִי כִּי הִקִּיפוּ יְמֵי הַמִּשְׁתֶּה וַיִּשְׁלַח אִיּוֹב וַיְקַדְּשֵׁם וְהִשְׁכִּים בַּבֹּקֶר וְהֶעֱלָה עֹלוֹת מִסְפַּר כֻּלָּם כִּי אָמַר אִיּוֹב אוּלַי חָטְאוּ בָנַי וּבֵרֲכוּ אֱלֹהִים בִּלְבָבָם כָּכָה יַעֲשֶׂה אִיּוֹב כָּל־הַיָּמִים:

("counsel"), a leading concept in the Wisdom literature (*Story of Job's Beginning*, 23; also Crenshaw, *Defending God*, 216, n. 37).

5. The Hebrew word here is ברך ("to bless"). See the explanation in the following section.

The narrator depicts Job as the epitome of the whole man, possessing a great number of animals, a full and vivacious household (ten children).[6] He is characterized as "blameless and upright" (תָּם וְיָשָׁר)[7] and he "feared God and turned away from evil" (וִירֵא אֱלֹהִים וְסָר מֵרָע) (1:1). This valuation is certified by his regular offering of sacrifices simply in the odd chance (אוּלַי) that his children may have sinned against God "in their hearts" (בִּלְבָבָם) (1:5). Job's way of life is depicted as the life of perfect righteousness. His fortune is perfect bliss. The description of Job's full life here is presented in Hebrew through the use of a modal nuance of a *waw consecutive*, indicating a casual relationship in which Job's character (v. 1) is the precondition of his wealth in descendants (v. 2) and possessions (v. 3). Thus, the text in verses 2 and 3 should read: "*and so* there were born to him;" "*and so* he possessed seven thousand sheep . . ."[8]

The idea of this sort of description is simply the concept of *do ut des* ("I give in order to receive"). The narrator portrays a divine blessing as the image of the righteous man blessed by God. God shows his gracious face upon those who "fear him and turn away from evil." This kind of blessing reflects also in the accuser's response to God (1:9–11). The description intentionally establishes the views of the relationship between God and man implicit in the retribution principle, an oversimplification of the Deuteronomistic theology.[9] Job's reputation as "the greatest man among all the people of the

---

6. The numbers used in the narrative obviously present the notion of completeness: seven sons and three daughters, 7,000 sheep and 3,000 camels, 500 yoke of oxen and 500 female donkeys (1:2–3); seven days and seven nights (2:13); seven uses of the Hebrew verb "bless" (in the prose frame); and seven bulls and seven rams (42:8). These numbers are telling the reader that Job's blessing is a perfect blessing. Notice also the four disasters (1:14–19) which correspond to the four reports (1:15, 16, 17, 19).

7. See Klaus Koch, "תמם *tmm* to be complete," *TLOT* 3:1424–1428. Koch notes an interesting observation that "only in Job and Ps 37:37 does תָּם approach תָּמִים and become synonymous with יָשָׁר (Job 1:1, 8; 2:3) and antonymous to 'qš 'to pervert.'" Here the word תָּם ("blameless") points to Job's character, the term יָשָׁר ("upright") to his actions.

8. This is what Paul Joüon calls a "*energic et*" waw (*Grammar of Biblical Hebrew*; § 115, 379). See also Clines, *Job 1–20*, 13; Balentine, *Job*, 47; Newsom, *The Book of Job*, NIB, 345; etc.

9. Weiss, *Story of Job's Beginning*, 43, perceives the description is intentionally to show that the land of Uz stands on a false foundation of the doctrine of wisdom. However, reading Job only the first five verses does not give the reader that this description is the false doctrine conducting in the land of Uz. This understanding must be gained only after reading the prologue as a whole setting of the story together with the rest of the book, where the retribution principle is portrayed as a conceptual problem between Job and his friends.

east" (1:3) not only made Job as an epitome of a righteous man,[10] but also made God appear to be a deity who merely responds to man according to the divine mathematics of retribution.[11] This establishes the theology of retribution as the "given," the presupposition that will be put to the test as Job's story unfolds. It also becomes the conceptual problem of the rest of the book, and more importantly the conceptual problem of Job's expectation for divine justice.

This blessed life of Job as holistic and theocentric in chapter 1 is reflected elsewhere as well. In chapter 29, Job reminisces on "the months of old," he describes those days as "when his lamp shone upon my head, and by his light I walked through darkness . . . when the *Shadday* was yet with me, when my children were all around me" (29:3, 5). As a result, "I [Job] thought, 'I shall die in my nest, and I shall multiply my days as the sand'" (29:18). The perspective on life and death in Job 29, as well as in the prologue here, encompasses a right relationship with God, peace and serenity of life (e.g. the uninjured and healthy life), including an accepted and peaceful death, full of years and in the presence of family.[12]

Scene 2

Then God takes initiative, asking the satan:

> "Have you considered my servant Job, that there is none like him on the earth, a blameless and upright man, who fears God and turns away from evil?" (1:8)

---

10. Job is defined by comparison with "the people of the east," where wise men live. Thus, it is possible that this phrase may imply that it refers to wisdom (cf. וַתֵּרֶב חָכְמַת שְׁלֹמֹה מֵחָכְמַת כָּל־בְּנֵי־קֶדֶם in 1 Kgs 5:10 [Eng 4:30], "And Solomon's wisdom was greater than the wisdom of all the men of the east"). If this is implied, Job is not only honored and respected by the people of the east for his righteousness but he is wise.

11. The term "divine mathematics" is of Edouard Dhorme, *Commentary on the Book of Job*, trans. Harold Knight (Nashville, TN: Nelson, 1967), cxxxiv.

12. Interestingly, the friends similarly enunciate life of blessings that God will grant a repentant Job with security, prosperity, a full family, rescue him from (untimely and violent) death, and Job will "come to the grave in ripe old age" (5:25–26). Also Elihu speaks of a repentant sinner whom God will redeem his soul "from going down into the pit" and his life will "look upon the light" (33:28). The repentant sinners will be able to "complete their days in prosperity, and their years in pleasantness" (36:11). Thus, this view of blessed life comes along with an accepted and peaceful death. There is no idea of untimely or unfair death in this view of blessed life.

The satan does not answer God's question. But he takes up Job's characterization as one who fears God by responding God with a rhetorical question in Job 1:9, "Does Job fear Elohim for no reason?" (הַחִנָּם יָרֵא אִיּוֹב אֱלֹהִים). As its emphatic position indicates the importance assigned to it, the word חִנָּם, "for nothing/without reason," not only signals doubts about Job's integrity as an individual, but also questions a basic view of a wisdom theology which assumes an inevitable nexus between reward and righteousness. The accuser doubts not only that Job's loyalty to God is due only to all the beneficence God bestowed on him, but also that God's way of rewarding the righteous that is not right. The adversary insists that if God removes his protective hedge (שׂוּךְ, v. 10a) then Job will curse[13] him to his face (1:11; 2:5). The accuser receives permission from God to "lay hands" (שׁלח יד) on Job (1:11, 12a; 2:6), and a crescendo of suffering is inflicted on him by the Sabeans, the fire of God, the Chaldeans, and a great wind.[14]

Scene 3

Having been informed of the loss and the sudden death of his children, Job remarks,

| And he said, "Naked I came from my mother's womb, and naked shall I return there. YHWH gave, and YHWH has taken away; blessed be the name of YHWH. | 1:21 | וַיֹּאמֶר עָרֹם יָצָתִי מִבֶּטֶן אִמִּי וְעָרֹם אָשׁוּב שָׁמָּה יְהוָה נָתַן וַיהוָה לָקָח יְהִי שֵׁם יְהוָה מְבֹרָךְ׃ |

---

13. The text in 1:11 reads: וְאוּלָם שְׁלַח־נָא יָדְךָ וְגַע בְּכָל־אֲשֶׁר־לוֹ אִם־לֹא עַל־פָּנֶיךָ יְבָרֲכֶךָּ. The Hebrew verb בָּרַךְ ("to bless") is used instead of קָלַל ("to curse," which usually occurs in the Piel, קִלֵּל). It is possible that this usage is (a) a euphemism usage instead of קְלָלָה, or (b) a sarcastic use, or (c) a scribal correction (i.e *Tiqqune sopherim*, the traditional eighteen scribal changes, in which the scribes made in order to ease a reading viewed as portraying God in a too human or negative manner). The term בָּרַךְ occurs seven times in the entire book of Job. The reader must decide on the basis of context which meaning to apply in each instance. Within Job 1–2, there are six occurrences of the word בָּרַךְ (1:5, 10, 11, 21; 2:5, 9), the seventh and last appearance of the word occurs in Job 42:12, where "Yahweh בָּרַךְ the latter days of Job more than the beginning . . ." As the prologue begins with Job's full life with the ambiguous meaning of "to bless" and "to be blessed," the epilogue ends Job's story with his peaceful death as a crowning bless of his life. For further discussion on this term, see Tod Linafelt, "The Undecidability of בָּרַךְ in the Prologue to Job and Beyond," *BibInt* 4 (1996): 154–172.

14. These tragedies befall upon Job are from moral harm (i.e. Sabeans; Chaldeans), the power below, and natural harm (i.e. fire, great wind, and disease), the forces above (2:7).

In this initial reaction to the onslaught of suffering and death, Job's speaking of returning to "mother's womb" (בֶּטֶן אֵם) is not only applied to the notion of the birth of humanity from earth (Gen 3:19) but also the idea of death in the grave, Sheol (see a parallel word "there" [שָׁם]; also in 3:17, 19). The term "naked" (עָרֹם) is also used metaphorically to reflect the comparison of the property and human relationship to clothes, and the concept of exposure. Thus, Job is comparing his miserable present experience of loss as like death, for he has been stripped of all that clothes his human life.[15] In the second half of the verse, Job also reflects a sense that death is not an irrational, intruding enemy, but part of ordered, controlled, creation. "One is naked, and YHHW gives those things that clothes life; YHWH takes those things, and one returns naked to death."[16] Therefore, both life and death here are viewed as coming from God.[17] The latter, either bad or good death, is not something intruding to frustrate Yahweh's design. It comes from the hand of Yahweh himself. It is what it is. In the context of the prologue, death is submissive. Job seems to be able to acknowledge his complete dependence on Yahweh, who both gives and takes. His first response to his calamities (1:21) presents his complete trust in Yahweh. Here he is in the position of one who is in faith and simply receives whatever comes from God without questioning "why" (i.e. he does not question why God gave or why God took it away). Death seems to have been acceptable here in the sense that it is from Yahweh. Although the death of Job's children and his servants seems to be cruel and violent (1:15–17, 19), it is described in an offhanded manner.[18] Contextually, while they are introduced as they "were born" to

---

15. See Carol Newsom, *The Book of Job: A Contest*, 51–65, for moral imaginations in the prologue and the epilogue of the book of Job. Newsome points out that the use of metaphorical speech helps to construct the meaning of Job's moral imagination in the prologue. Job's words refer his horrible experience of loss to a horizon of meaning framed by birth and death.

16. Newsom, 59. Newsom also observes that "Although the text does not take direct issue with the traditional ancient Near Eastern depiction of death as the land of nothingness, the rhetoric of these sayings implicitly challenges such understandings."

17. Lloyd, *Biblical Perspectives*, 57–58, notes that "life and death are bound together as part of a singular divine will for his creatures. To accept one is to accept the other, to despise one is to despise the other." His statement is too general in the context of the prologue of the book. It is true that Job does not despise death, but in the sense that death is viewed as resignation.

18. Rowold, "Life and Death," 14, n. 6. Their death, thus, is not integral to the narrative flow of the story.

Job in 1:2, the narrator presents another group of Job's children in 42:13 as: "He [Job] had also seven sons and three daughters." Weiss suggests that the significance of the word "were born" emerges from a comparison to the word "had" in 42:13. That is, "the verse at the beginning of the story relates only that these children were 'born' to Job, and not that he 'had' them, for the story proceeds to tell of their death."[19] In the context of the prologue, their death is not the primary focus of the story; rather it is in its implication for life with God.[20] However, Job seemingly views the death of his children and servants as submissive in the hands of Yahweh (cf. 12:10; 30:23; 34:14). He does not question God why it happened. He simply accepts it. In fact, nowhere in the book of Job documents that one can escape death. Even in words of lament and accusation, Job reflects the reality and normality of death: "I know you that you will bring me to death and to the house appointed for all living" (30:23). Hence, death does not only happen, but also is part of the human condition under the design of God. It is recognized as part of life, no matter how it happens. Moreover, in the midst of catastrophe, Job articulates his grief (i.e. "Job arose and tore his robe and shaved his head and fell on the ground") with the doxology (i.e. "and Job worshiped") (1:20). Job's words point that Job will not curse God, even in the face of loss, and untimely and violent death of his beloved ones. In the midst of suffering and loss, Job accepts God's will and can praise God. This is Job's starting point, and the point to which he returns in the end.

Scenes 4, 5 and 6[21]

At another meeting of a celestial court God proudly responds to the accuser, "he [Job] still holds fast his integrity (תֻּמָּה), although you incited me against him to destroy him without reason" (2:3; cf. 1:9). Job's wife also recognizes Job's תֻּמָּה, as she asks him: "Do you still hold fast your integrity?" (2:9). In fact, not only Yahweh twice proudly boasts about Job (1:8; 2:3), the narrator also praises Job's integrity in the opening verse. This theme of integrity will develop more in the rest of the book.

---

19. Weiss, *Story of Job's Beginning*, 27.
20. Rowold, "Life and Death," 14, n. 6.
21. The description of scene 6 will be discussed more in the introduction of the dialogues between the three friends and Job in chapter 3 of this book.

As the accuser responds with a knowledge that "all that a man has he will give for his life (נֶפֶשׁ)" (2:4), he proposes a more severe test of Job's integrity with a shift to focus on Job's body as a locus of the test. Here the accuser increases the level of suffering in order to "break" Job's faith. Here the term "life" (נֶפֶשׁ) in the mouth of the accuser denotes the uninjured and healthy life.[22] He challenges God: "But stretch out your hand and touch his bone and his flesh, and he will curse you to your face" (2:5).[23] The accuser is granted permission, with the provison that he spares Job's נֶפֶשׁ, and smites him with "loathsome sores from the sole of his foot to the crown of his head" (2:7). This tormenting and dangerous skin disease attacks Job's whole body. Job later on enunciates his painful ulcers as worse than death (7:4–5, 14–16; 19:20; 30:17). This physical pain is real, malignant, and recognized as from the hand of God. The only thing Job, who once was a whole man, can do now is sit in the ashes, scratch himself with a broken piece of potsherd and accept the "evil" at the hand of God,[24] as he has accepted the good that precede it (2:8). In other words, Job accepts personal suffering as he has previously accepted losses as something that comes from the hand of God, until his wife appears into the scene and says something to him.

When Job's wife asks: "Do you still hold fast your integrity?" She suggests that he should "curse God and die" (2:9).[25] She envisions death as the result of blasphemy.[26] If Job would reject God, then God would swiftly finish him off. Yet this kind of death would be better than a present painful suffering. She, like the friends, perceives Job's affliction as proof of God's hostility.[27] On the literary level, she serves as the first foil of the story to Job's position.

---

22. Wolff, *Anthropology*, 20. See also the idea of uninjured and healthy life in the friends' view of life in 5:25–26; 36:11; etc.

23. Again, note that in Hebrew, instead of the term "to curse," the word בָּרַךְ, "to bless" is used in 2:5 (אִם־לֹא אֶל־פָּנֶיךָ יְבָרֲכֶךָּ).

24. Note that here in 2:10 רַע is used in the sense of "harm," not moral evil.

25. Note again that the Hebrew text has the word "bless (בָּרֵךְ)," not "curse" as rendered in English translation (בָּרֵךְ אֱלֹהִים וָמֻת).

26. Although her words echo what the accuser has predicted for Job (2:5), the prologue does not focus on her character or the motivation behind her words. So she is not the "Satan's" subordinate, as understood by Fyall et al. Interestingly, she is the only character who is vocal in the book, but has no name.

27. See Christopher Wright Mitchell, *The Meaning BRK "To Bless" in the Old Testament*, SBL Dissertation Series 95 (Atlanta, GA: Scholars Press, 1987), 163.

Her words (as well as the friends' and Elihu's) lead Job into the wilderness of struggling. She cannot sustain life in the face of calamity and dreadful suffering. For her, there is no retribution for being faithful. She raises, for the first time, the question of God's justice as not keeping the doctrine of retribution in this world. It seems that for her a God, who does not keep divine retribution, is not reliable for man.[28] Thus, she suggests that Job "curse God." Her last advice for Job is "to die." Death is seemingly viewed as an escape from suffering life. God is seemingly viewed as an unjust God. On the contrary, Job responds,

| "Shall we receive good from God, and shall we not receive evil?" | 2:10 | גַּם אֶת־הַטּוֹב נְקַבֵּל מֵאֵת הָאֱלֹהִים וְאֶת־הָרָע לֹא נְקַבֵּל |

Job acknowledges that what Yahweh gives is not simply life but life inevitably with "good" and "evil."[29] The incidents of "evil/harm" cannot break his relationship with God. For Job there is no "accident" in the ultimate sense. God is the only one who is responsible for all things. This is the view of a monotheistic religion.[30] Job has this idea of God and absolutely accepts God's governance. Even though Job "turns away from evil (רַע)" (1:1, 8; 2:3) (i.e. he does not walk after the path that leads to evil deeds [moral evil]), he recognizes that it is possible, and even acceptable, that evil/harm (רָעָה) may "come upon him" (2:11). In other words, "injustice" or "harm" may happen to him. Part of Job's righteousness lies in the fact that he transcends the concept of justice inherent in the retribution principle and held "in the land of Uz." The text points to the misunderstanding associated with the retribution principle; namely, the righteous man will only be blessed. Job response to his wife here is not a declarative statement like his confession of

---

28. Also Fischer, "How God Pays Back," 36.

29. C. Dohmen, "רעע," *TDOT* 13:560–587. Dohmen (562) notes that this term covers the most varied aspects of everything not good or negative; making no distinction between "bad" and "evil" (in a moral sense), and so the exact meaning of the word in each instance can be determined only from contextual clues. The term "evil" (רַע) here contextually is not moral evil but rather the painful suffering in contrast to Job's pervious blessings. Thus, the text should read: "Shall we receive good from God, and shall we not receive harm?"

30. Note that the concern of the book is to show the reaction of the perfectly righteous man to the unexpected events which affront the belief in divine justice, and not to teach merely the universality of the fear of God.

faith in 1:21, but a rhetorical question. In addition, there is a shift from the use of the first common singular pronoun "I" in 1:21 to the first common plural pronoun "we" here in 2:10. The shift points to a change in Job's language. According to Janzen, it signals the beginning of the loss of confidence in confessional contexts.[31] Janzen also suggests that when his wife counsels him to "curse God and die," the sharpness of his retort [2:10a] implies that in fact she has voiced his own unspoken feelings.[32] If so, at least Job has not openly reached this point. At least outwardly he "keeps his integrity." Following Job's second response in 2:10a, the reader finds more hints in the narrator's comment on Job that "In all this Job did not sin with his lips" (2:10b, בְּכָל־זֹאת לֹא־חָטָא אִיּוֹב בִּשְׂפָתָיו).

In 1:22, the narrator comments that "In all this Job did not sin or charge God with wrong." The narrator again brings Job's action to a pause and declares that Job has now undergone terrible physical suffering and still has not cursed God. The phrase "in all this" does not refer to just his conversation with his wife, but to all the preceding events. However, the comment in 2:10b recalls Job's pious concern in 1:5 that his children may have sinned, and cursed God "in their hearts." The narrator leaves it an open question between what Job is saying (with his lips) and what Job is thinking in his heart.[33] As already mentioned, as the book aims to build the divine truth, which is not that of the wisdom principle in the land of Uz, it is necessary to see Job's reactions not only in the prologue but the rest of the book as a whole. Here in the prologue, though Job refuses to curse God in 2:10 as his wife has suggested, Job does not utterly bless God as he did in 1:21. Thus, the narrator's comment on Job in 2:10b invites the reader to ponder upon what is in Job's mind: He did not sin with his lips; but does he sin in his

---

31. Janzen, *Job*, 52.

32. Janzen, "Lust for Life," 154. In a similar conclusion, Weiss, *Story of Job's Beginning*, 73, states, "Psychological observation would suggest that the rational claim which Job presents in order to reject his wife's suggestion is actually directed toward dispelling those thoughts that are in his own mind. This suggestion is not only the logical result of psychological considerations, it is, more importantly, implied in Job's own words [2:10]."

33. Janzen, *Job*, 51. See also Weiss' investigation on a comparison of Job 1:21 with 2:10 (*Story of Job's Beginning*, 71–74). Weiss, 72–73, proposes that the intentional difference in the style of the narrator's comment makes it clear that Job cannot be stable after the second attack from God. After the second stage of his trial, and after his wife's words, Job may not sin "with his lips." But "in his heart – over which even Job has no control – he will sin, will raise questions about God's ways."

heart? Is it possible that Job will raise questions in his heart about God's way of dealing with the righteous man? It is significant to see the movement of the story that Job starts off in the right response to God in 1:21 then begins to move away from it in 2:10 only to return at the end of the book (i.e. after the two speeches of Yahweh). By the change from Job's first response to his second response, the Joban author masterfully connects the prose prologue to the following poetic section. After seven days of silence, instead of cursing God, Job curses the day of his birth. Attempting to make sense out of his suffering, Job asks the "why" questions in Job 3.

Summary of the Prologue

The prologue of the book of Job functions as an introduction to what follows. Two issues appear in the prologue: (a) the retribution principle idea that blessing corresponds to righteousness (ch. 1), and (b) the notion that death is an escape from suffering (ch. 2). Job rightly rejects both at the outset. Thus the prologue serves as a microcosm of the position of the book as a whole. It also lays out the position which Job will return at the conclusion of his struggle at the end of the book.

Job 1. Chapter 1 sets significant issues in the book. The first issue is the contrast between two explanations of Job's sufferings. The Joban author intentionally aims to present two different explanations: the wisdom understanding of retribution principle (i.e. the righteous man is blessed by God) in the land below and the truly divine trial in heavens above. The remainder of the book forces Job and the reader to question the human understanding of divine justice in the doctrine of retribution. For Job this question is based on his knowledge of his own righteousness. For the reader it is rooted in the dramatic irony of the reader's knowledge that Job's suffering is part of a divine trial rather than God's judgment upon Job's sin. This divine trial is about God's ways of treating the righteous person.[34] This trial will be affirmed as the book unfolds that the understanding of divine justice reflected in the theology of retribution is under attack in the following sections of the book as a false principle in explaining of why people suffer in this life. As

---

34. Also John H. Walton, "Job 1: Book of," *Dictionary of the Old Testament: Wisdom, Poetry, and Writings* (IVP) (Downers Grove, IL: IVP, 2008), 333–346.

the narrator acclaims Job's righteousness from the beginning of the book, it is made clear that Job is not on trial. Rather, it is the understanding of the relationship between God and man represented by the retribution principle that is on trial.[35] In order to destroy this false worldview, all that Job has must be destroyed. And in order to gain full recognition of divine truth, "it must first be seen how Job will react when reality delivers an unexpected blow."[36] All Job's reactions must be investigated through the rest of the story. The fact that God accepts the accuser's challenge affirms that God is beyond being judged by human standards (i.e. the retribution principle). It is God's claims and his will to test Job, his righteous servant.

The second issue in Job 1 is about the accuser and his question. The prologue explicitly affirms a freedom of God. It is God who initiates the discussion and approves the test, even a horrendous test, on Job. This fact stands against the simple solution that what happens to Job is simply "Satan did it."[37] Some scholars argue that the accuser (satan) in the prologue is not the same figure as the so-called "Satan" in the New Testament.[38] He is the accuser, the heavenly subordinate who is a "spy roaming the earth and

---

35. Walton, "Job 1," 340, also notes that "the charges are made by the adversary and by Job against God, and it is his [God's] policies that are on trial." Contrary to Walton's view, the present author sees believes instead that since although there is some truth in the retribution principle, it is misapplied in the case of Job. The Joban author attempts to present that we cannot use or apply this traditional worldview in every case of man; thus, it is not God's policies, but the retribution principle that is on trial in the book of Job. As the book unfolds, we see that the Joban author uses the retribution principle as a device to serve the purpose of the book and to articulate its argument in the narrative flow of the book. This principle is presented as: (a) false at the beginning of the book, (b) conceptually wrong in the dialogues, and (c) is eventually rejected at the end of the book.

36. Weiss, *Story of Job's Beginning*, 43.

37. Some scholars (e.g. Weiss, *Story of Job's Beginning*, 43) see a rival figure emerges to take responsibility for the test, becoming an extension of God through personification of a doubting thought. However, as Crenshaw, *Defending God*, 70, points out, "the adversary cannot act apart from the deity's permission. This dependence of the subordinate figure means that responsibility for its acting rests ultimately with God."

38. Another view of the satan in the book of Job is perceived as the so-called "the Satan." For instance, Dirk Kinet views that "the figure of Satan seems to have an exculpatory function. It is not God's own idea to inflict vicissitudes on Job in order to test his religious devotion. Satan is the real instigator . . . [H]e acts more or less as an independent agent, thereby exonerating God from sole responsibility." ("The Ambiguity of the Concepts of God and Satan in the Book of Job," in *Job and the Silence of God* [New York: Seabury Press, 1983]), 30–35; Tromp, *Primitive*, 213; Fyall, *My Eyes*, 137; etc.

reporting to God on the evil he found therein."[39] After the second scene in the heavens, the accuser disappears from the rest of the story. On a literary level, the accuser serves only to set up the conflict of the story; that is, the question of Job's integrity, and that as a way of exploring the concept of divine justice held by the theology of retribution. Since his appearances are purposefully introduced for the setting of the story, his role, thus, is insignificant from the perspective of the book as a whole. However, his role provides an important theological twist in the challenge against God's policies. While a man (i.e. Job's wife, the three friends, and Job himself) can contend that it is not a good policy for God to allow righteous man to suffer, the accuser views it differently and doubts God's confidence in Job's motivation for being upright and blameless. The accuser does raise an important question of the existence of human's disinterested righteousness, and thus of the theology of retribution. It is this question that sets the drama of Job into motion. The question reflects the common view of ancient Near Eastern religion that the divine-human relation is based on quid pro quo.[40] The accuser, thus, challenges God's ways of rewarding the righteous. Later on, the reader will see that this question concerning divine justice becomes Job's main struggle as he attempts to understand God's way in terms of human reason. The purpose of the prologue (as well as of the rest of the book), thus, is to dispute the conventional claim of divine justice, specifically the point of view which primary principle is expressed in the wisdom notion that the righteous man is blessed by God. To accomplish this purpose and to answer above question, Job must undergo a horrendous test, being taken

---

39. Pope, *Job*, 9–10.

40. In his *Religion in Ancient Mesopotamia* (Chicago: University of Chicago Press, 2001), 216, Jean Bottérro points out the concept of quid pro quo that "the cult [in the ancient NE] . . . was therefore necessarily anthropomorphic: if the gods had created human beings, . . . it was, from the gods' point of view, out of necessity, out of the need for material goods that humans alone were able to produce and present to them. Through their industry, their technology, and their work, humans not only met their own needs but, above all, out of natural vocation and by virtue of the will of their creators and masters, functioned as servants and providers for the gods. From such perspective, religious behavior focused on that fundamental duty of "maintaining" the gods: of providing them with all the goods and services, and luxury, that were indispensable to them; not, of course, to keep them alive – were they not by nature immortal? – but to guarantee them, like the subjects their kings, and existence that was not only bearable but opulent and pleasant, as befitted the masters of the universe."

away all the blessings he previously has and having the real physical pain. The account of Job's suffering, thus, is an attack on the retribution principle as an explanation of why people suffer in this life. It is in this context that death becomes an important question for Job, specifically within the framework of *this* lifetime.

The third issue in chapter 1 is Job's right response to God in 1:21. Life in the first scene of the story (1:1–5) is so orderly, uninjured and highly healthy, including a full and happy family. Significantly, it is life with God. Job is presented as a whole man who lives his life in wholeness. Death under this blessed life is predicted as a good and peaceful death (cf. 29:18). The blessing upon life is viewed one-sidedly only through "good" (e.g. blessings upon materials and households) that comes from God. Under this blessing, there is no room for "evil" (e.g. harm, injustice, suffering, etc.). However, when "evil" falls upon Job (1:13–19), Job expresses his faith, accepting God's governance (1:21). He accepts even the premature and violent death of his servants and children. His first response is vital to the narrative of the story. Here Job does not ask God a "why" question. He continues to live his suffering life in his faith without questioning the seemingly unjust way of God. His first response is not to ask "why," but simply to say, "YHWH gave, YHWH took it away; blessed be the name of YHWH." At this point (ch. 1) Job does not try to figure out why God allows "bad things" to happen to him, a righteous man. He simply lives in faith and trusts in God's way, in what God gave and took away. In the midst of suffering, he does not curse God. Thus, he has demonstrated his disinterested piety already that he has not served God for the sake of only "good/blessings." Job's first response, therefore, is the right response. It is the response that God will lead him back to at the end of the book. But before he returns to this right position (i.e. trust in the truly divine truth), Job will undergo horrendous suffering and doubt about God's justice through the process of the dialogues with his friends. From the prologue, once his wife (and later on the friends and Elihu) gets involved and challenges this position, she forces him to ask the "why" question. Job is pushed into the realm of spiritual chaos.

Job 2. Chapter 2 of the prologue not only presents the shift of Job's position but also the connection between the prose and the dialogue that follows. After the second test on Job's body, his wife appears as the first foil to Job's position (2:9). Her words initially lead Job into the realm of spiritual chaos. The narrator's comment on Job in 2:10b affirms this hint of Job's inner struggle. It is the struggle not against God per se, but against the expectation of God that his wife's suggestion implies: God seemingly appears to be unjust for he does not keep divine retribution (i.e. he does not bless the righteous Job). From her perspective, death is viewed as an escape from this suffering life.[41] Her expectation is a kind of the accuser's expectation as well but from a different angle in viewing the divine justice. God's justice now apparently becomes unpredictable. Job's second response (2:10a) has become ambiguous.[42] It is not a declarative statement as in 1:21, but the negative rhetorical question which signals the loss of confidence in confessional contexts. In the first response (1:21), his words are personal, and tangible; in the second response, they are general and abstract. In 2:10, Job speaks of "good" and "evil" that we must accept; but previously neither good nor evil was mentioned but rather God's giving and taking away. In addition, the phrase "from God" does not recur after "evil" as it does after "good." Significantly, Job's earlier utterance was a reaction not to the words of those around him but directly to the action of God. Here in 2:10 they are a reaction to the words of someone present (i.e. his wife's). Thus, this second response is "part of Job's newly awakened, uncertain, questioning reticence."[43] The change in Job's first and second response marks the narrative contrast in the prologue. Through Job's second response (2:10), the reader sees the profound connection between the prologue and the dialogue that follows.

The prologue implicitly affirms what will be the conclusion of the book. Specifically, it calls into question God's justice in terms of the mathematics retribution principle. This question concerning divine justice is firstly introduced to the reader by the accuser. It is not Job, but rather the accuser who asks the question in Job 1. The fact that God appears to be unjust establishes

---

41. If the suggestion "Curse God and die" carries the idea of committing a suicide, this may be what James refers to Job as being "patient" (James 5:11); for Job, during the process and at the end of the story, does not kill himself.

42. The shift of using the pronoun "I" in 1:21 to "we" in 2:10 suggests that Job is not only pairing himself with the reader, but his individual "I" "is hidden anonymously among the 'we'" (Janzen, *Job*, 52). It is possible also that Job is merely articulating a general principle – and one that stands in opposition to the retribution principle.

43. Janzen, *Job*, 52.

the retribution principle as the "given," the presupposition that will be put to test in the rest of the story. This presupposition becomes the conceptual problem of the story, specifically and importantly the conceptual problem of Job's expectation in divine justice. His first response to his calamities (1:21) is to accept whatever comes from the hand of God without questions. And so, he confesses "the Lord gives and the Lord takes away; blessed be the name of the Lord." He accepts loss, and even the unmerited and untimely death of his children in faith and without the need of an explanation. Job perceives no connection between his loss and God's justice.

Soon, however, he is led into the wilderness of doubt, beginning with the question and the suggestion of his wife (2:9). Job's questioning reticence in 2:10 signals his inner struggle against the expectation of God's justice in terms of the retribution principle. After seven days of reflection Job begins to ask the fatal question "why?" This is his first step into the spiritual chaos and despair that follows. His three friends each attempt to help Job find an answer to this question of why. Their counsel is shaped by the retribution principle. As discussed in chapter 1, the retribution principle is rooted in a clear biblical truth that God promises to bless those who keep his word in faith and promises to punish those who reject his word. The friends, however, make the mistake of applying this principle backward. They assume that all blessing is explained by the recipient's righteousness and all suffering is explained by the sinfulness of the recipient. But underlying this is a more insidious mistake, the assumption that all blessing and all suffering are functions of divine justice, and that the ways of divine justice are knowable by man (i.e. there is no room for the notion of *deus absconditus*).

Therefore, the position of the friends implies that the ways of God can be comprehended by human reasons, as reflected in the retribution principle, and Job accepts their presuppositions. This creates a crisis: Job rejects their counsel because he knows that he is righteous and that his suffering cannot be explained by this principle that they have persuaded him to adopt. Indeed, the reader knows (in exquisite dramatic irony) that Job's sufferings have nothing to do with his having sinned because the prologue has told us that not only is Job righteous but also his suffering is a result of the challenge of the accuser to God and not as a result of Job's unrighteousness. But as Job listens to his friends and attempts to find an explanation for his suffering he plunges further and further into a realm of spiritual chaos, "the wilderness of why." Job's struggle produces intense inner turmoil. As he attempts to reconcile the concept of divine justice inherent in the retribution principle with his own knowledge of his righteousness, he cannot find an answer. God appears to be unjust because he appears to be punishing a righteous man. And Job rebels against God's apparent injustice. Job's wandering in this wilderness leads to vacillating and contradictory reflections on death. Sometimes Job views death as an escape from his situation. Other times he accepts the view of death implicitly in the retribution principle, namely that it is punishment for sin. At still other times death appears to be an inevitable result of his inexplicable sufferings. He cries out, sometimes in hope, sometimes in despair, sometimes for a helper or intermediary who could plead his case before God and seek justice on his behalf. But once Job begins to ask the question "why" there is no escape from the wilderness into which it leads him. Thus, Job and his friends go around and around without reaching any conclusion: there is no escape from the contradiction because the retribution principle in Job's specific case is fundamentally wrong. The workings of divine justice are not comprehensible to human reason. Elihu offers a variation on the same idea, that suffering can be a warning to prevent sin. But Elihu also operates within the general framework of the retribution principle, and his perspective does not lead Job in a closer to a resolution to his crisis.

Finally, God himself intervenes. God challenges Job's fundamental assumption, which he has adopted from his friends, that the ways of God are comprehensible to human reason. They are not, as God's speeches make clear. The ways of God are hidden from man unless God himself chooses to reveal them. The question "why" can never be answered by human reason. In this way God's speeches bring Job back to the place where he began before posing the fatal question. And at the end of the book Job is where he was at the beginning: at peace with accepting whatever comes from the hand of God without the need to understand it in terms of human reason.

In this way, the book of Job offers the same conclusion that God gives to Habakkuk. Habakkuk considered one side of the coin: why do the unrighteous prosper? Job ponders the other side of the coin: why do the righteous suffer? In each case God's answer is the same, the answer that he gives to

Habakkuk in chapter 2: the question "why" can only be answered from the perspective of the eschaton. Until then the righteous must live by faith.

Job's First Lament[44] (Job 3)

Chapter 3 marks a remarkable shift from the prose narrative of the first two chapters. It establishes the terms, literally and figuratively, of Job's complaint against God. Many terms used in this lament will reappear in chapters 38–41, when God finally appears to Job. The first verse continues the prose style from Job 1 and 2, introducing the content of the chapter. The following poetic section contains two themes expressed by means of curses and laments.[45] This first poetic section of the book is an emotional outburst. On the emotional level, it is Job's (first) death wish. The study will investigate how Job exploits his death wish as his implicit argument against the unjust way of God.[46]

After seven days and nights of silence, Job deeply falls into bitterness of his soul and feels the enmity of God. Instead of cursing God, Job curses (קלל) the day of his birth (3:1, in Hebrew, simply "his day.")[47] He wishes that his day and his life could revert to the formless and empty . . . darkness

---

44. Instead of "monologue," the designation "lament" is used here for Job 3 for it is a self-lament (*Ichklage*). It carries components of the lament: the cursing of Job's own birthday (3:3–9), the self-lament (or self-complaint) (3:11–19, 24–26), and the lament directed to God (3:20–23). See Westermann, *Structure of the Book*, 37–38, 60, n. 5. However, unlike the laments of the Psalms, Job 3 is not directed to God personally by employing the second person singular form of address (31).

45. See Alter, *Biblical Poetry*, 76–83. Alter points out that the Joban author masterfully uses a system of poetic intensifications. Poetic intensification means the build-up of feeling from line *a* to line *b* in semantically parallel lines. His investigation is helpful and is able to lead the reader to see the movement from the general point to the specific matter. This movement builds the focusing effect which makes Job's confession of fear powerfully emphatic.

46. From the structure of Job 3 as a whole, the argumentative nature of the text is highlighted, for example, by usage of כִּי ("because," "for what purpose;" in 3:10, 12, 13, 22, 24, 25), מָה ("why;" in 3:11, 12(x2), 20, 23), and an emphatic negative particle לֹא ("no," "there is none;" in 3:10, 11, 16(x2), 18, 26).

47. The Hebrew term קלל in Piel is normally used for cursing a person not a thing or an event (see L. Koehler and W. Baumgartner "קלל," *HALOT* 2:1103–1104). Some scholars suggest that Job may be cursing God implicitly in this lament. However, the Joban author may put in Job's mouth a conventional term with ambiguity in its carrying of meaning. Thus, the Joban author presents that Job comes as very close to "curse" God as the satan has predicted or as Job's wife has suggested. See a further discussion of this term in W. J. Urbock, "Blessings and Cursings," *ABD*, 1:755–761.

of Genesis 1:2.⁴⁸ Job's first lament here is not strictly a death wish per se,⁴⁹ but a forlorn and futile wish that God would press the delete button on his life, so that he would never have to deal with and try to make sense of his unbearable suffering. Job speaks out of the depths of his pain. It is Job's verbal reaction or a lament, where the "why" existential questions are expressed.⁵⁰ He curses the day and night of his birth in 3:3–10,⁵¹ and expresses a lament with a repeating "why?" of existence in 3:11–26. With struggling despair, Job learns that life is now inexplicably ruled by "trouble" (עָמָל, v. 10) and "turmoil" (NIV, רֹגֶז, v. 26).

In macabre eloquence, Job cites three splendid opportunities for such pre-emptive death: in the womb, in the birthing process, in infancy (3:10, 11, 12, with summary in v. 16).

---

48. As it has been long explored, the use of terminological and thematic parallels connects the curse section (3:3–10) with the creation account of Gen 1. See those thematic parallels, for instance, in Habel, *Book of Job*, 104. For the sequences of incantations, which follow the progression of events in the creation account, see Michael Fishbane, "Jeremiah 4:23–26 and Job 3:3–13: A Recovered use of the Creation Pattern," *VT* 21 (1971): 151–167.

49. Job does not really wish to die. He has no idea of committing suicide. In addition, for Job life is not evil or negative as the real pessimist maintains.

50. See Claus Westermann, "The Literary Genre of the Book of Job," in *Sitting with Job: Selected Studies on the Book of Job* (Grand Rapids, MI: Baker, 1992), 51–63. Westermann rightly proposes that the lament is widely and fundamentally attested in the book of Job and helps the readers to understand the book as a whole. Structurally, the encompassing confrontation is that between Job and God (ch. 3, and chs. 29–31), while within this confrontation stands the one between the friends and Job (chs. 4–27). The dialogue, therefore, is framed by Job's laments (Job 3 and 29–31).

51. Structurally, in Hebrew the first unit, a curse (3:3–10), has eight lines, the following unit, a lament (3:11–26), is longer, containing twice the length of the first unit – 16 lines. Images of light and darkness prevail throughout the former unit, where Job calls forth the complete reversal of creation to snuff out his own life. The focus of his curse moves backward from the day of his birth to the night of his conception. Deep darkness is described as a predator, ready to destroy (3:5–6). He finally names the mythic sea monster Leviathan, symbol of the primordial chaos waters that threaten to destroy the orders of creation (3:8b). Next to Job himself, this is the only reference to a living creature in his execration of the cosmos. Another reference to Leviathan in the book appears, with a lengthy description, in the second speech of YHWH (41:1–34 [MT 40:25–41:26]). Notice that while in 3:8 Job invokes Leviathan to destroy the world, in the second speech of YHWH God commends Leviathan to Job as one of the two representatives (the other is Behemoth) from whom Job can learn something of God's world. Thus, this mythic monster has its literary function within the context of the book as a whole, not a menacing force as Fyall et al suggests. A further discussion of Leviathan will follow in chapter 4 of this book.

Because it did not shut the doors of my mother's womb, nor hide trouble from my eyes.	3:10	כִּי לֹא סָגַר דַּלְתֵי בִטְנִי וַיַּסְתֵּר עָמָל מֵעֵינָי:
Why did I not die at birth, come out from the womb and expire?	3:11	לָמָּה לֹּא מֵרֶחֶם אָמוּת מִבֶּטֶן יָצָאתִי וְאֶגְוָע:
Why did the knees receive me? Or why the breasts, that I should nurse?	3:12	מַדּוּעַ קִדְּמוּנִי בִרְכָּיִם וּמַה־שָּׁדַיִם כִּי אִינָק:
Or why was I not as a hidden stillborn child, as infants who never see the light?	3:16	אוֹ כְנֵפֶל טָמוּן לֹא אֶהְיֶה כְּעֹלְלִים לֹא־רָאוּ אוֹר:

By using a כִּי clause at the end of the first unit (3:3–10) Job ceases his curses and gives a reason for not wanting to be born (v. 10; cf. vv. 24–26 in second unit): "Because it did not shut the doors of my mother's womb." The word "it" refers to "that night," which has been the object of his curses in verses 6–9. The term "my mother's womb" in Hebrew is only "my womb" (בִטְנִי). Job does not make a direct reference to his parents. He refers to the womb from which he came.[52] The idea here refers to the conception of a child. That is, God is the one who allows conception to take place (e.g. Gen 29:31) and who prevents the conception (e.g. 1 Sam 1:5; cf. Job 1:21).[53] Job is implying that God, the Creator of the night of his conception (3:3), is the one who is responsible for his "trouble" (עָמָל) outside the womb.[54] His implicit argument is that a just God should not have created human being for such a fate. Job's "why" questions, thus, address God indirectly. Job's cry and his "whys" are equivalent to a death wish in the sense that he would like to make death retroactive. Verse 11 is the start of the second unit (3:11–26). He begins by asking the first of five "why" questions (3:11, 12 [x2], 20, 23),

---

52. From what Alter calls poetic intensification, the image of "shut the doors of my mother's womb" also looks back to the imagery of darkness (vv. 3–9) and forward to the grave of verses 13–19.

53. Rick D. Moore, "The Integrity of Job," *CBQ* 45 (1983): 17–31, suggests that Job 3 is "a step-by-step rebuttal of Job's manifesto of faith in 1:21" (26). Moore also notes that Job's first words in chapter 3 signal a complete turn around in his character and worldview.

54. With this idea in mind, the friends will argue Job later that "trouble" is what a man reaps for the sins he sows (4:8; cf. 5:6). But Job keeps contending in 7:3 that "trouble" is assigned to him in the same way that a master assigns hard labor to a slave (cf. 3:19).

which are repeated to emphasize Job's wish that he could have died. This sort of question is typical of a complaint. Obviously, Job could not prevent his own birth; he now wishes he had died (מוּת) at birth (רֶחֶם, "from the womb,") in verse 11a.[55] In verse 11b, the term for death is repeated, with synonymic emphasis, denoting the idea of "breathe out a last breath" or "expire" (גוע). Then Job wonders why, if he had to leave the womb, were there "knees" (בֶּרֶךְ) to receive him as a newborn (v. 12). And once received into this world, why were there "breasts" (שָׁדַיִם) to feed and nurture him for a life that he now wishes had never begun (v. 16).

If Job could die at one of these three stages, he would have found "rest"[56] with those greatest people (3:13–15):

For then I would have lain down and been quiet; I would have slept; then I would have been at rest,	3:13	כִּי־עַתָּה שָׁכַבְתִּי וְאֶשְׁקוֹט יָשַׁנְתִּי אָז יָנוּחַ לִי׃
with kings and counselors of the earth who rebuilt ruins for themselves,	3:14	עִם־מְלָכִים וְיֹעֲצֵי אָרֶץ הַבֹּנִים חֳרָבוֹת לָמוֹ׃
or with princes who had gold, who filled their houses with silver.	3:15	אוֹ עִם־שָׂרִים זָהָב לָהֶם הַמְמַלְאִים בָּתֵּיהֶם כָּסֶף׃

Job wishes that unmaking his birth day would unmake his life and all the anguish it contains. That is, if the events in verse 12 had not occurred, then Job would have died, and verse 13a, which is a consequence, would have been true. Using four different metaphors for death: lie down (שָׁכַב), be quiet (שָׁקַט), sleep (יָשֵׁן), and rest (נוּחַ),[57] Job is intensely longing for

---

55. For similar laments asking "why" questions, see Pss 10:1; 22:1; Jer 20:18; Lam 5:20.

56. Notice the thematic word "rest" (נוּחַ) will reappear again in verse 17 and will be reiterated along with the term "quiet" (שָׁקַט) in verse 26.

57. John E. Hartley, *The Book of Job*, NIBC on the Old Testament (Grand Rapids: Erdmans, 1998), 95, Hartley is right in applying this term "rest" (נוּחַ) with the biblical Sabbath notion in the creation account. His recognition also reminds us how important this biblical term (נוּחַ) is. Instead of the term שָׁבַת, it is the Hebrew term נוּחַ which Job uses here three times in his opening lament. While the term שָׁבַת is used as the end of God's creative activities, the term נוּחַ, found more in the Former Prophets and the Deuteronomistic literatures, is used more in redemptive activities. Both terms are used to connote the idea of the proper and expected end of the shalomic life in the presence of God (cf. Exod 20:11; Deut 5:14). The Old Testament views rest as a God-given gift. Rest is viewed as cessation of activity (e.g. Gen 2; Exod 20:11; Deut 5:14), or as cessation from movement and trouble

death as complete peace and rest from this turmoil. Job has lost everything: his properties, his honor, his children, and his wife (i.e. to side with him in truth searching). He is overwhelmed with grief, loss, meaningless, and hopelessness. Job is anxious and restless. He speaks out of the depth of his pain and welcomes death as the most desirable. "Job imagines a radically different form of existence, one without trouble and fear, as inclusive as it is liberating."[58] In addition, it is the peaceful land, where kings/rulers, the great men, lie down in peace. Job, as the "greatest of all the people of the east" (1:3), will be reunited with them enjoying their end in peaceful land of the dead. Job characterizes the land of the dead as a place of gloom, darkness, and deep darkness in 10:21–22, and acknowledges the ugly side of the underworld, for instance, in 13:28 and 17:12–16. Yet he prefers the rest of death to a life of suffering and loss on this earth.[59]

Returning to his theme of death as a resting place, Job continues:

There the wicked cease from troubling, and there the weary are at rest.	3:17	שָׁם רְשָׁעִים חָדְלוּ רֹגֶז וְשָׁם יָנוּחוּ יְגִיעֵי כֹחַ:
There the prisoners are at ease together; they hear not the voice of the taskmaster.	3:18	יַחַד אֲסִירִים שַׁאֲנָנוּ לֹא שָׁמְעוּ קוֹל נֹגֵשׂ:
The small and the great are there, and the slave is free from his master.	3:19	קָטֹן וְגָדוֹל שָׁם הוּא וְעֶבֶד חָפְשִׁי מֵאֲדֹנָיו:

(e.g. Gen 8:4; Num 14:22–35). In the wisdom literature, the term נוּחַ is used frequently to express the wisdom principle of retributive justice (e.g. Prov 14:33; 21:16; cf. Eccl 7:9). The concept of rest (נוּחַ) also plays a role in Job's critical dispute with this ideology. In light of his suffering, Job longs for death as the ultimate rest – life's final and lasting cessation from action and trouble. In addition, the term נוּחַ involves the state of "satisfaction, joy, calm," which is reflected in the deuteronomic expression that rest is "from your enemies." If this connation is applied here, Job is longing for death, the ultimate rest, as not only a cessation from his suffering but also as searching for satisfaction or the ultimate calm of his life. Death, thus, is not the enemy, but the state of freeing him from his "enemies" (e.g. suffering). For further discussion of the term נוּחַ, see, for example, H. D. Preuss, "נוּחַ," *TDOT* 9:277–286; P. A. Barker, "Rest, Peace," *Dictionary of the Old Testament: Pentateuch* (Downers Grove, IL: IVP, 2003), 687–691.

58. William P. Brown, *The Ethos of the Cosmos: The Genesis of Moral Imagination in the Bible* (Grand Rapids, MI: Eerdmans, 1999), 323.

59. The idea of one should prefer the underworld as a place of rest to life is virtually unprecedented in the Hebrew Bible (cf. Eccl 6:3–6). See Clines, *Job 1–20*, 91–92; Balentine, *Job*, 89–90.

Why is light given to him who is in misery, and life to the bitter in soul,	3:20	לָמָּה יִתֵּן לְעָמֵל אוֹר וְחַיִּים לְמָרֵי נָפֶשׁ:
who long for death, but it comes not, and dig for it more than for hidden treasures,	3:21	הַמְחַכִּים לַמָּוֶת וְאֵינֶנּוּ וַיַּחְפְּרֻהוּ מִמַּטְמוֹנִים:
who rejoice exceedingly and are glad when they find the grave?	3:22	הַשְּׂמֵחִים אֱלֵי־גִיל יָשִׂישׂוּ כִּי יִמְצְאוּ־קָבֶר:
Why is light given to a man whose way is hidden, whom God has hedged in?	3:23	לְגֶבֶר אֲשֶׁר־דַּרְכּוֹ נִסְתָּרָה וַיָּסֶךְ אֱלוֹהַּ בַּעֲדוֹ:

The Hebrew term "there" (שָׁם) is used metaphorically for the underworld where the dead resides (3:17, 19; cf. 1:21). Job projects that death is a resting place not only for those who are great (3:14–15), but also for those who are powerless will find rest (3:17–19). The egalitarian sense seemingly includes the wicked and weary, captives and slaves, small and great.[60] The prospect of death unleashes imaginative possibilities for communal existence, no hierarchy and free from all burdens.[61] Job identifies himself strongly with those who are oppressed, suggesting a kind of liberation for the wearied powerful. Thus, life which comes with "trouble" (or "turmoil," רֹגֶז, v. 17; cf. v. 26) will be liberated by death itself. That is, only death can free the sufferer from the injustice of existence.[62] Contemplating the bitterness of his soul, Job expresses that "there . . . a slave is free from his master" (v. 19). If "master" there (אֲדֹנָיו) carries the echo of one of the referents for God (אֲדֹנָי) – and the Joban author uses parody and irony regularly and masterfully – then

---

60. In Job 21, Job argues against the friends that too often the wicked "spend their days in prosperity and in peace they go down to Sheol" (21:13). This contention of Job contributes an interesting connection with Job's pondering on death as escape in chapter 3, since both mention the wicked in the context of rest. In chapter 3, Job speaks of death as escape from the misery of life under God, which places him with the wicked (3:17), and in chapter 21 Job refers to the casual walk of the wicked through life into death, without judgment by God. In neither case does death seem to hold threat or fear for the wicked.

61. Cf. Johnston, *Shades of Sheol*, categorizes the theme of death in Job 3 as a friend (27–28).

62. Habel, *Book of Job*, 111.

Job is not only seeing himself as a slave before God, but also is yearning for a place of freedom from God.[63]

Job's recognition of other suffering in the world (i.e. of the prisoners, of the weary, of the slaves, etc.) leads him to ask another "why" question (3:20). Interestingly, the Hebrew verb יִתֵּן ("give") is in active form, not passive as rendered in ESV (also NIV, NRSV, NIB, etc.). The pronominal presence of God is indicated in the Hebrew by the conjugated form of verb "to give" in the third person singular.[64] The text, thus, should read: "Why does he [God] give light to those who are in misery?" Though Job does not explicitly mention God's name,[65] the tone of his language also points that he acknowledges that God is an active agent behind his suffering. For Job, "it is cruel wrong to create people who are destined to suffer and be embittered."[66] In verses 21–22, Job speaks of himself (and of other sufferers) as those

> who long for death, but it comes not,
>   and dig for it more than for hidden treasures,
> who rejoice exceedingly
>   and are glad when they find the grave? (Job 3:21–22)

Instead of "yearning for" (חכה) Yahweh and his counsel (Pss 33:20; 106:13), Job is longing for death as "a welcome savior."[67] The yearning ("digging") of death and the joy of finding it, as if it were a hidden treasure, ironically resemble the quest for wisdom (also in 28:1–19, 22; Prov 2:4; 3:13–18; 8:18–19). In verse 23, Job thinks: "Why is light given to [i.e. Why he gives light to] a man whose way is hidden, whom God has hedged in (יָסֶךְ)?" In Hebrew "why is light given" is left implicit. The question is supplied from verse 20a. Job calls himself "man" (גֶּבֶר),[68] the same Hebrew word he imag-

---

63. Also Rowold, "Life and Death," 5; Balentine, *Job*, 92. The imagery of God as "master" and human as "slaves" will be repeated again in 7:1–6.

64. Alter, *Biblical Poetry*, 82.

65. As already mentioned of the lament frame of the book (chs. 3 and 29–31), Job addresses to God indirectly here in chapter 3, but in chapter 31 Job mentions God's name directly, presenting his own relationship with God. See a discussion of Job 31 in chapter 3 of this book.

66. Aron Pinker, "Job's Perspectives on Death," *JBQ* 35 (2007): 73–84.

67. Habel, *Book of Job*, 111; Clines, *Job 1–20*, 100.

68. The term גֶּבֶר does not simply mean a man like אָדָם or אֱנוֹשׁ, neither of which indicates a particular sex, nor does it mean man in general. The word connotes the idea of a young, strong man, or a particular man. See K. Kosmala, "גֶּבֶר," *TDOT* 2:377–382. The

ined in verse 3, being cried out on the night of his conception. Job clearly implies that God is the one who hides a man's way of (blessing) life. This is the first and only time that God is mentioned in the opening lament. It must have been painful to Job to mention God as the source of his suffering.[69] Since God is the one who hedges Job in, thus, God is the cause of his painful suffering. The idea of "hedging in" here is echoing what the accuser has asked Yahweh in the prologue (1:10) that God showed his favoritism by setting up a protective "hedge" around Job and his household. The Hebrew word in 1:10 is שׂוּךְ, which commonly refers to performing a protective function. For Job, the hedge functions in reverse. That is, the hedge is here to strangle and to stifle him. Without God's hedge Job would be safe and happy; with it, his life turns up side down and is filled with despair.

Notice that Job is aware of the cause of his suffering, which is God and not the traditional idea of cause-effect relation. Here Job, a man of faith, experiences a conflict between faith and experience: the conflict between trust in God's grace and justice, and the reality of pain, suffering, and imminent death in this life. His cataclysm suggests to him that God does not operate justly. Perceived from the perspective of the retribution principle God appears unjust and arbitrary. Thus, this marks Job's adoption of the retribution principle as a starting point for understanding his life in relation to God, and the results are not salutary. Job's lament reflects that the primary belief in the land of Uz bases on a false foundation concerning divine justice, namely that suffering is a sign of punishment from God. But since he is aware of his own integrity, the reader sees the painful conflict in Job's belief. What Job is describing is an angry despair in which there is no

---

term גֶּבֶר occurs fifteen times in the book of Job (3:3, 23; 4:17; 10:5; 14:10, 14; 16:21; 22:2; 33:17, 29; 34:7, 9, 34; 38:3; 40:7). The term appears for the first time in 3:3 as a newborn child, a גֶּבֶר. Kosmala suggests that its usage in 3:3 is very unusual (*TDOT* 2:380–381). The Joban author may intend to point that the child (i.e. Job) was already determined from his birth to be a particular man, in the context of Job 3, as far as Job's opinion of himself is concerned. Note also that Job's friends do not call Job גֶּבֶר (e.g. אָדָם or אֱנוֹשׁ, or one born of a woman in 5:7; 15:7, 14), and when they use this word in referring to Job, it is only to carry the idea *ad absurdum* (e.g. 15:7–10). To the extent that Job refers to himself as גֶּבֶר, it is interesting that in his two responses to the speeches of Yahweh at the end of the book, Job is not a גֶּבֶר as he insists during the dialogues.

69. Also Alter, *Biblical Poetry*, 82.

escape, no future, no life, but only further torment. Job has lost everything and would prefer death to this present devastated life.

Job concludes the nature of his horrible anguish explicitly in 3:24–26 that

For my sighing comes instead of my bread, and my groanings are poured out like water	3:24	כִּי־לִפְנֵי לַחְמִי אַנְחָתִי תָבֹא וַיִּתְּכוּ כַמַּיִם שַׁאֲגֹתָי:
For the thing that I fear comes upon me, and what I dread befalls me.	3:25	כִּי פַחַד פָּחַדְתִּי וַיֶּאֱתָיֵנִי וַאֲשֶׁר יָגֹרְתִּי יָבֹא לִי:
I am not at ease, nor am I quiet; I have no rest, but trouble comes.	3:26	לֹא שָׁלַוְתִּי וְלֹא שָׁקַטְתִּי וְלֹא־נָחְתִּי וַיָּבֹא רֹגֶז: פ

In 1:5 Job was very considerate and feared of missteps or punishments that his children may have done even in their hearts. Now what he has feared comes upon him. His cry in verses 24–26 is based on the belief that God's actions should be understandable, or even predictable, within the framework of divine justice in the retribution principle. Job summarizes his tragedy here. He has mentioned the threefold of exultation that those who find grave will rejoice and be glad (v. 22). Here he endures a threefold absence of peace, rest, and quiet (v. 26). Job finishes his lament with the Hebrew word "trouble" (רֹגֶז; "turmoil," NIV; as in v. 17). This noun and its cognate verb and adjective connote the idea of "intense emotional agitation."[70] The word "sums up what for Job is wrong with life and what is desirable about Sheol."[71] The overall perception of life at this very moment contrasts to the portrayal of the tranquility of life in the prologue. Life now has no quiet (3:13, 26), and no rest (3:13, 17, 26). As narrated in the prologue, the "trouble/turmoil" (3:10, 13, 17, 20, 26) has come.[72]

In summary, in his introductory lament (ch. 3), Job expresses his serious desire to die because death is viewed as a release from his suffering, and unjust life (3:11, 12, 16; cf. 10:18). Here, death is not negative, but

---

70. Newsom, *Job: A Contest*, 94. Clines insightfully renders the word as "raging." (*Job 1–20*, 95–96). See also biblical instances in 2 Sam 19:1; Jer 33:9; Joel 2:1; Ps 99:1.

71. Clines, *Job 1–20*, 104.

72. Brown, *Ethos of the Cosmos*, 324, 325, n. 20, points out that the term "trouble" positioned at the end of Job's lament serves as the transition to Eliphaz's discourse, which marks the first fight between Job and his friends. That is, "trouble" comes in the arrival of Job's friends, who are ready to offer "consoling" advice.

desirable because it equalizes unjust social structures (3:13–19), brings injustice to an end, and gives peaceful rest to the sufferer (3:13, 17; cf. 7:15). Job's view of death does not seem to anticipate extinction. Rather, it is imagined as another form of existence, where freedom and equality reign. Job is wondering why he has lived to suffer. If God creates man in order to make them suffer; this purpose cannot be understood in the framework of the retribution principle. Job's death wish, thus, is an emotional expression of hopelessness, a reach to an escape from the unjust God. It is seemingly as separation from God. This view of death, thus, stands in stark contrast to the *misery, bitterness, sighing, groans, fear, dread, no peace, no quietness, turmoil* (3:20, 24–26) which characterize the present life that God has allotted him (3:23).[73] It is also opposite to the normal, natural fulfillment of a shalomic life in chapter 1. It is shared with the wicked among others. And it "speaks of nothing after death other than simple cessation of suffering – no heaven or hell."[74] However, at this point of the story death is not a natural fulfillment of a shalomic life in a sense that it is an escape from the suffering. In this sense, death here, therefore, is viewed as positive rather than as negative.

Job's lament does not express any conclusion about the failure of the theology of retribution, nor is it a death wish per se, but it is the voice of a despairing person. It is a lamentation and not an accusation. The world of his blessed life has come to a crashing end: everything is falling apart. He loses everything, seemingly including the justice of God. The seven-day-and-night period of silence is not only from men but from God. God who was once "with me" (29:5; cf. 1:1–5) is now silence. Job is anxious to know the true explanation of the cause of his suffering and imminent death. Significantly, Job wants an answer from God, for God is the one who is the cause of his (and of other sufferers') suffering. He is aware that something is wrong in his relationship with God. Job's "why" questions, thus, reflect a shift of focus to the message of the book (i.e. the relationship between God and man). And takes up a theme common to Old Testament wisdom literature, they also reflect a transitional stage of his view of death, from accepting death to questioning it.

---

73. Rowold, "Life and Death," 4.
74. Rowold, 4.

CHAPTER 3

Views of Death and the Retribution Principle in the Dialogues and in Elihu Speeches of the Book of Job

The study in this chapter will mainly focus on the dialogue section of the book of Job. It will follow the flow of the story and deal selectively with those texts that illustrate the relationship between the ideas of death and the retribution principle. The focus of this chapter will be on three perspectives on death and the retribution principle of the three friends, of Job, and of Elihu.

The dialogue in the book of Job presents the confrontation between the friends and Job. The three friends present their main argument, the retribution principle, which portrays the fate of the sinner. Thus, the study will address the three friends' common understanding of divine retribution, their views of death in the dialogue, and how their views of death reflect the two faces of Yahweh.[1] The three friends' view of death is addressed as a group for they have the same basic presupposition that suffering and death are punishment from God. While there are strong similarities between the speeches of Job's three friends, each of them does represent his own distinctive viewpoints. However, as the concern of the book is more specific, the study will first treat those retributive elements that are relevant to the questions of death in their similarities, and will then note some of their general concerns about death for their distinctiveness only as necessary. As they

---

1. As noted previously, in terms of the retribution principle the two faces of Yahweh are knowable and predictable by man. The three friends posit that everyone can know how a man encounters God: if a man is good, he is rewarded; if not, he will be punished. There is no room for the notion of *deus absconditus* in this worldview.

have the same basic assumption on divine justice, only Eliphaz's speeches particularly in the first and second cycles of the dialogues will be examined in detail but parallels from other speeches will be cited in notes.[2] Eliphaz's ideas and words will be held as representative of the group.

Collectively, the three friends strongly defend the idea of divine retribution. While Job's integrity is questioned by the accuser in the prologue, the friends' primary concern is the vindication of divine justice. They maintain that the righteous are rewarded and the wicked are punished by a righteous God in this earthly life. Although there is some truth in this premise, the three friends go far beyond the generally true proposition that sin leads to suffering. They work the logic of this theory backward: suffering is a sign of wrongdoing on the part of the sufferer; prosperity is a sign of virtuous action. Job suffers; therefore, he has sinned. Given their perspective, death is understood to be the ultimate recompense for sin. Significantly, in their retributive worldview, it is not a natural death, but a terrified death Job is experiencing that represents the ultimate recompense from God (e.g. 4:9; 8:3–6; 11:20).

The retribution principle as a theme is explicitly generated from the friends, not from Job. Job's view of death, then, changes significantly and dramatically, not in the prologue, not even in the trial of Job nor in Job 3, but in the disputation speeches with the friends. After Job's wife challenges his position, and after seven days of reflecting, Job begins to ask the question "why": why did I not die at birth, why did I not die in the process of birth, why, and why? As Job starts to ask this question "why?," he enters into a realm of spiritual chaos. The friends, with good intentions, think they have the answer to Job's question: Job must have sinned. Job, however, cannot accept their answer because he knows that he is righteous. Job is certain that their answer is wrong. Nevertheless, Job cannot find any other answer to the problem. This leads Job to attempt to question God, and particularly God's justice, on the basis of human reason informed by the retribution principle. The more he attempts to understand God and his ways, the more

---

2. In the first round of the dialogues, the three friends emphasize the negative side of the retribution principle. In the second round, they all express only the judgmental face of God, portraying only on the horrible destiny of the wicked. In the third round, they still portray the fate of the wicked, but are more specific by directly and explicitly charging against Job with some specific sins. Thus, there is nothing new in the third round of the dialogues.

he struggles. As these arguments unfold, his understanding of death vacillates between a negative and positive attitude toward death.

In analyzing Job's understanding of death, the study will follow the narrative flow of Job and see that Job, in effect, also has two faces: he is alternately defiant and faithful.[3] Sometimes it is the struggling or defiant Job who speaks of death as the dismal termination of life (e.g. 10:18–22). At other times the faithful Job struggles to look beyond physical death and has hope in Yahweh (e.g. 14:14; 16:18–21; 17:6–16; 19:25–27). This vacillation between the defiant/despairing Job and the faithful Job is crucial to the literary development of the book and recognizing it helps the reader understand why Job speaks about death in different ways in different parts of the book. Hence, Job's understanding of death in the dialogues does not develop in a linear way but emerges from the tension between Job as a man of defiance and as a man of faith.

The last character to be considered in this section is Elihu. Most commentators may prefer to link Elihu's section to Yahweh's speeches, and some may view him separately as a transitional figure. However, Elihu, like the three friends, interprets Job's dreadful suffering and death from the perspective of an understanding of God's holiness and justice rooted in the theology of retribution. He affirms, as do the three friends, that God's desire is to deal mercifully and lovingly with people. However, when people violate God's holiness and justice, God will punish with intent to bring the sinner to repentance. On the other hand, if the sinner does not repent, his rejection will lead him to the ultimate recompense – death (e.g. 36:8–12). For this reason, Elihu's views of death and the retribution principle belong together with those of the three friends and Job in this chapter.

The Dialogues: The Three Friends and Job

The mission of the three friends (רֵעַ),[4] Eliphaz, Bildad, and Zophar, is to "console and comfort" Job, the greatest man of the east (2:11; cf. 1:3). The

---

3. These two characteristics of Job may be categorized as "*simul iustus et peccator.*"
4. For the meaning of the word "friend" and the friendship theme in the book of Job, see Norman C. Habel, "Only the Jackal Is My Friend: On Friends and Redeemer in Job," *Int* 31 (1977): 227–236.

prologue presents them as performing pastorally toward Job. Their gestures suggest their sympathetic sorrow and intention to help Job come out of his affliction with renewed energy for moving on with his life. After they "lifted up their eyes" to see Job, they were shocked to discover that Job was scarcely recognizable. They "wail," "tear" their robes, and "throw dust over their heads toward heavens"[5] (2:12). Then they "sit with Job" for seven days and seven nights in silence (2:13). The length of time intensifies their sorrow and is the traditional period of mourning at the death of a most notable figure (cf. Gen 50:10; 1 Sam 31:13). The kind of "ritual" they perform signifies that they have come not only to encourage Job to move on with his life but also to acknowledge a journey that has ended in death.[6] The prologue ends at 2:13. The seven-day period functions as a turning point in the dramatic action of the story. What remains is the sound of silence, waiting for something to happen.[7] Job's pain is visibly unbearable. It grows greater and greater with each passing day and moment.[8] Later on, after Job breaks the silence, the attempts of the friends in the following dialogue to bring Job comfort and compassion are taken by Job as something different.

The First Cycle of the Dialogues
Eliphaz's First Speeches: Chapters 4:6–11; 5:8–25, 26–27. In the first speech of the friends, the reader encounters for the first time the retribution principle as a theme from the mouth of Eliphaz (4:6).

---

5. It is possible that the act of throwing dust over the head and toward heaven signifies not only the friends' sympathetic identification with Job but also an appeal to God to cover the sources of Job's affliction with dust. For the former idea, see, for instance, Janzen, *Job*, 58–59; Habel, *The Book of Job*, 97; etc. For the latter thought, see Cornelis Houtman, "Zu Hiob 2:12," *ZAW* 90 (1978): 269–272.

6. Balentine, *Job*, 68. See also the Old Testament's general view that one who has illness, persecution, despair, and nonparticipation in the life of the community is metaphorically anticipating in death for example, Wolff, *Anthropology*, 111; Bailey, Sr., *Biblical Perspective*, 39; etc.

7. Alter, *Art of Biblical Narrative*, 114–130, suggests that when the biblical narrative is selectively silent, it has a purpose either about different personages, or about different aspects of their thought, feeling, and behavior. The art of reticence in the biblical narrative reflects "a sense of the unknowable and the unforeseeable in human nature."

8. Janzen, *Job*, 59–60, notes an insight on the shift of the theme of "greatness." In 1:3 and 1:19, the *lemma* appears in adjectival form גָּדוֹל. However, in 2:13 the verb גָּדַל is used, which intensifies the process of Job's pain which keeps "growing, becoming great." So now Job's "greatness" is defined by what he has lost not by what he possessed.

Is not your fear [of God] your confidence, and the integrity of your ways your hope?	4:6	הֲלֹא יִרְאָתְךָ כִּסְלָתֶךָ תִּקְוָתְךָ וְתֹם דְּרָכֶיךָ׃

This is the substratum of Eliphaz's theology: those who fear God and are pious will enjoy God's favor and deliverance. The retribution principle, thus, is explicitly generated from the friends. Job's view of death, then, starts to change significantly and dramatically here in the first speech with the friends. As Eliphaz begins with a rhetorical question, "Is not . . . ?" (הֲלֹא), Eliphaz takes for granted that Job also accepts this basic traditional principle. The answer to this question brings 1:1 back into the conversation. Here the idea of "fear of God"[9] and the term "integrity" are specified. Eliphaz's question turns the whole shape of the book for it requires Job to defend himself. It is critical for Job because Job's fear of Yahweh and his integrity are Job's confidence (כִּסְלָה) and his hope (תִּקְוָה). The friends drive Job to defend his integrity and question God's justice. Eliphaz continues,

Remember: Who that was innocent ever perished? Or where were the upright cut off?	4:7	זְכָר־נָא מִי הוּא נָקִי אָבָד וְאֵיפֹה יְשָׁרִים נִכְחָדוּ׃
As I have seen, those who plow iniquity and sow trouble reap the same.	4:8	כַּאֲשֶׁר רָאִיתִי חֹרְשֵׁי אָוֶן וְזֹרְעֵי עָמָל יִקְצְרֻהוּ׃
By the breath of God/Eloah they perish, and by the blast of his anger they are consumed.	4:9	מִנִּשְׁמַת אֱלוֹהַ יֹאבֵדוּ וּמֵרוּחַ אַפּוֹ יִכְלוּ׃
The roar of the lion, the voice of the fierce lion, the teeth of the young lions are broken.	4:10	שַׁאֲגַת אַרְיֵה וְקוֹל שָׁחַל וְשִׁנֵּי כְפִירִים נִתָּעוּ׃
The strong lion perishes for the lack of prey, and the cubs of the lioness are scattered.	4:11	לַיִשׁ אֹבֵד מִבְּלִי־טָרֶף וּבְנֵי לָבִיא יִתְפָּרָדוּ׃

Elihphaz's point is not that the innocent never suffer, but that they never "perish" (אבד) or are "cut off, destroyed" (כחד). Eliphaz uses the word אבד three times (vv. 7, 9, and 11) as a refrain for the death of the wicked. In chapter 3 Job says, "Let the day perish (אבד) on which I was born." The

---

9. Literally, it is "your fear" (יִרְאָתְךָ). The phrase "fear of God" is appropriately rendered for it is an ellipsis form which echoes, for instance, יִרְאַת אֱלֹהִים in Gen 20:11 or יִרְאַת יְהוָה in Prov 1:29; also in the mouth of Eliphaz in 15:4; 22:4.

word is used for the death of Job's birthday. Here Eliphaz uses it three times to warn that if Job does not repent, Job's wish may soon be fulfilled. Eliphaz is affirming that the upright (יָשָׁר, cf. 1:1, 8; 2:3, where Job is designated with this same word) do not die prematurely; Job is not dead yet; therefore, Job is among the righteous and can afford to have hope (v. 6).[10] The wicked, on the other hand, will be certainly punished. This assertion is hurtful for it implicitly attributes the death of Job's ten children (1:19) to some kind of sinfulness.[11] They have been killed because of God's anger (cf. 4:9). In verse 8, Eliphaz speaks of his own experience ("As I have seen") and expects Job to accept that his experience is universally true. He affirms that the wicked will be certainly punished, and it is God who is active in this moral execution. While Job seems to blame God for the trouble (עָמָל in 3:10, 20) that now defines his life, Eliphaz implies that the guilt may be found in Job alone because of his wickedness (עָמָל in 4:8). Eliphaz does make a casual connection between all "trouble" and "iniquity" (אָוֶן). Eliphaz completes his initial review of the notion of retribution with a portrait of the destruction of lions as connected with the fate of the wicked.[12] Despite its power, the lion is doomed to perish. As Job is among the righteous (v. 6); the innocent and upright are not cut off (i.e. die in their prime, v. 7); the wicked, on the other hand, are suddenly brought to an end (vv. 8–9). It is the "breath (of God)" (נְשָׁמָה) and the "blast" (רוּחַ; lit., "wind, spirit;" cf. 1:19) of his anger that consummates the destruction of the wicked (v. 9). So it is the

---

10. Cf. Driver and Gray, *Critical and Exegetical Commentary*, 43; Clines, *Job 1–20*, 124; Balentine, *Job*, 107.

11. Bildad also has a strong idea that suffering is punishment. He presses this idea one step further by asserting that the untimely death of Job's seven sons and three daughters is proof of that punishment (8:4, "your [Job's] children have sinned against him [God], he has delivered them into the hand of their transgression"). Unless Bildad knows something about Job's children that the narrator does not share, he, like Eliphaz, is constructing an accusation to fit the retribution principle. Since God does not pervert justice (8:3), so if there is suffering and dreadful death, there has been sin. As Bildad applies to Job who has not been struck dead, it is possible that Job is "pure and upright" (8:6). Job, then, will be delivered from his affliction (8:7, 21–22).

12. Note that Eliphaz uses five different words for lion in verses 10–11: אַרְיֵה, שַׁחַל, כְּפִיר, לַיִשׁ, and לָבִיא. Job once speaks for himself in 10:16 as שַׁחַל, which God hunts for him. See similar usages of this symbol for the wicked in Pss 7:2; 17:12; 58:6; Prov 28:15; Nah 2:10–12; etc. For the comparable usage of the lion as a symbol of the impious in the "Babylonian Theodicy," see James B. Pritchard, ed., *Ancient Near Eastern Texts Relating to the Old Testament*, 3rd ed. (Princeton, NJ: Princeton University Press, 1969), 602.

wicked, and not Job, who come to such ultimate destruction. Eliphaz does not condemn Job directly in this speech.[13] However, without attending to Job's complaint, he has already subtly judged Job and found him guilty.

Eliphaz makes a positive recommendation to Job by asserting that

As for me, I would seek God, and to God would I commit my cause.	5:8	אוּלָם אֲנִי אֶדְרֹשׁ אֶל־אֵל וְאֶל־אֱלֹהִים אָשִׂים דִּבְרָתִי׃

Eliphaz is trying to put himself in Job's shoes, and to suggest what he would do in the same situation. Eliphaz uses a strong adversative word, "As for me; Indeed" (אוּלָם),[14] followed by an emphatic אֲנִי to emphasize his good counsel. He speaks with confidence in his doctrine. The word דרשׁ ("to seek") is found earlier in 3:4, where Job wishes that God may not "seek" that day, the day of his birth. Here Eliphaz encourages Job to have a formal approach to God for assistance. Eliphaz speaks of how God will bless the righteous and how God will punish the wicked. He supports his idea by documenting (in 5:9–27) many reasons why Job should seek God: God will give life and safety world of nature and humans (vv. 10–11), God will turn schemes of craftiness into darkness (vv. 12–14), and God will save the needy and poor from the mighty and unjust (vv.15–16). Eliphaz comments further that God may use suffering as a reprove or a discipline for his children (vv. 17–18).[15] He speaks eloquently of how God will provide security, prosperity, and a full family, how God will rescue a person from untimely and violent death and will turn fear into laughter in the face of destruction. Eliphaz's words of encouragement in 5:19–26 assure Job that he will not die until he has reached a "ripe old age" (5:26). This kind of death would be a sign of God's blessing upon Job's life. These are descriptions of life in terms of what Job can expect after he repents and makes his relationship right with

---

13. For an investigation of the coherence of the speeches of the three friends and the distinctive viewpoints of each friend, see Clines, "The arguments of Job's Three Friends," in *Sitting with Job: Selected Studies on the Book of Job*, ed. Roy B. Zuck (Grand Rapids: Baker, 1992), 265–278.

14. In Job 2:5, the accuser also uses this same emphatic adversative word אוּלָם.

15. Note that in Job 5:17 Eliphaz does speak of suffering as discipline (מוּסָר), a positive act of *Shadday* for the education of the sufferer. But this is not a dominant theme in the speeches of the three friends. Later on, Elihu picks up this idea and expands more on this theme (Job 33).

God again. Eliphaz uses the term *shalom* (שָׁלוֹם) (5:24) to describe such life with complete peace. Thus, a shalomic life is life, including a peaceful death, with and under God.

Note that the divine name *Shadday* (שַׁדַּי) occurs here (5:17) for the first time in the book of Job. It is interesting that out of forty-eight of its occurrences in the Hebrew Bible as a whole, this divine name appears thirty-one times in the book of Job.[16] Of the seventeen instances outside of the book of Job, seven appear in the patriarchal narratives (e.g. Gen 17:1; cf. Exod 6:3). We may have a better understanding of the significance of this name in the context outside the book of Job. In Genesis, *Shadday* is not only a God who promises abundant children to those who are childless and fruitful land to those who are landless (e.g. Gen 28:3; 35:11; 48:3) but is also a God of protection (e.g. Gen 17:1; 43:14). The idea of protection appears again in Psalm 91:1, "He who dwells in the shelter of the Most-High will abide in the shadow of *Shadday*." From these usages, *Shadday* connotes the idea of a God of conception, birth, nurture, and protection.[17] Eliphaz encourages Job to bear confidently his "pain" (v. 18; cf. 2:13, where a nominal form of this same word is used [בְּאֵב]). The two-sided divine character[18] used by Eliphaz here in 5:18–26 is for Job to hope for divine protection and safety and the divine blessings of offspring. That is, those who experience the discipline of *Shadday* and his subsequent deliverance from death (cf. 33:18, 28–30) can expect a secure and prosperous future.[19] For them, death is under the hand of God and ultimately a payment for sin.

---

16. Habel, *Book of Job*, 135, observes that the frequent usages of this divine name may suggest that the poet deliberately chooses titles typical of the patriarchal times to identify the world of the characters.

17. In his article, "Lust for Life and the Bitterness of Job," *ThTo* 55 (1998): 152–162, Janzen notes, especially in 155–160, the twofold focus of this term *Shadday*: on the fertility of the human family and on the fertility of the whole creation.

18. See the similar two-sided character of God – positive and negative – for instance, in Deut 32:39, "I kill and I make alive; I wound and I heal"; and in Hos 6:1, "He has torn us, that he may heal us; he has struck us down, and he will bind us up" (cf. also Isa 30:26).

19. In his first speech, Zophar starts from the same presupposition as the other friends that suffering is deserved. He concentrates wholly upon the fact that Job is suffering, so Job is a sinner. For Zophar, God's mercy has already been taken into Job's account (11:6, "God exacts of you less than your guilt deserves"). Job needs to forsake his present (and secret) evil-doing. Zophar places also the emphasis on the promise of restoration (11:15–19); if Job repent there is hope, but if Job does not, his fate will be no different than that of the wicked (11:20, "But the eyes of the wicked will fail/come to an end; all way of escape will be lost to

Eliphaz ends his first speech with the promise of a crowning blessing on a life protected by God – death at a ripe old age. He says,

You shall come to your grave in ripe old age, like a sheaf gathered up in its season.	5:26	תָּבוֹא בְכֶלַח אֱלֵי־קָבֶר כַּעֲלוֹת גָּדִישׁ בְּעִתּוֹ:
Behold, this we have searched out; it is true. Hear, and know it is for your good.	5:27	הִנֵּה־זֹאת חֲקַרְנוּהָ כֶּן־הִיא שְׁמָעֶנָּה וְאַתָּה דַע־לָךְ: פ

Though the meaning of the noun כֶלַח ("ripe old age") is obscure, it connotes the idea of "strength (with body vigorous, powers unimpaired)."[20] The word is found in this sense also in 30:2. Eliphaz suggests that in God's wounding and in his binding up (5:17, 24), Job has experienced the fulfillment of the promise.[21] Therefore, Eliphaz points that the death of an old man whom God has not corrected in vain is counted as reaching a high fulfillment (v. 26). In addition, death at "the right time" (lit. בְּעִתּוֹ, "at its time;" 5:26b) is viewed as a blessing. The text seemingly points to the blessing of death at the right time. As being governed by the retribution principle, the

---

them, and their hope is to breathe their last.") Zophar's portrait of life of the forgiven person is similar to Eliphaz's sketch in 5:17–20. Note that the fate of the wicked in Zophar's view is the absence of security of the blessed life. So it is not death, not even premature death, nor divine punishment, nor physically illness that is the true punishment the wicked endure. Rather it is that the wicked lose the joy of living ("their eyes fail," cf. Deut 28:32, 65; Ps 69:4[3]), a place of refuge ("ways of escape perish from them," cf. Jer 25:35; Amos 2:14), and loss of hope ("breath their last," cf. 31:39 and Jer 15:9 where the phrase means "despair, solemn sadness"). It is the sphere of security that is reckoning as the retribution in this life: Guilt will find its punishment, and right doing its reward (11:11, 13–16, 20). Therefore, nothing can stay the hand of inflexible justice. Death, in Zophar's view, is the end of all suffering, for life with absence of security is so bad. The wicked does not look for death, but it is the best choice for them. This theology leaves no room for God to exercise further mercy or forgiveness. See Clines, *Job 1–20*, 271–273; Hartley, *Book of Job*, 203.

20. BDB, 480. Some scholars (e.g. Clines, *Job 1–20*, 153) see a connection between this word and the term לֵחַ in Deut 34:7 ("Moses was 120 years old when he died. His eyes was undimmed, and his vigor (לֵחֹה) unabated"). If the word is a mixed form of כֹּח and לֵחַ, then death "at ripe old age" or "in its full strength" in Job 5:26 comes with a bonus of power unimpaired. With this connotation, death in its fulfillment of life, thus, comes without the loss of strength and fading of powers that usually accompany extreme old age. See *HALOT* 2:478; cf. Habel, *Book of Job*, 118.

21. Wolff, *Anthropology*, 111–112, comments that "yet being old may mean not to have enough 'life,' which would not be good. But the reverse is bad too; that is, to have had enough life, but not to be old."

three friends have the idea that death before the proper time (e.g. Zophar in 20:11; Eliphaz in 22:16) or being "cut off" before life has run its full course (e.g. 4:8) is a punishment and a divine disapproval. While the book of Proverbs affirms death after a long life as a blessing to those who heed the teaching of the wise (i.e. Prov 3:2, 16; 4:10; 9:11; 10:27), the death of the patriarchal heroes who were "gathered to their people" (i.e. Abraham, Gen 25:8; Ishmael, Gen 25:17; Isaac, Gen 35:29; Jacob, Gen 49:33; Moses, Deut 32:50) is counted as the final blessing. Here Eliphaz points out to Job the blessing of death at the right time. The poet uses images from nature (כַּעֲלוֹת גָּדִישׁ) to depict death as the gathering of grain for harvest in due season. "Life is not only to be lived at one with nature but to be experienced as part of its very cycle."[22] Death at the right time, thus, denotes death at "the proper time for an event,"[23] a natural progression to fulfillment in death. It is the fitting conclusion to a life that has run its full course (cf. Deut 11:14; Jer 5:24; Hos 2:11; Pss 1:3; 104:27; Prov 15:23). This perspective on life in Eliphaz's view is strikingly positive: it is peaceful (cf. vv. 23, 24), reflecting the life-giving power of God, the *Shadday*. That is, God can renew a person even in calamities. This strength from God can not only hold a person who is nearly dead from breaking apart entirely, but also enable that person to become healthy and prosper again. This idea implies that Job can flourish again after his great suffering if he repents. However, at this moment life, for Job, is not peace but torment (3:26). Death, by contrast, is a place where Job can "rejoice exceedingly and be glad" (3:22). Ironically, what Eliphaz has promised Job (5:25–26) is fulfilled at the end of the book where Job has seven other sons and three other daughters (42:13–14), lives for one hundred and forty years (42:16), and dies an old man sated with days (42:17).

In this first speech, Eliphaz closes his counsel with the wisdom tradition exhortations "hear" (שׁמע) and "know" (ידע) (5:27; cf. Prov 1:8; 4:1; 24:14). With this closing, he concludes that the description of the one protected by God according to the retribution theology (5:19–26) has been verified by the wisdom of the sages. Therefore, it has been spoken for Job's own sake (lit. "for yourself"). Job should accept his counsel as valid. Significantly,

---

22. Habel, *Book of Job*, 136.
23. *HALOT* 2:899–901.

Eliphaz emphasizes the negative side of the retribution principle, the certain punishment of the wicked (4:8–11), rather than its positive side, the good fortune for the righteous who suffers (4:7). His theology leaves no room for the possibility that righteous persons might perish in innocence.[24] Eliphaz points to Job that the "breath of God" (מִנִּשְׁמַת אֱלוֹהַּ, 4:9) brings death not life, which is contrary to what the creation tradition affirms in Genesis 2:7 (נִשְׁמַת חַיִּים). In addition, as observed by Balentine, the allusion to the formation of man out of the dust of the ground in Genesis 2:7 connects humans intimately to God ("the man of dust," הָאָדָם עָפָר) and to the commission to image God's dominion and stewardship of creation (Gen 1:26–28; 2:15).[25] Thus, Eliphaz's views of "clay" and "dust" as merely symbols of human's intrinsic corruption invalidate the possibility of being righteous and pure in relation to God (4:17, 19). Eliphaz is right in arguing that God is the cause of Job's misfortune. God is involved in human affairs (4:9; 5:8–27). However, his emphasis on God's involvement in human affairs is only a one-sided projection of God namely, the wrathful face of God that will condemn a sinner if he does not repent. What Eliphaz has suggested is the critical factor that not only disturbs but also drives Job to a desire for the vindication of his case.

Job's First Response to His Friends: Chapters 6:8–10; 7:1–6, 20–21; 10:18–22. In the first cycle of the discourses, Job's first responses to the friends are in Job 6–7; 9–10; 12–14. In their first speeches, Job's friends lead him to the point where he can only see the judgmental face of God, and Job responds to that judgmental face of God. As a result of the argument, Job is forced to attempt to reconcile his suffering with his knowledge of his own righteousness when the latter is questioned by the accusations of his friends. As Job reacts to the friends' insistence on death as the (eventual) deserved punishment for sin, and as Job comes to terms with what seems to be imminent and undeserved death, he no longer speaks of death as escape as in Job 3.

In his *vexation* and *calamity* (6:2), Job says if his anguish and punishment were measured quantitatively, then his friends would see how inexplicable

---

24. See, for instance, 2 Kgs 21:16; 24:4; cf. Ps 106:38; Isa 59:7; Jer 22:17.
25. Balentine, *Job*, 121.

the extent of his suffering was. Because of this, his words have been rash (3:1, 11). The core of his anguish lies not in the fact that he is suffering physically and emotionally, but rather in the fact that no reason can be found for his suffering. God is silent (cf. 23:3–7). If this were punishment, then Job could accept it, but it is not. Job starts his speech by comparing God to an archer (6:4). The image of God as an archer is common in the Old Testament (Deut 32:33; Ezek 5:16; Lam 3:12–13; Ps 7:13). Eliphaz asserts that disaster is either the harvest of evil that a person has sown (4:8) or the result of discipline from *Shadday* (5:17). Job does not accept his theory. Job cannot accept these arrows as God's discipline or justified punishment (v. 4). These arrows, thus, are poisonous.

Job is not crying out for nothing. Just as simple beasts will cry out only when they do not have what they need for life (v. 5), so also Job cries out in his despair. He sees no reason or resolution. In verses 6 and 7 Job announces that the suggestion of the friends is worthless. Their arguments are without consolation or comfort. They do not try to understand Job's existential anguish. Job then expresses his inability to go on. He gropes for ways to articulate aspects of the murky, ominous reality of death. Among his first words in this discourse with the three friends is Job's stunning prayer that God would bring his agony to an end and simply snuff him out (6:8–9):

Oh that I might have my request, and that God would fulfill my hope,	6:8	מִי־יִתֵּן תָּבוֹא שֶׁאֱלָתִי וְתִקְוָתִי יִתֵּן אֱלוֹהַּ:
that it would please God to crush me, that he would let loose his hand and cut me off.	6:9	וְיֹאֵל אֱלוֹהַּ וִידַכְּאֵנִי יַתֵּר יָדוֹ וִיבַצְּעֵנִי:

In chapter 3, Job has expressed his futile wishes that he should not have been born (3:3–10) and that he should have died at birth (3:11–19) and has asked why the lives of those who would rather be dead are prolonged (3:20–23). But here Job, for the first time, states explicitly his desire for death. Job's hope (תִּקְוָה)[26] is not a "blameless way," as Eliphaz has encouraged

---

26. The Hebrew term תִּקְוָה derives from the verb קָוָה, which may mean "thread," or "hope." The verb form appears forty-seven times in the Hebrew Bible, including five times in the book of Job (3:9; 6:19; 7:2; 17:13; 30:26; all in Piel stem). The noun תִּקְוָה occurs thirty-two times in the Bible, with thirteen times in Job (4:6; 5:16; 6:8; 7:6; 8:13; 11:18,

Job in 4:6, but death itself. The friends' understanding of hope is based on the retribution principle; namely, that the righteous can have confidence that God will reward or restore Job's persistent hope for vindication (cf. Prov 10:28; 11:23; 23:18). On the contrary, Job knows that his case is outside the realm of the retribution principle. His wish for death is connected to his understanding of his relationship to God and that understanding of his relationship to God has been perverted through the friends imposing upon him the notion of divine justice in terms of the retribution principle. As a result of the argument with the friends, he can only think of God in terms of justice and not in terms of graciousness and mercy. Job can see only God's judgmental face. And not only that, but God's justice seems to have gone awry, so that God himself appears to Job as unjust. Since he knows that he is innocent, Job is willing to stand before the judgmental face of God. But how shall he stand before God if God himself is unjust? God's justice appears to Job to be perverted. This is what leads Job to despair. Job, then, has lost his sense of hope in God's graciousness. Therefore, he prefers to die rather than to live. At this point, all he can think of is to escape. With his body in extreme pain, Job perceives hope differently from the friends; that is, death at the hand of the one who brings his suffering (cf. 7:2, 6; 17:13, 15).[27] Thus, Job prefers to die than to live with only dispirited hope.

Significantly, Job is not contemplating committing suicide.[28] God is the one who initiates these circumstances, so it is only God who can put an end to it. Job pleads that God is willing (יאל) to "crush" (דכא) him, not as a punishment but as end to his life. Job would gladly be crushed as his own children were in the prologue (1:19). The same word "crush" is used by Eliphaz literally in 4:19, "crushed like a moth," but here (and in 5:4) it is used figuratively that God would let loose his hand and "crush" him as

---

20; 14:7, 19; 17:15, 25; 19:10; 27:8). See C. Westermann, "קוה qwh *pi.* 'to hope,'" *TLOT* 3:1126–1132. Job's life, therefore, is literally hanging by a fast disappearing thread.

27. Newsom insightfully points out that the images of hope (e.g. the double meaning of תִּקְוָה: "hope," and "thread") and of the wounded and invaded body are used in relation to the understanding of the body of time. Thus, while the friends encourage Job to have "hope" in the future time, the time for Job whose body is in pain is a time of urgency. These images serve as an integrative figure that allows life to be grasped as a whole. For a further discussion on the narrative time and the time of a body in pain, see Newsom, *Job: A Contest*, 133–136.

28. Also Walter Riggans, "A Note on Job 6:8–10: Suicide and Death-Wishes," *Dor le dor* 15 (1986–87): 173–176.

a creature of dust, as Eliphaz maintains (4:19). The picture, thus, is that of God freeing his hand so that he can cut Job loose. The image of a hand echoes also the event in the prologue where the accuser has asked God to put his hand on Job. However, God's preservation of the suffering life of Job is, from Job's perspective at this point, the most terrifying act of God, for it serves only to prolong his unendurable suffering. In addition, the Hebrew word "cut off" (בצע) literally means to cut the thread so a fabric can be removed from the loom.²⁹ King Hezekiah uses a similar phrase when he laments his impending death by saying that "like a weaver I have rolled up my life; he cuts me off from the loom" (Isa 38:12b; cf. Job 7:6; 27:8). This image depicts God cutting Hezekiah (and also Job) out of the thread of the fabric being woven on the loom. In Job's case, the act of "cutting off," must be done by God himself, and not by Job taking his own life.³⁰ Death could be a comfort rather than going on with terrified dying. Job, thus, hopes seemingly to experience a kind of severe wounding that should bring immediate death and thus relieve him of pain.³¹

Job is not simply viewing death as surcease (6:8–9), for in verse 10 Job expresses:

| This would be my comfort; I would even exult in pain unsparing, for I have not denied the words of the Holy One. | 6:10 | וּתְהִי עוֹד נֶחָמָתִי וַאֲסַלְּדָה בְחִילָה לֹא יַחְמוֹל כִּי־לֹא כִחַדְתִּי אִמְרֵי קָדוֹשׁ׃ |

---

29. See D. Kellermann, "בצע," *TDOT* 2: 206–207.

30. In the whole book of Job there is no idea of committing a suicide. In other Old Testament passages, the reader may see the thought of suicide in, for instance, the stories of Israelite heroes: Saul, who eventually has to fall on his own sword (1 Sam 31:3–4); Abimelech, who is wounded by a woman, has his armor-bearer kill him out of male pride (Judg 9:53–54); Zimri, who burns his citadel down upon himself when he sees his capital taken by Omri (1 Kgs 16:18); and Ahithopel, who hangs himself (2 Sam 17:23).

31. Job's wish for death, specifically death by divine violence, is an ironic plea parodying those psalmists who pray for God's hand to be lifted from them (Pss 32:4; 39:10[11]), who pray not to be cut off (Ps 88:5; Isa 38:12), and who pray for relief from being crushed by God (Ps 38:2, 8[3, 9]). See, Newsom, *The Book of Job*, NIB, 387; Habel, *Book of Job*, 147.

Job concludes his request to God that if he died, his death would be his "comfort" (נֶחָמָתִי) again (10a). Death would indeed be a friend.³² Death is much more welcome here, for Job will "jump for joy" ("exult," סלד, a verb found only here).³³ Thus, death is preferred to a life of *pain unsparing* – pain that has no mercy on the one suffering. It seems that Job is not merely wishing for death, but a swift death. Such a sudden death would be bliss when compared to his present painful life. However, since death comes undeservedly at the hand of God, Job maintains at least the comfort that he would not die due to recompense for gross sin. Thus, Job will not have "concealed" (כחד)³⁴ "the words (אִמְרֵי) of the Holy One (קָדוֹשׁ),"³⁵ who

---

32. Also Habel, "Only the Jackal," 229. Interestingly, Job's initial response to Eliphaz in chapter 6 is not explicitly disputation about a theological issue (i.e. the friends' defense of God), but a very human lament – a call for his friends to be true to their function. Habel notes further that as the friends fail from showing the art of "comfort" (נֶחָמָה), Job prefers death who would be a fellow traveler in the land of no return, the land of endless despair. Job feels betrayed and yearns for a meaningful compassion from the friends and genuine hope (229).

33. The root סלד is a *hapax legomenon* in the Old Testament. The traditional rendering to this word is "to exult, to leap (for joy)" (LXX, Targum). However, the post-biblical meaning suggests "to draw back," as a hand to recoiling from the heat of a fire (BDB, 698). Riggans, "A Note on Job," 176, prefers the latter meaning and suggests that in 6:10 Job does not leap for joy. Rather Job "is constantly recoiling in fear and horror from this God and this world." Riggans' point is that suicide is viewed as a grave sin in the Jewish tradition. Though Job does not commit suicide, his death wish may make him commit the sin of despising life anyway. So, he proposes that Job does not wish for death (i.e. not leaping in joy for being death), but "merely wishes a swift, painless death" because Job springs back in fear or the like. Riggans concludes, in 176, that Job is not actively seeking death, but in the state of pathos where swift death would be preferable to long anguish. However, as the word סלד occurs only once in the Hebrew Bible, there is no support from other passages. From the context of Job 6 itself, the traditional meaning still makes sense. Job's death wish does not make him commit a sin of despising God or life. In addition, as the story unfolds the reader will see that after chapter 6 Job continues to make several wishes for death. Significantly, at the end of the book God does not only affirm that Job is the one who speaks what is right, but also implicitly declare to Job not guilty.

34. The root כחד, does not really mean "deny." Literally, it means to "hide," or to "conceal" the truth (e.g. 15:18; 27:11). The context of Job's mood seems to support its basic literal meaning. That is, Job has not "concealed" the truth in the sense that he has exposed the decisions of God (i.e. in the prologue) for what they are (e.g. unfair, unholy) in Job's life (Habel, *Book of Job*, 140, 147; also Dhorme, *Commentary on the Book of Job*, 82).

35. The singular form of the Hebrew term "the Holy One" (קָדוֹשׁ) occurs only here in the book of Job. The term is an epithet for God (also in Isa 40:25; 57:15; Hos 11:9; Hab 3:3; Sir 45:6). However, the plural form, קְדֹשִׁים, appears in Job 5:1 and 15:15 rendering as "angels." Here (6:10) if Job is going to expose how the decisions or the truth of God affecting his life as he states in the preceding clause, clearly the term "the Holy One" is used as satirical.

has decided to "destroy him without reason" (2:3).³⁶ The sentiment of the text is expressed well by Riggans, "If there is no longer *justice* with God, Job says, at least I pray (v. 8) that there is still *mercy*. Finish me off quickly, Lord."³⁷ Job, thus, completely rejects Eliphaz's idea of repentance. Although his words may seem to be disrespectful from the friends' point of view, he will bemoan and boldly accuse God.

In this obvious death wish (6:8–10), Job's view of death is outside the realm of the retribution principle. It would not be an act of judgment (i.e. in the retribution principle) but of mercy if God were to "crush" Job. Thus, to be cut off by God would not be punishment, as the friends implied (4:9), but freedom from the terror of Eloah (6:4). His implicit argument is that he is innocent; therefore, he prefers death to the acceptance that he has sinned. In addition, as he is experiencing a tortuous living death, Job expresses his wish for a swift death that could end his pain immediately. This lament is a desire to leave this world suddenly by God's hand. Ironically, as Job does not know that Yahweh has given him into the "hand" of the accuser to afflict him without taking his life (2:5–6), Job here wishes that God would no longer withhold his hands but exterminate Job.

Job shifts the target of his speech from the friends in chapter 6 to God in chapter 7. He laments in distress over God's treatment of human life, which is ephemeral (7:1–10). While the friends express death as the ultimate recompense for sin (e.g. 4:7–11), Job, placing his particular distress into the broad perspective of human futility, now speaks of death in terms of the generic, systematic (and miserable) reality of human life. Job says:

> Has not man a hard service on earth,
>   and are not his days like the days of a hired hand?
> Like a slave who longs for the shadow,
>   and like a hired hand who looks for his wages,

---

36. In his dissertation, "The Function and Significance of the Klage in the Book of Job with Special Reference to the Incidence of Formal and Verbal Irony," (Southern Methodist University, 1975), John C. Holbert, 139, sees that Job 6:10 is a parody of Ps 119:50, "This is my comfort in my affliction, that your אִמְרָה gives me life." In the prologue of Job the literal "word" God has spoken has been his word to the satan to "not kill Job." Though Job does not know of the heavenly wager, in his faithful to God, and far from God's word giving Job life, Job wants only death from God's word.

37. Riggans, "A Note on Job," 176.

> so I am allotted months of emptiness,
> > and nights of misery are apportioned to me.
> When I lie down I say, "When shall I arise?"
> > But the night is long,
> > > and I am full of tossing till the dawn.
> My flesh is clothed with worms and dirt;
> > my skin hardens, then breaks out afresh.
> My days are swifter than a weaver's shuttle
> > and come to their end without hope. (Job 7:1–6)

Job's day are nearly spent. He, at the same time, is mocking Eliphaz's word to accept *Shadday*'s discipline (5:17). Job has no time to wait for any alleged divine wounding or healing at 7:6. As Job mourns that his life is an insubstantial breath that will rapidly be spent (7:7–8), he realizes that he is facing the imminent end of his life (7:9–10). Sheol is a place from which the dead do not return (also 10:21) and regain former recognition. Job suffers from physical illness.[38] His deeper anguish is that he is not able to escape. God continues to persecute him even in dreams (7:13–14). In repeated negative terms,[39] Job's sentiments connote the emptiness and helplessness. These phrases also bring out the idea of the irreversibility of descent into Sheol, the realm of the dead: it is final. Job, then, continues complaining against God (as in 7:7–8) by rejecting life and preferring death:

So that I would choose strangling and death rather than my bones.	7:15	וַתִּבְחַר מַחֲנָק נַפְשִׁי מָוֶת מֵעַצְמוֹתָי׃
I loathe my life; I would not live forever. Leave me alone, for my days are a breath.	7:16	מָאַסְתִּי לֹא־לְעֹלָם אֶחְיֶה חֲדַל מִמֶּנִּי כִּי־הֶבֶל יָמָי׃

---

38. Habel, *Book of Job*, 159, notes that in the OT the physical illness is viewed as a symbol of death. Job described his body as attired in "dust" and "worm," therefore, "he is apparently asserting that his body is clothed with the marks of mortality, death, and corruption."

39. For example, "לֹא־תְשׁוּרֵנִי עָיִן" ("not noticed," 7:8), "לֹא־יַעֲלֶה" ("not come up," 7:9), "לֹא־יָשׁוּב" ("not return," 7:10), and "וְאֵינֶנִּי" ("and I am no more," 7:8, 21).

Job wishes again for death. Literally, the text in verse 15 reads, "my soul/throat chooses strangling." The Hebrew "my soul/throat" (נַפְשִׁי) can be used as a substitute for the personal pronoun "I."[40] Job would rather die than continue living on miserable body. Job is expressing his own exhaustion and despair: "I loathe my life; I would not live forever" (7:16; cf. 9:21; 10:1).[41] He is also struggling to understand the assumption that remarkable suffering is from the action of God, particularly as a response to sin. Thus, Job bitterly asks God:

If I sin, what do I do to you, you watcher of mankind? Why have you made me your mark? Why have I become a burden to you?[42]	7:20	חָטָאתִי מָה אֶפְעַל לָךְ נֹצֵר הָאָדָם לָמָה שַׂמְתַּנִי לְמִפְגָּע לָךְ וָאֶהְיֶה עָלַי לְמַשָּׂא:
Why do you not pardon my transgression, and take away my iniquity? For now I shall lie in the earth; you will seek me, but I shall not be.	7:21	וּמֶה לֹא־תִשָּׂא פִשְׁעִי וְתַעֲבִיר אֶת־עֲוֺנִי כִּי־עַתָּה לֶעָפָר אֶשְׁכָּב וְשִׁחֲרְתַּנִי וְאֵינֶנִּי:

Job's words of protest arise from his painful sense that God has betrayed their relationship.[43] Job is not admitting that troubles have come on him because he has sinned. The phrase חָטָאתִי, "if I sin," establishes a hypothetical

---

40. In poetry or ornate discourse, the term נפש may be used as the essential of man stands for the man itself. Thus it is a paraphrase for personal pronoun. See BDB, 659.

41. Habel, *Book of Job*, 163–164, suggests that Job is making a mock rejection of God's offer of eternal life. His idea is from a comparable situation in the Canaanite Aqhat legend. However, it is not necessary to walk outside the text. Contextually, Job may not want to always remain alive. He is expressing the simple fact that we all die one day.

42. The MT reads a burden "to me" rather than "to you." The change is generally acknowledged as one of the eighteen "scribal corrections" (*tiqqune sopherim*) where the original text was altered out of reverence to God. See, for instance, Terrien, *Job*, 968; Harold H. Rowley, *Job*, eds., Harold H. Rowley and Matthew Black (Thomas Nelson & Sons, c. 1970) 82; etc.

43. The same sentiment may be found in the mouth of the prophet Jeremiah, who voices a sense of having been betrayed by God, that "O YHWH, you have deceived me, and I was deceived; you are stronger than I, and you have prevailed. I have become a laughingstock all the day; everyone mocks me" (Jer 20:7).

condition⁴⁴ which is used to get relief from God, who is now Job's tormentor. Since Job is going to die soon (cf. עַתָּה "now," 7:21), he is asking God that any sin he may have committed is hardly worth recompense. So how should that alleged sin affect God? Job calls God as "watcher of mankind," alluding to 7:12, "you set a guard over me."⁴⁵ In Psalm 8 (i.e. 8:4) the attention of God is positive, presenting God's interesting concern and compassion. It is a gracious face of God that the psalmist is reacting to. However, here Job is put in the position to encounter the judgmental face of God. Thus, God's watching over mankind, particularly over Job, is no longer a good thing but a bad action. Job is satirically twisting the understanding of God as protector (נֹצֵר) who is now performing the "satan-like surveillance role"⁴⁶ (1:7) upon Job. He is God's target (מִפְגָּע, 7:20; cf. 6:4, where Job complains of being shot by God's arrows; and 16:12, where God has set him up as his target). Job's terrified and imminent death is evidence to the eyes of the friends, and presumably of God, that Job is guilty of some sin. In response, Job wishes some of his suffering back on God by suggesting that God will be the loser if Job slips off into the void of death, seemingly beyond God's retrieval (אֵינֶנִּי, 7:21; cf. 7:8; Ps 39:13[14]).⁴⁷ The phrase "I shall not be" here completes the sense of Job's willingness to die.

In chapter 7, death is not only viewed as the imminent, shriveled end to Job's empty life (e.g. 7:1–4, 6), but also an escape from God. This is because

---

44. Instead of taking Job's opening words here as hypothetical, Andersen (*Job*, 132) is among the few who sees the phrase as confessional. It is more likely that Job's words carry the thought of sarcasm, not confession. Contextually, the reader sees that Job contends throughout that he is innocent (e.g. 12:4; 27:2–6), God also declares that Job is blameless and upright (1:8; 2:3), the narrator comments that he did not sins with his lips (2:10). Thus, the logic of Job's mourning suggests rather that the sin in which Job is speaking about is only hypothetical. In addition, the fact that Job has acknowledged his own innocence in 6:29–30, gives the reader a hint that Job is far from admitting any real sin here. See also Clines, *Job 1–20*, 194.

45. The full impact of God's terrible "watching" of 7:20 should be noted. It contrasts sharply with the alleged protective "hedge" of the prologue, and is a continuation of Job's point of view, expressed by his opinion of God's hedge at 3:23, including God's muzzle at 7:12, and the parody of Ps 8 and the continual presence of God in 7:17–18.

46. The term is from Habel, *Book of Job*, 155.

47. Habel, 161, 167, insightfully notes that the expression אֵינֶנִּי, "I shall not be" is not only a statement of nonexistence, but also an idea of absence, referring back to a former presence, where Job has been God's past target of object of scrutiny (cf. 8:22; 24:24). Thus, when God seeks for Job, his victim, to pardon him, Job will be safely beyond God's power. The land of the dead is the only place of freedom, the only escape.

Job is not able to behold the gracious face of God at this moment. He views God as his enemy, as the unjust Judge. His understanding of his relationship with God has been changed because of the friends' questioning. As a result, his view of death has been changed. What he once viewed as a wholesome natural end to a life lived before a gracious God he now views as a bitter, shriveled end of an empty life. The change in his view of death reflects the change in Job's understanding of his relationship with God, which has been led to that point by the question of his friends and their imposition of the retribution principle as a controlling theology of Job's relationship with God. And Job has accepted that, at least, as a working principle, which in turn led him to despair, and to desire to die as an escape from his suffering. Death now appears to be a bitter pill to be swallowed at the end of the suffering of his life, because from his point of view it is undeserved. His horrible death should not be happening, because he knows that he is innocent. There is a tremendous irony here. Later on, Job recalls in 29:5 that one thing that made the "months gone by" joyful was that the "*Shadday* was still with me" (בְּעוֹד שַׁדַּי עִמָּדִי). The irony is that God is with him now and God has not changed. What has changed is Job's perception of what God is doing. In the former happy days when God was with him, Job perceived God as the *Shadday,* the One who protects and cares for life. Now God is still with him, but Job can not perceive that gracious, protective *Shadday*. He can only perceive God as the Eye that watches over him, the judgmental God. Therefore, the shift here is not in whether God is or is not with Job, but in how Job perceives God, namely what face of God Job is encountering. As Job attributes his pain and suffering to what appear to him to be the capricious deeds of God, Job begs for escape from God and from Immanuel, from being with God, "Leave me alone, for my days are a breath . . . How long will you not look away from me, nor leave me alone till I swallow my spit?" (7:16, 19; cf. 10:20).[48]

Job had spoken of death (including his own terrified and imminent death) as the ultimate and absolute termination of all existence (7:9, 21; also 10:21; 14:10, 12; 16:22). In his speech in chapter 8, Bildad rebukes Job in the following speech and declares that it is only the tents of the wicked

---

48. Cf. in Job's opening lament, he speaks of one of the ways death brings rest is that it frees the slave (i.e. Job) from the master (i.e. God) (3:19).

that "will be no more" (אֵינֶנּוּ, 8:22; cf. 7:8, 21; 24:24). For Bildad a terrified death will come only to the wicked (cf. Pss 84:10; 118:15). While Bildad, in his concluding speech in 8:20–22, argues that God is on the side of the one who is blameless and will reward the good and punish the wicked, Job sees in his imminent death only the injustice of God (9:22–31; 10:1–7, 14–17).

Job responds to Bildad in chapter 9 by wishing for an arbiter/umpire to make his case before God.[49] In chapter 10, Job expresses another explicit wish for death (10:18–22). He loathes his life (10:1; cf. 9:21). His disappointment enables him to speak fiercely ("speak in the bitterness of my soul," 10:1) to God. Job does not understand God's justice (cf. 9:30–31). He does not want to be condemned in advance, at least not until he knows the reason why; and so he asks God to specify the accusations God has against him (10:2). It seems to Job that God is not satisfied with oppressing and despising Job, a righteous man, but even prefers the schemes of wicked men (10:3). How does God not see his innocence and rush to help (10:4)? Job also doubts in God's mercy for God appears to want to keep him alive in order to harm him repeatedly (10:12–16). His anger and resentment lead him into emotional agony and a desire to die. He regrets his birth and pleads with God to let him die in peace in 10:18–22:

Why did you bring me out from the womb? Would that I had died before any eye had seen me.	10:18	וְלָמָּה מֵרֶחֶם הֹצֵאתָנִי אֶגְוַע וְעַיִן לֹא־תִרְאֵנִי׃
And were as though I had not been, carried from the womb to the grave.	10:19	כַּאֲשֶׁר לֹא־הָיִיתִי אֶהְיֶה מִבֶּטֶן לַקֶּבֶר אוּבָל׃

---

49. See discussion of Job 9 together with Job 14, 16, and 19 in the later section of this chapter.

Are not my days few? Then cease,[50] and leave me alone,[51] that I may find a little cheer	10:20	הֲלֹא־מְעַט יָמַי יֶחְדָּל [וַחֲדָל] יָשִׁית [וְשִׁית] מִמֶּנִּי אַבְלִיגָה מְּעָט׃
before I go – and I shall not return – to the land of darkness and deep shadow,	10:21	בְּטֶרֶם אֵלֵךְ וְלֹא אָשׁוּב אֶל־אֶרֶץ חֹשֶׁךְ וְצַלְמָוֶת׃
the land of gloom like thick darkness, like deep shadow without any order, where light is as thick darkness.	10:22	אֶרֶץ עֵיפָתָה כְּמוֹ אֹפֶל צַלְמָוֶת וְלֹא סְדָרִים וַתֹּפַע כְּמוֹ־אֹפֶל׃ פ

Job strongly insists that he is innocent (10:14–15).[52] In other words, Job again rejects the way in which the friends are attempting to apply the retribution principle to his case. At the same time he is struggling to understand his impending ugly death and the fact that God appears to be acting unjustly. Theologically, Job is struggling because he does not know how to deal with these things and so he asks God to leave him alone as he is near death (10:18–22). There is a difference between this statement and the similar one in chapter 3. In chapter 3 Job did not ask why God allowed him to be born, but in 10:18a he directly blames God for his sorrowful existence (cf. 3:11).[53] This is an indication of Job's angry determination to hold on a merciful God against a judgmental God. In 3:16, Job responds to God's apparent injustice by envying babies who had never lived to see the light of day, and wishing

---

50. The study, following the ESV, understands this verb as an imperative (i.e. the MT Qere), "then cease." Some translations may read the verb as indicative (i.e. the MT Kethib), for instance, "Are not the fewness of my days soon cease?" In either case, the meaning of this line is the same; that is, Job is rhetorically asking God that he has only a short period of time left to live.

51. Again, the study will follow the Qere reading of the MT. Literally, the Hebrew is "put from me." This reading may expect the reader to understand "God's hand" (cf. 1:11–12; 2:5) or "God's attention" (cf. 7:17). As parallel to the first line, Job is asking God to leave him in peace.

52. Job 10:14–15: "If I sin, you watch me and do not acquit me of my iniquity. If I am guilty, woe to me! If I am in the right, I cannot lift up my head, for I am filled with disgrace and look on my affliction."

53. Notice the shift from "I" to "you." While in 3:11, Job asks, "Why did 'I' come out from the womb?" in 10:18, Job states, "Why did 'you' bring me out from the womb?" See Westermann, *Structure*, 53.

that nobody had ever seen him alive (10:18b; cf. 7:8, 12).⁵⁴ Job wishes that he had never lived but had died at birth and been buried (10:19; cf. 3:16a).⁵⁵ Verse 20 begins and ends on the same term of "few" or "little" (מְעַט). The sentiment is the same as in 7:16,⁵⁶ where Job expresses his depression and hopelessness that since his "days are a breath," he would not live forever. So the phrase "leave me alone" implies that whatever comfort Job can gather is found without God, and that he will soon die. As the only face of God Job can see is the judgmental face of God and that judgmental face of God seems to be unjust, there is no comfort in God. The only comfort Job can find is being away from God.

The words for "darkness" in verses 21–22 recall 3:4–6, and the description of death recalls Job's lament in 7:9–10, 21. Job refers to death as the land of no return (10:21; cf. 7:9–10). Death is the absolute termination of all humans. Once a person enters this land, there is no possibility of returning to earth. The designated term אֶרֶץ "land/earth, here referring to the underworld,"⁵⁷ is characterized by five different terms communicating the sense of darkness: חֹשֶׁךְ, "darkness;" עַלְמָוֶת, "deep shadow" (x2);⁵⁸ עֵיפָתָה, "(thick) darkness;" אֹפֶל, "gloom" (x2); לֹא סְדָרִים, "without order." These are traditional ways of describing Sheol, the land of the dead, (cf. Ps 88:7, 13; Isa

---

54. In light of the surveillance motif in the book of Job, Habel, *Book of Job*, 200–201, suggests an ironic allusion to the "Seeing Eye" or the "Watcher of human" (7:8, 17–22; 10:4, 6, 14) that "to be born and live beneath that "Eye" is the ultimate humiliation for Job."

55. TEV translates this verse very clearly with a noun clause as subject: "To go from the womb straight to the grave would have been as good as never existing." In addition, the archetypal connection between the womb and the tomb (i.e. grave) seems to be perfectly and beautifully expressed by the Joban poet.

56. In 3:17 Sheol is a place where the wicked will "cease" (חדל) from troubling. In 7:16, Job sarcastically says to God to "cease from me." There is a time for the wicked to eventually "cease," but is there a time when God will "cease" his "terror?" (חתת; cf. 6:21; 7:14). See Holbert, "Function and Significance," 148.

57. Magnus Ottosson, "אֶרֶץ," *TDOT* 1: 399–400. In *Shades of Sheol*, 99–114, especially 109, Johnston suggests that the term אֶרֶץ alone does not identify it as the underworld. However, as the term is used in 10:20–21 with other qualifying terms (i.e. gloom, darkness, chaos), contextually it denotes the earth below.

58. See David Winton Thomas, "עַלְמָוֶת, in the Old Testament," *JSS* 7 (1962): 191–200. Thomas, 197, decisively points out that the Hebrew term עַלְמָוֶת incorporates the term מָוֶת "death" used as a superlative, and thus means "a very deep shadow, thick darkness"; there is "no intrinsic reference in עַלְמָוֶת to physical death, or to the underworld of Sheol." This literary reading is in contrast to those proponent of mythological reading (e.g. Fyall, *My Eyes*, 106, 113) who see the word עַלְמָוֶת as the menacing sinister Job has already summoned in 3:5 and now is back again in 10:20–21 with its pair (i.e. חֹשֶׁךְ) denoting "the presiding genii of Sheol."

45:18–19).⁵⁹ Job understands death to be the realm of deep darkness, having no order (i.e. chaos; cf. Gen 1:2), specifically it is the land of no return.

Here we see that Job's attitude toward death has changed. This is because the friends' questioning has led Job to the point where he can only think of God in terms of God's judgmental face and that judgmental face seems to be unjust. And that in turn has led Job away from viewing death as a positive end to a good life to something that is either despair or a longing for death that is the response of Job's despair when all he can behold is the judgmental face of God and the unjust of the judgmental face of God. In 3:17–18, 21–22, Job described death in highly desirable terms, something to be actively sought. Even in chapter 7, Job spoke of death as a kind of protection from the relentlessness of God (7:21). Now, however, Job's description of death is more negative.⁶⁰ The sense of "no return" reflects Job's melancholy. Job realizes that if he is going to find relief, it must be in this life. The irreversibility of death (v. 21a), thus, confronts Job. The gloomy state of the realm of the dead, intensified by images of darkness, moves him to despair.

Job's Speeches Continued: Chapters 13:13–16; 14:7–15, 18. In Job 11, starting from the same presupposition as the other friends, Zophar emphasizes that suffering is deserved. He concentrates entirely on the fact that Job is suffering. Since the friends could not find Job's obvious sins, Zophar argues that Job is a secret sinner.⁶¹ In response to Zophar, Job's speeches in chapters 12–14 bring the first cycle of discourses to a close.⁶² The emphasis on the wrathful face of God in the retribution concept described by the friends in the first cycle of dialogues (chs. 4–5; 8; 11) naturally is of no comfort to the suffering Job, especially as God appears unjust. Instead, their counsel frustrates and further infuriates Job. Job's response in chapter

---

59. Tromp, *Primitive*, 95–98.

60. Newsom, *The Book of Job*, NIB, 415.

61. Although the three friends have the same presupposition that suffering is punishment from God, each of them has its own distinctiveness in their argument. Briefly, Eliphaz argues from the pious life of Job in order to offer hope and consolation (Job 4–5). Bildad speaks of the contrast between the fates of Job and Job's children in order to offer Job a warning. Zophar argues from Job's obvious suffering in order to denounce Job. See detail analysis of the distinctive viewpoints of the three friends in Clines, "Arguments of Job's," 274–276.

62. They are also the longest of Job's speeches in the first cycle of discourses, totally seventy-five verses.

12 is, thus, the mockery of the friends (12:2–12) and their view of God (12:13–25). Job, a man of faith, is not renouncing his faith in God and in God's beneficence, but rather is responding to the view of the friends that would appear to make God unjustly wrathful. Job claims to be equal to his friends in knowledge. He insists on his knowledge from experience, from what he has seen, and what he has heard (13:1–2). Job, then, comes to a different conclusion: the wrathful face of God only condemns man, and not encourages man as the friends affirm (e.g. Eliphaz 5:8–17; Bildad 8:20–21; Zophar 11:13–19).[63] The wrathful face of God only drives man, including the innocent sufferer like Job, to despair.[64]

Job's conclusion leads him to a bold confession of faith, including his view of death which is inherent in it:

Let me have silence,[65] and I will speak, and let come on me what may.[66]	13:13	הַחֲרִישׁוּ מִמֶּנִּי וַאֲדַבְּרָה־אָנִי וְיַעֲבֹר עָלַי מָה:
Why should I take my flesh in my teeth and put my life in my hand?	13:14	עַל־מָה אֶשָּׂא בְשָׂרִי בְשִׁנָּי וְנַפְשִׁי אָשִׂים בְּכַפִּי:
Though he slay me, I will hope in him;[67] yet I will argue[68] my ways to his face.	13:15	הֵן יִקְטְלֵנִי לֹא [לוֹ] אֲיַחֵל אַךְ־דְּרָכַי אֶל־פָּנָיו אוֹכִיחַ:

---

63. Habel, *Book of Job*, 215–217, points out that Job understands that God's alien intervention in 12:13–25 deprives society's leaders and nullifies the efficiency of their administration.

64. Christopher W. Mitchell, "Job and the Theology of Cross," *Concordia Journal* 15 (1989): 161.

65. Literally, the Hebrew is "Be silent from me."

66. The Hebrew ends with "what," which may be taken as "come what may," or "let be what will be."

67. It is of interest to note that the RSV, for instance, follows the consonantal text, the Kethib, and translates this phrase, "I will *not* hope in him," which is an obvious aural error. However, this study follows the Qere annotation of the MT. The fact that Job speaks of God as his salvation in verse 16a supports the Qere. Cf. Habel, *Book of Job*, 225, 230, agreeing with Gordis, sees the nuance meaning of the verb יחל as "be silent," as in 32:11, 16; thus, he proposes the rendering "I will not wait," in which Job will not "wait" silently for God to speak. For a further discussion of the evidence for the antiquity of the variant reading, see Bruce Zuckermann, *Job the Silent: A Study in Historical Counterpoint* (New York: Oxford University Press, 1991), 170–174. For a discussion of keeping both the Kethib and the Qere in understanding the text of Job, see Newsom, *The Book of Job*, NIB, 434–435.

68. The term אוֹכִיחַ is rendered as "argue" in 13:15b. It is the verbal form of the noun מוֹכִיחַ, "umpire" used in 9:33, where Job longs for an umpire, a referee, to equalize the

This[69] will be my salvation, that the godless shall not come before him.	13:16	גַּם־הוּא־לִי לִישׁוּעָה כִּי־לֹא לְפָנָיו חָנֵף יָבוֹא׃

In 7:11 and 10:1, Job expressed the view that the bitterness of his soul forced him to speak. Here Job petitions again to the friends to be silent in order that he may keep speaking without any interruption from them (13:13a).[70] Job is ready to pay the price for whatever may happen to him for speaking out (13:13b). He is ready to risk even his life (בָּשָׂר and נֶפֶשׁ; 13:14). However, as Job is a man of trust, he continues with his bold trust in the merciful God as a rebuttal against the wrathful God of the friends (13:15–16). For the friends, who strongly hold to the retribution doctrine, God is strictly just according the divine retributive principle and a man cannot stand in God's presence. In their view, thus, there is no room for a merciful God who is gracious enough to forgive all sins of sinners. On the contrary, Job asserts his striking idea of God that God will ultimately be his salvation notwithstanding death. His bold confession implicitly answers his own question to his wife in 2:10 ("Shall we receive good from God, and shall we not receive evil?").[71] Job knows that there is no salvation or deliverance (יְשׁוּעָה) outside God. He must gain it from God or not gain it at all. Job, therefore, abandons his friends' encouragement to find a restored life through Job's repentance and their idea to trust in God's eventual justice (4:5–7; 11:18). If Job were an ungodly person, he would not dare to appear before God to argue his case. But because Job remains confident in God, he believes that he will be able to come face to face with God, and that God must eventually acquit him of wrongdoing. As no one can see God's face and live (Exod 33:20), Job is willing to take the ultimate risk of presenting

---

discrepancy between the dread power of God and fearful Job (9:34). However, in chapter 13, Job is willing to argue his own case before God.

69. Instead of "this," the pronoun in 16a "he" should be rendered. The translation "he" is appropriate for it most likely refers to God, the referent of the pronominal suffixes in verses 15a, b, and 16b. Nevertheless, the theological message is virtually identical with both translations.

70. By using a cohortative אֲדַבְּרָה, "Let me speak," with the first-person pronoun אֲנִי, "I myself," Job presents his determination to speak whether the friends will approve or not.

71. Balentine, *Job*, 211.

his case before God's face.⁷² Job is taking a major step in his faith. Job's hope is not in a God who is wrathful, alien, and tormenting him, but in a God who is merciful and compassion. It is in a gracious God who ultimately will be his salvation, even though this same God should take his life. Job's hope, therefore, transcends even death.

Chapter 14 continues Job's hope and introduces a new element into Job's struggle. The broad sketch of this chapter can help us to understand Job's vacillation between hope and despair. It is possible to view the whole chapter as having three discourses on despair alternating with two on hope. In verses 1–6 Job speaks of the inevitability of death for everyone. In verses 7–9 Job looks to nature and sees hope for the tree stump that it may sprout again. In verses 10–12 Job's mood switches back to despair when he compares man's death to a dried-up river/lake. In verses 13–17 he regains hope, imagining how God could hide him in Sheol until God's wrath is past and God would call him to resume their relationship. However, in verses 18–22 Job switches back to lament that God destroys a man's hope to live.

Job laments the brevity of man's life (14:1–6, also 14:10–12), which makes birth inescapably linked with death (14:1–2).⁷³ As Eliphaz contends that mortals, as being not "pure" (טהר), have no hope of being acquitted (4:17), Job, on the contrary, attempts to prove his innocence in spite of his apparent impurity as a miserable mortal (4:3–4; cf. 9:30–31). Job recognizes that it is impossible for a self vindication: "Who can bring a clean thing out of an unclean? There is not one!" (14:4). Thus, the brevity of man's life compounds the problem of vindication.

For there is hope for a tree, if it be cut down, that it will sprout again, and that its shoots will not cease.	14:7	כִּי יֵשׁ לָעֵץ תִּקְוָה אִם־יִכָּרֵת וְעוֹד יַחֲלִיף וְיֹנַקְתּוֹ לֹא תֶחְדָּל׃
Though its root grow old in the earth, and its stump die in the soil,	14:8	אִם־יַזְקִין בָּאָרֶץ שָׁרְשׁוֹ וּבֶעָפָר יָמוּת גִּזְעוֹ׃

---

72. While Job expresses his longing for an umpire who should stand between him and God in 9:33, Job here resolves to plead his case directly to God's face (13:13–16).

73. Newsom, *The Book of Job*, NIB, 441, notes that the phrase "few days and full of trouble" in 14:1b reverses the traditional phrase "old and full of days" (Gen 25:8; 35:29; 1 Chr 29:28).

| yet at the scent of water it will bud and put out branches like a young plant. | 14:9 | מֵרֵיחַ מַיִם יַפְרִחַ וְעָשָׂה קָצִיר כְּמוֹ־נָטַע׃ |

Job, then, compares man's sad destiny of death with the fate of a tree (14:7–9).[74] The Hebrew term כִּי, "for," is a conjunction used to refer to verse 5 and the time limits set on human life by God.[75] It is ironic that only the tree, and not human being, who can truly lay claim to hope,[76] for only the tree has the power of regeneration. The dead tree, like the dead mortal, lies in the "dust" (עָפָר, 14:8), the domain of death and the underworld (cf. 7:5; 17:16; 21:26). However, the tree has an amazing capacity to return to life at the mere scent of water (v. 9).

But a man dies and is laid low;[77] man breathes his last, and where is he?	14:10	וְגֶבֶר יָמוּת וַיֶּחֱלָשׁ וַיִּגְוַע אָדָם וְאַיּוֹ׃
As waters fail from a lake and a river wastes away and dries up,	14:11	אָזְלוּ־מַיִם מִנִּי־יָם וְנָהָר יֶחֱרַב וְיָבֵשׁ׃
so a man lies down and rises not again; till the heavens are no more he will not awake or be roused out of his sleep.	14:12	וְאִישׁ שָׁכַב וְלֹא־יָקוּם עַד־בִּלְתִּי שָׁמַיִם לֹא יָקִיצוּ וְלֹא־יֵעֹרוּ מִשְּׁנָתָם׃

Human beings,[78] by sharp contrast (וְ, "but," v. 10), do not lie dormant, but lie forever lifeless. In his despair Job rejects the tree for another natural

---

74. In 8:12–20, Bildad compares one plant that withered and died like the godless with another having deep roots that sent forth new shoots like the righteous. For Job here the comparison lies between mortals that wither like flowers and actual trees that have the "hope" to send forth shoots of new life.

75. Job 14:5 says, "Since his days are determined, and the number of his months is with you, and you have appointed his limits that he cannot pass."

76. Notice that Job repeats Zophar's idea of hope in 11:18–19. The idea of the hope for the tree here is that being cut down is not the end of its life. By contrast, human death is the final end of his existence.

77. The root meaning of the Hebrew word חלשׁ, "laid low," is "be weak" or "dwindle away" (*HALOT* 1:324). Thus, the expression "laid low" does not mean "laid in the grave." The idea is that a strong man (גֶּבֶר) has become weak or powerless (cf. Joel 3:10).

78. Ironically, the Hebrew term for man here is גֶּבֶר in which the meaning is associated with the root meaning "be strong, powerful" (cf. 3:3; *HALOT* 1:175–76). The following parallel term is אָדָם, already used in 14:1 as "every human being" who is born to a life "full of trouble."

phenomenon: water. Man's death is irreversible like lakes and rivers which vanish and do not reappear (v. 11). Job concludes human destiny with a connective *waw* (וְ) in verse 12 and characterizes death as a sleep (שׁכב, "lie down"),[79] from which one does not rise (לֹא קוּם),[80] awake (לֹא), or is aroused (לֹא עוּר),[81] or live again (חיה, v. 14) on earth.

Oh that you would hide me in Sheol, that you would conceal me until your wrath be past, that you would appoint me a set time, and remember me!	14:13	מִי יִתֵּן בִּשְׁאוֹל תַּצְפִּנֵנִי תַּסְתִּירֵנִי עַד־שׁוּב אַפֶּךָ תָּשִׁית לִי חֹק וְתִזְכְּרֵנִי׃
If a man dies, shall he live again?[82] All the days of my service I would wait, till my renewal should come.[83]	14:14	אִם־יָמוּת גֶּבֶר הֲיִחְיֶה כָּל־יְמֵי צְבָאִי אֲיַחֵל עַד־בּוֹא חֲלִיפָתִי׃

Yet another fascinating perspective on death is the glimpses of life with God which are precisely in the face of what seems an inevitable and unfair

---

79. The verb denotes the meaning of lying down in bed or "laid to rest" in the grave as a state and not a process (cf. 3:13; 7:21; 20:11; 21:26). See Louvain W. Beuken, "שׁכב," *TDOT* 14: 664–665.

80. The phrase "rise not again" emphasizes the timelessness of death or lying down in death. See, Beuken, "שׁכב," 664–665.

81. Once a person dies, he will not awake or be aroused. Beuken, "שׁכב," 664–665. The idea is that death is the finality of human being. In the OT, for instance, Isa 26:19 and Dan 12:2, obvious resurrection passages, use similar expressions for resurrection idea that the dead: יְחָיוּ, "they will live;" יְקוּמוּן, "they will rise;" הָקִיצוּ, "they will wake up." For the biblical reference, see Hartley, *Book of Job*, 235. At this point the text shows that Job is not thinking about the possibility of life after death.

82. The LXX reads the affirmation, "He will live!" (ζήσεται), instead of the obvious Hebrew interrogative, "Will he live again?"; thereby paraphrasing and offering a resurrection idea in this passage.

83. Some scholars (e.g. C. Mitchell) see that Job 14:14 gives hint to the possibility of an afterlife. The evidence of this idea of an afterlife is from the noun חֲלִיפָה, which comes from the same root חלף as the verb is used to describe the tree sprouting again in 14:7, suggesting that with the term "renewal, change" Job is thinking of an afterlife. However, the rhetorical question in 14:14a expects a negative answer "no." Therefore, Job does not contemplate a life after death, but is rather speaking of his emerging from being temporarily hidden in Sheol. The sentiment of the idea reflects the relational problem between God and Job. Newsom, *The Book of Job*, NIB, 442, rightly observes that "when Job thought in legal terms, he demanded disclosures of his alleged sins, offenses, and iniquities, so that he could refute them (13:23). When he thinks in the relational terms of personal religion, images of concealment provide the resolution (14:16–17)."

death. Job, who is trapped between the anger of God and the irreversibility of death, expresses a hope that God could hide him temporarily in Sheol,[84] seemingly without Job undergoing death. It could become Job's temporary refuge, and he could be protected from God's wrath until it had passed. Job cannot enter Sheol on his own; that act would have to be of God.[85] In the following verse, Job asks the rhetorical question that expects a negative answer ("If a man dies will he live again?" v. 14). Job is reflecting on the arrangement he would like God to make with him in verse 13 (i.e. to hide him in Sheol). It seems that such an idea with God would mean that Job would live again.[86] What Job is saying here is not the reality, but his hope that Sheol is seemingly not a final destination but instead a temporary asylum. The time in Sheol is viewed as the days of "my service" (צְבָאִי).[87] As Job has "hope in him [God]" (לֹו אֲיַחֵל, in 13:15), in the hiding in Sheol Job could also "wait/hope" (אֲיַחֵל) for a renewal (חֲלִיפָה).[88] Job here does not see death as a refuge from God, as he did in 3:13–19 and 7:8–10, 21. Job's imminent death has become part of the problem, because his desire has changed. Job wishes that God in time would call for Job, Job would answer (14:15; cf. 13:22; 19:27a), and their relationship could resume in the mutual care and love that characterized life in Job 1. Death, thus, threatens the restoration of this relationship.[89] Job is very confused. Along with despair, Job is also yearning for the right relationship with God. Since God determines death, Job is dying because God is bringing him to death (14:5). Death, therefore,

---

84. Again, the term Sheol here as well as in chapter 3 is used to denote the general realm of the dead.

85. Newsom, *The Book of Job,* NIB, 442, notes that "the contradictions in Job's image of God are here projected into God's very will; God would hide Job from God's own anger, which seeks to destroy Job."

86. Cline, *Job 1–20*, 331–332; Hartley, *Book of Job*, 236.

87. The Hebrew term צָבָא refers to military service as in an army, with a set of time and an occasion for release. See the term in H. Ringgren, "צָבָא," *TDOT* 12:211–215.

88. Cf. Habel, *Book of Job*, 238–239, thoroughly analyzes chapter 14 and proposes that the brilliant pivot piece of the chapter lies in verses 13–17. In addition, 14:14b–c stands in diametric opposition to Job's statement of intent in 13:15, where Job declared that he "would not wait [in silence]" to present his case even if God should slay him in the process. Now Job is announcing his hope that he would wait patiently if he had the same hope of resurrection as a tree and a final opportunity for an impartial trial.

89. Death in ancient Israelite thought is a realm cut off from God's presence (cf. Ps 88:5[6]).

is not the biggest problem here, but the relationship with God which is now not right. Though Job has hope, it is short-lived.

In 14:18–22, there is no evidence for a bold hope, for God destroys man's hope. Job muses on the erosion images, that is, mountains, crags, stones, and dust are destroyed by water (vv. 18–19a). God destroys every hope with the same irresistible forces. In the end, death is the final fate of all human beings. Job's concluding images of death are governed by the language of separation. Death as the realm where one is separated from God is presented in Job's use of verbs for departure, for instance, "and he passes," renders the Hebrew וַיַּהֲלֹךְ, "and he goes" (v. 20a), which is an indirect manner of speaking about death (i.e. "pass away"). The phrase is paralleled with וַתְּשַׁלְּחֵהוּ ("and you send him away," v. 20b). Death is also a separation from his own family. That is, those in the world of the dead know absolutely nothing about those matters which most closely concern them, such as the welfare of their families – neither their sons' good fortune ("to be honored," יִכְבְּדוּ) nor their bad ("brought low," וְיִצְעָרוּ, v. 21; cf. Eccl 9:5–6, 10). His last verses (14:22) does not describe a postmortem pain, but moves back to the process of dying.[90] This process, which separates the dying from their family and community even before the last breath is taken, becomes for Job the symbol of death as utter isolation.

To summarize chapter 14, what Job longs for is a resumption of a relationship with God. Though Job yearns for his relationship with a merciful God (i.e. life with God in ch. 1), which transcends death, his experience and reason testify to the universal rule of death over man. Death, thus, becomes part of the problem here. It is not only threatening the restoration of this relationship, but also a symbol of utter isolation. Job concludes his last speech in the first cycle in the same manner as he has done in each of his previous speeches; namely a portrait of death or despair (14:21–22; cf. 3:20–26; 7:19–20; 10:18–22). As Job still insists on asking "Why?" there remains no answer. As Job dares to hope for a life beyond this life (i.e. temporary in Sheol), and for a God beyond this God, "there is only the deepening conviction that the boundaries imposed on humankind render

---

90. Cf. D. Clines, *Job 1–20*, 336; Georg Fohrer, *Das Buch Hiob*, 261; also Pope, *Job*, 111; H. Rowley, "The book of Job and Its Meaning," in *From Moses to Qumran: Studies in the Old Testament* (London: Lutterworth Press, 1963), 107.

both yearning null and void."⁹¹ Job is destined to find nothing more than the dust and death that awaits him in Sheol.

After Job has responded to the three friends in the first cycle of the dialogues (chs. 6–7; 9–10; 12–14), more than anywhere else in the book the friends speak with one voice in the second cycle of speeches. Their concerns are narrowed to focus exclusively on one perspective of the retribution principle: the fate of the wicked (15:17–35; 18:5–21; 20:6–29), with no parallel statement of the fate of the righteous. In the first cycle of speeches, the friends address Job with respect, encouraging him to remember that he is innocent and can trust God to deliver him. Initially, the friends call upon the doctrine of retribution, arguing that God punishes the wicked (e.g. Eliphaz: 4:8–11; 5:12–14; Bildad: 8:4, 11–19; Zophar: 11:11, 20) and rewards the righteous (e.g. 4:7; 5:11, 15–16; 8:20–22; 11:13–19). But in the second cycle their tone is much sharper and stiffer in their response to Job (e.g. Eliphaz: 15:7–9; Bildad: 18:3; Zophar: 20:3). They become impatient with Job as they wish to convince Job that he will undergo greater hardship if he does not repent. The following study, namely, Eliphaz's speech in chapter 15, will exemplify and summarize the position he shares with the rest of the friends' speeches, that death is understood as an ultimate recompense from sin in the retribution principle.

The Second Cycle of the Dialogues

Eliphaz's Second Speech: Chapter 15:1–6, 25–30. In Eliphaz's second speech (ch. 15), he seeks to rebuke Job's claim to wisdom (vv. 2–16) and gives vivid instruction about the woes of the wicked (vv. 17–35). Eliphaz starts with:

Should a wise man answer with windy knowledge, and fill his belly with the east wind?	15:2	הֶחָכָם יַעֲנֶה דַעַת־רוּחַ וִימַלֵּא קָדִים בִּטְנוֹ׃
Should he argue in unprofitable talk, or in words with which he can do no good?	15:3	הוֹכֵחַ בְּדָבָר לֹא יִסְכּוֹן וּמִלִּים לֹא־יוֹעִיל בָּם׃

---

91. Balentine, *Job*, 221.

But you are doing away with the fear of God and hindering meditation before God.	15:4	אַף־אַתָּה תָּפֵר יִרְאָה וְתִגְרַע שִׂיחָה לִפְנֵי־אֵל:
For your iniquity teaches your mouth, and you choose the tongue of the crafty.	15:5	כִּי יְאַלֵּף עֲוֹנְךָ פִּיךָ וְתִבְחַר לְשׁוֹן עֲרוּמִים:
Your own mouth condemns you, and not I; your own lips testify against you.	15:6	יַרְשִׁיעֲךָ פִיךָ וְלֹא־אָנִי וּשְׂפָתֶיךָ יַעֲנוּ־בָךְ:

Eliphaz's opening verses (15:2–3) are introductory and concern the nature of Job's talk (i.e. Job's claim of being as wise as the friends in 12:3 and 13:2). He argues that Job's words are "windy" (דַּעַת־רוּחַ, v. 2),[92] "unprofitable" (לֹא יִסְכּוֹן) and "not useful" (לֹא־יוֹעִיל) (v. 3), even "arrogant" (הוֹכֵחַ, the hiphil infinitive absolute of יכח, which is used to echo Job's determination to contend with God in 13:3, 15). Eliphaz tries to present the consequences of Job's actions. Job "undermines" (פרר, "does away with") "faith" (יִרְאָה, "fear [of God];" lit. "fear," cf. 4:6). Job's heated words "hinder meditation" (תִגְרַע שִׂיחָה, v. 4).[93] Job deliberately chooses (בחר) to cover his iniquity with his mouth (v. 5), by complaining against his friends and his God with "a tongue of craftiness" (לְשׁוֹן עֲרוּמִים; cf. 5:12), with the result that it is Job's own tongue that condemns him (רשע, a hiphil form in v. 6), not God,[94] as Job contends in 9:29 and 10:2.

In sum, Eliphaz condemns Job that his words that express criticism, and challenge are the mark of one who would attack God and destroy the functioning of the true theology of retribution. As God and the narrator commend Job for his patience and his submission in the prologue (i.e. sitting patiently on the ash heap, seeming to be content to receive both the

---

92. Bildad also refers to Job's words as being "a great wind" in 8:2.

93. In his *The Book of Job: Commentary, New Translation, and Special Studies* (New York City: The Jewish Theological Seminary of America, 1978.) 160, Gordis sees the word for "meditation" (שִׂיחָה) as "conversation, communion with God." However, the term may refer to plaintive expression, that is, to complain, as in Ps 77:4 (cf. Pss 55:3, 18; 64:2; 142:3). It is this idea of "complain" that consistently denotes Job's "meditation" (i.e. Job 7:11, 13; 9:27; 10:1; 21:4; 23:2). See Balentine, *Job*, 232–233.

94. Grammatically, the accusation with the particle אַף ("Surely") and the personal pronoun אַתָּה ("you") in verse 4 are employed to underscore the fact that Job, not God, is responsible for breaking the fear of God.

good and the bad from God without complaint), Job becomes a perfect example of one "who fears God" (1:1, 8; 2:3). If Job could continue that posture, the friends would not have problems with him. But since Job starts to protest against God with destructive words in the dialogues, Eliphaz and the other two friends are convinced that Job has abandoned his piety that God expects and commends. They become mentally agitated that Job is destroying his own faith in God. Job's words also undermine the true meaning of the retribution principle as they have been taught according to the wisdom tradition. Since the three friends are distressed by what they hear in Job's responses and cannot come to understand that Job's complaint could possibly be true, they can only conclude that Job is guilty of speaking too harshly against God. Job's destructive words, thus, prove that Job is guilty and thus deserving of his present affliction.

In 10:7, Job has claimed not to be wicked (רשע).[95] Also in 10:15, Job said it was irrelevant whether he is wicked or not.[96] In 15:20–35, Eliphaz affirms (שְׁמַֽע־לִ֗י, "hear me," 15:17) that it makes a great difference. That is because one who is רשע has an evil life, sets himself against God (15: 25–26), and will consequently suffer much punishment from God.

Because he has stretched out his hand against God and defies the Almighty,	15:25	כִּֽי־נָטָ֣ה אֶל־אֵ֣ל יָד֑וֹ וְאֶל־שַׁ֝דַּ֗י יִתְגַּבָּֽר׃
running stubbornly against him with a thickly bossed shield;	15:26	יָר֣וּץ אֵלָ֣יו בְּצַוָּ֑אר בַּ֝עֲבִ֗י גַּבֵּ֥י מָֽגִנָּֽיו׃
because he has covered his face with his fat and gathered fat upon his waist	15:27	כִּֽי־כִסָּ֣ה פָנָ֣יו בְּחֶלְבּ֑וֹ וַיַּ֖עַשׂ פִּימָ֣ה עֲלֵי־כָֽסֶל׃
and has lived in desolate cities, in houses that none should inhabit, which were ready to become heaps of ruins;	15:28	וַיִּשְׁכּ֤וֹן ׀ עָ֘רִ֤ים נִכְחָד֗וֹת בָּ֭תִּים לֹא־יֵ֣שְׁבוּ לָ֑מוֹ אֲשֶׁ֖ר הִתְעַתְּד֣וּ לְגַלִּֽים׃
he will not be rich, and his wealth will not endure, nor will his possessions spread over the earth;	15:29	לֹֽא־יֶעְשַׁ֗ר וְלֹא־יָק֣וּם חֵיל֑וֹ וְלֹֽא־יִטֶּ֖ה לָאָ֣רֶץ מִנְלָֽם׃

---

95. Job 10:7: "Although you know that I am not guilty (כִּי־לֹ֣א אֶרְשָׁ֑ע), and there is none to deliver out of your hand?"

96. Job 10:15: "If I am guilty, woe to me! If I am in the right, I cannot lift up my head, for I am filled with disgrace."

he will not depart from darkness; the flame will dry up his shoots, and by the breath of his mouth he will depart.	15:30	לֹא־יָסוּר מִנִּי־חֹשֶׁךְ יֹנַקְתּוֹ תְּיַבֵּשׁ שַׁלְהָבֶת וְיָסוּר בְּרוּחַ פִּיו:

Eliphaz starts a vivid picture of the fate of the wicked in verse 17 and continues the details to verse 35. Eliphaz does not know the true meaning of the phrase "the stretching forth of the hand" in 1:11–12 and 2:3b–6,[97] and he reasons that Job's great anguish is from his defiantly "stretched out his hand" (יָד + נטה) against God (v. 25a).[98] (The phrase is in contrast to what Zophar has encouraged Job to "spread out the [Job's] hands" in 11:13.)[99] This phrase "he has stretched out his hand against God" (v. 25a), as Clines notes, appears nowhere else in the Hebrew Bible of human hostility to God.[100] It serves to heighten Eliphaz's point that it is foolhardy to "play the hero" (יִתְגַּבָּר) against *Shadday*.[101] Eliphaz has an idea that Job's "heroic" defiance is not only a sign of faithless but also wicked rebellion; thus, Job is deserved punishment.

Eliphaz continues to focus on the miserable future that is prepared for the wicked in verses 27–35. The fatness of the foolishly arrogant is a symbol of the material prosperity enjoyed by the wicked.[102] Therefore, despite his heath

---

97. The Hebrew phrase "stretch out your hand" used in 1:11, 12, 2:5 is "שלח + יָד," rendered as "touch" Job's possessions and (later) his bone and flesh with the purpose to test Job's faith in Yahweh. See Hossfeld-van der Velden, "שלח," *TDOT* 15:55–58.

98. The phrase "an outstretched hand" (יָד + נטה) is an image of warrior. It is used in the OT to describe a great act of God's power either in a positive sense (i.e. Yahweh led Israel out of Egypt [Exod 6:6; Deut 4:34; 5:15; Ps 136:12; etc]) or in a negative sense (i.e. Yahweh acted mightily against his people [Isa 5:25; 9:16; Ezek 6:14; 14:9; Zeph 1:4; 2:13; Jer 21:5]). In the mouth of Eliphaz, the subject of the phrase is human being, which means that one [Job] is ready to perform a hostile action against God. See H. Ringgren, "נטה," *TDOT* 9:381–382.

99. The phrase in 11:13, "כַּף + פרשׂ" indicates "a gesture of prayer," where Zophar suggests Job "spread the palms of his hands upward as if to receive God's gifts or to express his desire to union." See H. Ringgren, "פרשׂ," *TDOT* 12:122–123.

100. Clines, *Job 1–20*, 359.

101. In Yahweh's responses to Job (38–41), God calls and challenges Job twice to "gird his loins like a hero (גֶּבֶר)" (38:3; 40:7). Also Job has wondered in 3:3 why he, a "man-child" (גֶּבֶר), was born.

102. See Clines, *Job 1–20*, 360.

and prosperity, the wicked ends up as an inhabitant of ruined cities (v. 28).¹⁰³ What Eliphaz is focusing on here is that the wicked works for his prosperity (his "fatness"), but his fate is to lose his wealth – it will not endure.¹⁰⁴ The wicked can become rich, but he cannot remain rich.¹⁰⁵ Thus, his possessions will not spread over the earth/land.¹⁰⁶ They receive their retribution in this life time. Eliphaz, then, summarizes the fate of the wicked by repeating the darkness theme in verse 30 (cf. v. 22a). That is, the wicked will not escape "darkness" (חֹשֶׁךְ, i.e. death) (v. 30a),¹⁰⁷ in the sense that he has no hope for a long, peaceful life. He will not escape a terrified death, and will certainly die miserably, like a tree that will wither and die in the scorching heat (שַׁלְהֶבֶת, lit., "flame") (v. 30b; also 8:11–13). Note that it is Job's terrified death which is implied here. Furthermore, the phrase "and by the breath of his mouth he will depart" (וְיָסוּר בְּרוּחַ פִּיו, v. 30c) has been understood either as a reference of God's action or of personified death.¹⁰⁸ This phrase is a difficult clause.¹⁰⁹ Though God has not been mentioned since 15:26, the object of "mouth" can refer to the mouth of God. Because this phrase may be a reference to 4:9, in which Eliphaz claimed that the wicked, or Job as it is implied, will perish "by the breath of God." In this way, the MT is retained. Although

---

103. Clines, *Job 1–20*, 360, also notes that from the context of the pericopes, the initial כִּי in verse 27 should not be rendered "because," but "although." See also Andersen, *Job*, 178; also NIV, "though."

104. The term "לֹא־יֶעְשַׁר" should be rendered "no longer be rich" (NIV).

105. See Clines, *Job 1–20*, 362; Gordis, *Book of Job*, 165.

106. Some scholars understand the term "earth" here as "the underworld," describing the idea that the one who "יַד," against El in 15:25a, cannot "stretch forth" his possessions to the underworld, which is ruled by Mot, the King of Terrors. This translation receives its support from the parallel word "darkness" (חֹשֶׁךְ) in verse 30a. The terms Darkness, Flame, and its Mouth are also viewed as epithets of Mot, the gods of death, in the Ugaritic literature. See, for instance, Pope, *Job*, 112; Habel, *Book of Job*, 248, 260; etc. However, the context points to the rendering "earth." When Eliphaz mentions this fate of the wicked, he may assume that the wicked is a pastoralist-like. Eliphaz is aware that Job has already lost all his wealth in chapter 1. Thus, the possessions of Job (as the implied wicked) will not spread out over the land. This is an example of how to read the text literally within its own context. See, for example, Clines, *Job 1–20*, 362.

107. Job used the images of darkness to refer to death and Sheol in 10:21. So this is the idea, darkness as death, being expressed here. See also Ringgren, *TDOT* 5:255–256.

108. For the former interpretation, see, for example, NIV; Hartley, *Book of Job*, 253; for the latter understanding, see, for instance, Habel, *Book of Job*, 260.

109. See some comments on the textual notes in Habel, *Book of Job*, 248, 260; Clines, *Job 1–20*, 344, 362.

Eliphaz does not address Job directly (only in v. 17), he clearly uses this part of the speech, the fate of the wicked, as a warning to Job. Eliphaz ends this speech by connecting the idea that if Job insists on filling his "belly" (v. 2, בֶּטֶן) with wind, then Job's "belly" (v. 35; NRSV: "heart," בֶּטֶן) will bring forth deceit that leads him to destruction like the wicked.

Job's Speeches Continued: Chapters 16:18–22; 17. As in earlier speeches, the first part of Job's speeches here in chapter 16 express his disappointment with his friends (16:2–5). Their "windy words" are not helpful to Job. As they are "miserable comforters" (מְנַחֲמֵי עָמָל), their words add more pain to Job's suffering. Job could do a better job than they are doing. Job 16:7–14 is a lament in which Job addresses no one but speaks of God and his assaults on him (i.e. "he" and "I"). Job refers to God mostly in the third person (exception in 16:7b, and 8a, where God is referred to in the second person). Job does not refer to the friends at all after the first five verses in this chapter and speaks only of himself in 16:15–17. Job laments the attacks of God and characterizes God, his enemy, by depicting God's annihilating character as an oppressor (16:7–8), an angry beast (16:9), a traitor (16:11), a wrestler (16:12), an archer (16:12c–13a), and a swordsman (16:13b–14).[110] By contrast, Job characterizes himself as totally depressed, ruined, and defeated (16:15). The divine attacks have placed him in the sphere of the influence of death in which its deep darkness can be felt upon his eyelids (16:16; cf. 10:21–22). Job also protests to those who mock him as a man under divine punishment (16:10; 17:2, 4–6). However, Job's pleading accusation is against the source of his suffering; that is, God himself. "Because" (עַל; 16:17) it is not only the loss of his children and his own great pain, but also the fact that he is innocent. Thus, Job demands justice of God, specifically before his impending death. Job, in 16:18–22 moves from his deepest pain to hope,[111] states (cf. 9:33–35 and 14:13–17):

---

110. See Clines, *Job 1–20*, 376.
111. The legal, forensic language here (16:18–22) is explicit, see, for instance, Habel, *Book of Job*, 265; Sylvia Huberman Scholnick, "Lawsuit Drama in the Book of Job" (PhD diss., Brandeis University, 1975).

O earth, cover not my blood, and let my cry find no resting place.	16:18	אֶרֶץ אַל־תְּכַסִּי דָמִי וְאַל־יְהִי מָקוֹם לְזַעֲקָתִי׃
Even now, behold, my witness is in heaven, and he who testifies for me is on high.	16:19	גַּם־עַתָּה הִנֵּה־בַשָּׁמַיִם עֵדִי וְשָׂהֲדִי בַּמְּרוֹמִים׃
My mediator is my friend;[112] my eye pours out tears to God,	16:20	מְלִיצַי רֵעָי אֶל־אֱלוֹהַּ דָּלְפָה עֵינִי׃
that he would argue the case of a man with God, as a son of man does with his neighbor.	16:21	וְיוֹכַח לְגֶבֶר עִם־אֱלוֹהַּ וּבֶן־אָדָם לְרֵעֵהוּ׃
For when a few years have come I shall go the way from which I shall not return.	16:22	כִּי־שְׁנוֹת מִסְפָּר יֶאֱתָיוּ וְאֹרַח לֹא־אָשׁוּב אֶהֱלֹךְ׃

Job, encountering the imminent death, calls on the earth to allow his blood to cry out to God for vindication. A similar thought is in Genesis 4:8–15, where the blood of Abel cried from the ground, beseeching God to punish Cain (cf. Isa 26:21). As long as the blood is not covered over and hidden, it can cry out (Ezek 24:7–8). With this image, Job depicts himself as a murder victim whose blood is on the ground. He charges God for his violence, not for his justified punishment. His cry out is not for healing or restoration, but for justice or vindication which would be done after his death (16:18). Job has a strong belief in the power of עֵד, the "witness" (16:19). As God is the enemy in this lament, Job's request for the witness is addressed to the heavens.[113] Job still seeks vindication from God, for God is his enemy and is the only one who can reciprocate to the one whom he

---

112. The ESV reads, "My friends scorn me." The problem with this interpretation is that the Hiphil participle of ליץ elsewhere always denotes a mediator or intercessor; only other forms of the verb denote scoffing or mocking. In addition, to agree with a single witness or arbiter occurs in verses 19 and 21 (cf. 9:33), the immediate context of the plural form of מְלִיצַי should be slightly emended to the singular term מֵלִיץ as occurred in 33:23 ("mediator;" cf. Gen 42:23 ["interpreter"]; 2 Chr 32:31 ["ambassador"]; Isa 43:27 ["spokesman"]). The same line of thought is applied to the plural form of רֵעָי, "my friends." Because any reference to Job's three friends here seems alien to Job's idea of a celestial mediator, thus the singular rendering "my mediator is my friend" is favored and appropriated (cf. the LXX, though periphrastic, also supports the singular reading). See also Andersen, *Job*, 183; Habel, *Book of Job*, 265–266.

113. Andersen, *Job*, 182, notes that as the earth and the skies are the "sleepless watchers of men's actions and guardians of ancient covenants"; thus, Job appeals to them "as witness of his murder."

has wronged. However, since Job's adversary is infinitely mighty, a powerful "heavenly witness" is needed.[114] Thus, the MT reinforces the third answer to Job's problem.[115] The use of the verb יכח in verse 21 serves to remind the reader of the third party, "the מוֹכִיחַ," for whom Job longed in 9:33. As the figure is a heavenly one, Job hopes that he will certainly survive Job's imminent death (v. 22). This "witness" will bear Job's tears and plead his case before God on his behalf, even after Job has died, seeking Job's ultimate vindication, recognizing that Job is, and always was, a righteous man. This divine friend (רֵעַ) will also carry out the functions which Job's earthly friends failed to fulfill.[116] However, Job wonders if there is such a faithful witness or mediator. Job will soon die and his integrity will never be vindicated. Death becomes a problem again as Job thinks in terms of vindication. Although Job commences this section with words of hope (i.e. that someone will vindicate his case before God), he ends his impossible dream on a note of isolation and a cry of despair in verse 22 (cf. 9:35b; 19:27). Job is expressing the shortness of time left for him to live. He is expressing the urgency of his need for vindication in the face of his imminent death. For Job will be "walking" (הלך) to the land of no return (לֹא שׁוּב; cf. 7:9–10; 10:21), to the land of the dead. The expression emphasizes the fact that Job will not be able to return from the grave, where he will have no way to defend his reputation.

---

114. This figure adds a kind of a divine being quality to the hope for מוֹכִיחַ "mediator" of 9:33. Also Habel, *The Book of Job*, 275, 306, insightfully notes the possibility of a third party who is "the counterpart to the satan [i.e. the heavenly angel], one who can act in Job's defense." Within the Bible, a similar figure in Zech 3:1 is evident in the "angel of YHWH" who defends Joshua the high priest before the heavenly council against the baseless charges of the satan.

115. The identity concerning the figure of this "witness," as well as the "mediator" in 9:33 and the "redeemer" in 19:25, is a big debate. For example, Pope, *Job*, 125, sees that it is impossible to view "my witness" as referring to God, who is already seen by Job as Accuser, Judge, and Executioner. Gordis, *Book of Job*, special note 15, 527, leads the idea that in Job's oriental thought God can be viewed as both judge and witness at the same time. He proposes that Job is affirming his faith that behind the God of violence stands the God of righteousness and love – "both are not two but one." The present author agrees with Habel and others (e.g. Newsom, Balentine, etc.) who see this "witness" as a third party, who is Job's mediator and his friend. It is noteworthy that from the perspective of the book Job does not want to "see" the witness or the redeemer figure, instead Job wants to see God. However, the topic of the study does limit the scope of the study in which the concern of who is this figure is out of our scope here.

116. Habel, *Book of Job*, 275; Habel, "Only the Jackal," 227–236.

The reality of the separation and the finality of death (16:22) leads Job to lament over his loneliness and hopelessness in chapter 17. However, there is a turning point where Job's hopelessness turns into hope. Up to this point, God still does not speak, even though Job complains that God has totally exhausted his spirit, mind, and body in chapter 16. Job labels God as his enemy. Job is in a loosing battle with God. Although he longs for a heavenly witness, in reality it seems that there is no such figure who can come to defend his case. He appears to be approaching death in great pain. His days of life are coming to their end (17:1). The mockery of the friends adds insult to his pain (vv. 2, 6). Job appeals to God to be responsible for him (vv. 3–5). Then he describes his condition (vv. 6–9), concluding with an affirmation of himself as righteous (v. 9a). Job then addresses the friends with renewed vigor:

> The upright are appalled at this,
> and the innocent stirs himself up against the godless.
> Yet the righteous holds to his way,
> and he who has clean hands grows stronger and stronger.
> (Job 17:8–9)[117]

Job's statement here marks a significant change in Job. It is Job's next step, moving toward a new understanding in seeking the truth of God. It presents Job's hope for life amidst his despair and wishes for death.[118] It marks "a stage in Job's reconciliation with God, undercutting the climax in chapter 42."[119] The three friends betray their functions. They see Job's suffering as confirmation of their own righteousness. They reaffirm divine

---

117. These two verses are in wider disagreement. Some scholars consider them as an awkward intrusion in this context. Others think they are quite out of place. This study agrees with Jay S. Southwick, "Job: An Exemplar for Every Age," *Encounter* 45 (1984): 373–391. A literal reading of Job 17 leads us to see what Janzen, *Job*, 126–127, calls "the strange presence of the energy of hope."

118. Southwick, "Job: An Exemplar," 389, says, "It [17:9] is . . . pregnant with energy, comes across Job's lips totally unplanned. Once uttered, however, the energy of these words bursts forth bringing understanding from Job's subconscious to his conscious state of reality . . . A quantum leap has been made."

119. Moshe Greenberg also sees the sentiment of Job's complex speech in 17:8–9 as Job's affirmation of his own worth and the transcendent worth of unrewarded good. The sentiment is the same as in chapter 28. In spite of being forsaken by his God and his friends, Job still maintains his faith in the value of his virtue and in the absolute duty of man to be virtuous. Job, thus, reaffirms in chapter 28 that wisdom is inaccessible to man. See Moshe Greenberg, "Job," in *The Literary Guide to the Bible*, eds. Robert Alter and Frank Kermode (Cambridge, MA: Harvard University Press, 1987), 295.

justice at the expense of compassion. Job is frustrated. He cannot "find a wise man" among them (v. 10). Job now can do nothing, except cling to his belief in the rightness of his cause, of which he is more convinced than ever.[120] He, thus, declares to the friends with a renewed strength that he has hope for living. The following verses suggest this idea.

My days are past; my plans are broken off, The desires of my heart.[121]	17:11	יָמַי עָבְרוּ זִמֹּתַי נִתְּקוּ מוֹרָשֵׁי לְבָבִי:
They make night into day; "The light," they say, "is near to the darkness."[122]	17:12	לַיְלָה לְיוֹם יָשִׂימוּ אוֹר קָרוֹב מִפְּנֵי־חֹשֶׁךְ:
If I hope for Sheol as my house; if I make my bed in darkness,	17:13	אִם־אֲקַוֶּה שְׁאוֹל בֵּיתִי בַּחֹשֶׁךְ רִפַּדְתִּי יְצוּעִי:
If I say to the pit, "You are my father," and to the worm, "My mother," or "My sister,"	17:14	לַשַּׁחַת קָרָאתִי אָבִי אָתָּה אִמִּי וַאֲחֹתִי לָרִמָּה:
Where then is my hope? Who will see my hope?	17:15	וְאַיֵּה אֵפוֹ תִקְוָתִי וְתִקְוָתִי מִי יְשׁוּרֶנָּה:
Will it go down to the bars of Sheol? Shall we descend together into the dust?"	17:16	בַּדֵּי שְׁאֹל תֵּרַדְנָה אִם־יַחַד עַל־עָפָר נָחַת: ס

Job fears his life is terminating without any of his hope being realized (v. 11). In the first speeches with the friends, each one of the friends gives Job a hope of a reversal of fortune (e.g. 5:19–26; 8:21; 11:15–19), even Zophar uses the image of darkness encouraging Job that his life will be brighter than

---

120. Andersen, *Job*, 185.

121. The Hebrew of verse 11 is an unusual tricolon, where the third colon has no verb. Structurally, Job makes a complaint against God as his enemy in 16:6–17 and expresses his hope in 16:18–17:1. He then turns to make a complaint against his friends in 17:2–10 and expresses his new understanding of his situation; that is, he has hope for life in 17:11–16. This understanding finds its support from the text of 17:8–9 as mentioned above. See Southwick, "Job: An Exemplar," 388–389.

122. The Hebrew in verse 12 is obscure and is omitted in LXX. Some scholars understand the unidentified "they" in 12a as the friends whom Job is accusing them of failing to do their duty. In addition, the common rendering "they say" of verse 12b is not present in the Hebrew. Contextually, however, it is possible to understand "they" in verse 12a as referring to "desires" in the previous clause. Thus, the entire verse 12 contains a subordinate clause modifying "desires" in 11c. The text 17:11c–12 should read: "The desires of my heart, they would turn nigh into day: Light is near in the face of darkness." Also Habel, *Book of Job*, 264–267. Job is expressing his inner desire. He will cling to the possibility of hope.

the noonday and "its darkness will be like the morning" (11:17). The hope that the friends always present to Job is in a limitless future time.[123] But for Job, there is no time for hope for he is approaching death. Thus, death is a threat for it cut off the future with the result that it also destroys hope. Throughout the story of Job, Job repeatedly expresses the view that death puts an end to hope. For example, in 7:6 Job imagines that life speeds past faster than a weaver's shuttle, and consequently the shuttle is unable to keep supplying thread (תִקְוָה, "hope") for the cloth ("life"). The images of drained sea and dried-up river (14:11), the eroded mountain (14:18–19), and the uprooted tree (19:10) also present the destruction of hope by death.

However, Job does not want to merely wish for death. Now Job does not want to die. In spite of his painful suffering, he gains some strange vigor and has hope for life. The next line of verse 11 reads: "The desires of my heart, they make night into day: Light is near in the face of darkness" (vv. 11c–12). Job's words affirm to the friends that he actually increases in strength. The desires of his heart now turn hopelessness into hope. In the face of darkness (i.e. death), a new light (i.e. hope) is there (cf. 12:22, where God's light unveils the deep darkness). Hope makes a complete leap here. Job continues to affirm that if he dies, his hope would be gone. The repetitions of the root קוה, "hope" (vv. 13a, 15a, 15b), and the noun תִקְוָתִי, "my hope/my thread of life" (v. 15 [x2]) in relation to Sheol indicate that his hope will find its final resting place. Job expresses his emotional closeness of Sheol by those homely terms: "house," "bed," "father," mother," "sister" (vv. 13–14). Note also that the term Sheol and its synonyms are used in verses 13–14: שְׁאוֹל, "Sheol"; חֹשֶׁךְ, "darkness"; שַׁחַת, "pit"; and רִמָּה, "worm." These terms connote the idea of the nature of the land of the dead as the domain of destruction, filth, dark, and decay. Sheol is an utterly isolating place. Job acknowledges that if he dies, his hope will accompany him into Sheol.[124]

The rhetorical questions Job asks in 17:15–16, expecting a negative answer, reaffirm a new alternative of despair.[125] If "hope" is only in Sheol,

---

123. See Newsom's insightful reflection on Job's hope in Job 13–14 (*The Book of Job*, NIB, 443–445).

124. Habel, *Book of Job*, 279, sees that the text in 17:15–16 is ambiguous it can mean either that Job's hope will die with him, or that his hope will survive his death (cf. 14:7, 14).

125. Balentine, *Job*, 262–263, also sees that Job's rhetorical questions here "add a new note of despair, and a subtle new resolve, to what by now a familiar lament." They signal "a

then who can see it? So there is no hope in Sheol, and no one can see hope in Sheol (v. 15). Job's hope is to vindicate his case. He wants to see justice exercised somewhere on earth, where his cry can be heard (16:18). Sheol, thus, cannot be a place for vindication. Although Job's expressions of desire for death here are similar to what he has said previously (3:20–26; 7:19–21; 10:18–22; 14:18–22), his rhetorical questions in verses 15 and 16 reaffirm a change in Job. They are employed for driving some conviction.[126] Even though death is the enemy of hope, the fundamental problem is not death itself. The problem lies on the desire for vindication. Job cannot vindicate his case in Sheol, which is a place of utter isolation. His rhetorical questions give a hint to the reader that Job will not simply give up and will not be satisfied with any answer that equates hope with Sheol. Death is not Job's resolution to his problem. Combining with the certainty of his integrity, the rhetorical questions implicitly push Job into a new perspective on life, a new step to anticipate a new relationship with God.

Chapter 19:23–27. Bildad's characterization of the "evil-doer" in chapter 18 is certainly referring to Job's complaints in 16:11 that "El hands me over to an evil-doer." The Joban poet subtly reminds the reader of God's "handing-over" of Job to the accuser in the prologue. For Bildad, Job's words and his ugly appearance affirm to him that Job is evil and absolutely deserves all he has received, for the fate of the wicked cannot be otherwise. Job, thus, replies to Bildad with another description of the attacks Job thinks he is suffering at the hands of an angry God (19:1–12). Job accuses the friends of taking advantage of God's affliction of Job to add their own (19:2–6). Job concludes with the friends and starts to accuse God: "know then that God has put me in the wrong and closed his net about me" (19:6).[127] Following a reproach to the friends, Job laments and speaks to God in the third person, and not addressing the friends directly (19:7–12). Job also gives a pathetic

---

gradually strengthening resolve."

126. See examples of the impact of the usage of rhetorical questions, for instance, in C. J. Labuschagne, *The Incomparability of Yahweh in the Old Testament* (Leiden: Brill, 1966); Kenneth Kuntz, "The Form, Location, and Function of Rhetorical Questions in Deotero-Isaiah," in *Writing and Reading the Scroll of Isaiah: Studies of an Interpretive Tradition*, eds. Craig Broyles and Peter W. Flint, in *Formation and Interpretation of Old Testament Literature*, vol. 1, eds. Craig C. Broyles and Craig A. Evans (Leiden: Brill, 1997); etc.

127. Again the image of God made Job's life crooked (צוות) and has drawn a net around Job recalls picture of fencing Job in 3:23 (also 19:8), so that Job has no way out.

description of his rejection by his relatives and former friends (19:13–20). He makes a sarcastic appeal to his friends, with a simple but unlikely request:

Have mercy on me, have mercy on me, O you my friends, for the hand of God has touched me!	19:21	חָנֻּנִי חָנֻּנִי אַתֶּם רֵעָי כִּי יַד־אֱלוֹהַּ נָגְעָה בִּי׃
Why do you, like God, pursue me? Why are you not satisfied with my flesh?	19:22	לָמָּה תִּרְדְּפֻנִי כְמוֹ־אֵל וּמִבְּשָׂרִי לֹא תִשְׂבָּעוּ׃

Job's request here is a show of compassion on the part of the friends. The double plea for mercy in verse 21a here is used by Job as a parody of traditional piety, where the sufferer addresses חָנֵּנִי, "have mercy on me," to God.[128] Instead of performing their role as men of compassion, the three friends join with the judgmental God. The image of "God's hand" represents the action of God which is responsible for Job's suffering. The term נגע, "touched," is used in this same sense in 1:11, 19; 2:5; 4:5; and 5:19. It signifies the violence done to Job (cf. 19:7; 16:17–18). This line (v. 21b) gives the reason why Job calls for mercy. Job ironically calls the friends as "like God" (כְמוֹ־אֵל), who "pursue" Job (רדף, v. 22). The verb rendered "pursue" is not meant in the sense of follow or chase, but here it means "to afflict, persecute, punish, cause to suffer."[129] Job insists that it is God who afflicts Job. The friends also believe that God is the one who sends calamity upon Job. But their belief is based on the retribution principle in which the punishing/rewarding faces of God are actively operating. Job, on the contrary, rejects the basic assumption of the friends. Job knows that he is not sinful, and yet he is still experiencing the judgmental face of God. Job is struggling and sees only a capricious, and sometimes diabolical face of God (19:7–12; cf. 9:17–21).

As in the prologue, Job refuses to abandon his integrity. Job is searching for someone who will have sufficient faith in him to demand his acquittal

---

128. For instance, Pss 4:1[2]; 6:2[3]; 41:10[11]; 57:1[2]; 123:3; etc.

129. C. Frevel notes that the original usage of the term רדף is in military contexts. However, the word is often used for the adversaries of the individual, specifically in the poetry section of the Old Testament. Here Job is meeting with pursuit by God as well as by his presumptuous friends ("רדף," *TDOT* 13:340–351).

(19:23–27). He then resumes the idea of a witness which he developed already in chapter 16.

Oh that my words were written!	19:23	מִי־יִתֵּן אֵפוֹ וְיִכָּתְבוּן מִלָּי
Oh that they were inscribed in a book!		מִי־יִתֵּן בַּסֵּפֶר וְיֻחָקוּ׃
Oh that with an iron pen and lead,	19:24	בְּעֵט־בַּרְזֶל וְעֹפָרֶת
they were engraved in the rock forever!		לָעַד בַּצּוּר יֵחָצְבוּן׃

The pericope above is a continuation of Job's wish in 16:18. In both instances Job first thinks of inanimate objects as witnessing. He refers to his blood as crying out in 16:18. In 19:23–24 Job firstly thinks of physical, written evidence, rather than a person who would function as a witness. The purpose of the long-lasing (לָעַד) record (whether in a book/scroll or on a rock) of Job's words (i.e. his repeated protests of his innocence) is to testify to posterity that the claims of his friends that Job is an ungodly man are wrong. However, Job's sentiment quickly returns to the idea of a personal witness. The result is among the most touching words of faith in all of Scriptures:

| For I know that my redeemer lives,[130] | 19:25 | וַאֲנִי יָדַעְתִּי גֹּאֲלִי חָי |
| and at the last[131] he will stand upon the earth.[132] | | וְאַחֲרוֹן עַל־עָפָר יָקוּם׃ |

---

130. Cf. some scholars may see the resurrection idea in this text, for example, Michael L. Barré, "Note on Job 19:25," *VT* 29 (1979): 107–110, suggests the traditional word pair קוּם/חַי as "live/rise" used in the context of healing and resurrection. He then emends חַי into a Piel form and points the verb קוּם as a Hiphil, and translate the text as:
  I know that my redeemer can restore life/health,
  And that (my) guarantor can rise from the dust (= the netherworld).
However, the Joban author may have a specific purpose for this very choice of words pair. In the context of the book Job is longing for a vindication. The language used here is forensic; thus, the MT should be retained.

131. The Hebrew term אַחֲרוֹן is taken normally as an adjective (e.g. "last, latter," [with noun] in Exod 4:8; 2 Sam 23:1; Isa 30:8; etc.) or a noun (e.g. "the Last" in Isa 44:6; 48:12). The feminine longer form (אַחֲרוֹנָה), always preceded by proposition (בְּ, כְּ, לְ), is used as adverb (i.e. "afterwards, at the last") (BDB, 31; *DCH*, 195). However, the shorter form (אַחֲרוֹן) occurs five times adverbially in Qumran texts without a proposition. In addition, the context suggests that Job's vindication will take place at some future time (i.e. after Job's death; see the following line in 26a, "after [אַחַר] my skin has been destroyed"); thus, the term here should be taken as adverbial (i.e. "lastly, at the last").

132. In his dissertation, Holbert, "The Function and Significance of the Klage," 231, sees that the four Hebrew terms: גֹּאֵל, "redeemer;" חַי, "alive;" אַחֲרוֹן, "the last one;" and קוּם, "rise," are used conspicuously often in the Bible with God (cf. Isa 48:12; 44:6 Josh 3:10; Hos

And after my skin has been thus destroyed, yet in my flesh I shall see God,	19:26	וְאַחַר עוֹרִי נִקְּפוּ־זֹאת וּמִבְּשָׂרִי אֶחֱזֶה אֱלוֹהַּ׃
whom I shall see for myself, and my eyes shall behold, and not another. My heart faints within me!	19:27	אֲשֶׁר אֲנִי אֶחֱזֶה־לִּי וְעֵינַי רָאוּ וְלֹא־זָר כָּלוּ כִלְיֹתַי בְּחֵקִי׃

After it is introduced by verses 23–24, the text reaches its peak in 19:25–27 as its most well-known and well-beloved "redeemer" passage of the book.[133] The passage is one of the most difficult passages to translate in the Scripture. The strong emphasis on אֲנִי, "I," followed by the verb ידע (יָדַעְתִּי, "I know," v. 25a), is clearly significant.[134] There is a strong affirmation being made here. As Job tries to articulate, however unlikely, a possible solution to his situation, in his confidence Job expresses a note of defiance that his "גֹּאֵל lives" (v. 25a).[135] Though the word חַי is difficult to understand here, the parallel word קוּם (in v. 25b) may help to understand the meaning of this line that Job's גֹּאֵל will "rise up" (קוּם)[136] to testify his case against God.

2:1; Judg 8:19; Job 27:2), suggesting that the Joban author uses these words intentionally to indicate that God is now unwillingly to perform those things that these four words imply. That is, "God cannot redeem, God is not the Last, God will not appear, and thus God is not really alive." However, a summarized and correct counter notion may be seen from Habel, *Book of Job*, 305–306; Clines, *Job 1–20*, 465.

133. Although this periscope is widely used in the hymnody and in the funeral rites of the church with reference to the resurrection, it is most striking that nowhere does the New Testament cite or even allude to these verses.

134. See the movement of the theme "I know" in: "I know" a mortal cannot be just before El (9:2); "I know" that El will not hold me innocent (9:28); "I know" that you [God] have secret designs against me when I was created (10:13); and "I know" that I am in the right and I shall be vindicated only if I could present my case before an impartial court (13:18). Here Job has a strong conviction that someone will argue his case against God, his mighty enemy. This strong conviction, perhaps, arises from his conviction in his innocence.

135. Some scholars (e.g. Mitchell) may see from 19:25a an expression of an eschatological redemption after death from the mouth of Job, with a supporting clearer statement in the belief in bodily resurrection in 19:26–27. This idea may be an attempt to emphasize the fact that the theology of Job is uncompromisingly monotheistic. This trend of interpretation also ultimately interprets the identity of the redeemer figure as God himself, viewed from the perspective of the whole Bible. However, the immediate context of forensic appeal draws another alternative that since Job has already developed his idea of his heavenly witness in chapter 16, here in chapter 19 Job reaffirms his desire that his divine advocate is now alive. It is Job's strong expression of hope to have a divine defender to argue his case against his most powerful enemy, God himself.

136. The verb קוּם contextually carries the connotation of a legal expression for taking one's stand in court to testify (also in 30:28; 31:14; Deut 19:15–16; Isa 54:17; Mic 6:1; etc.).

While a גֹּאֵל is normally a kinsman,[137] the preceding argument of Job about an advocate seems to demand that this redeemer is the ultimate friend.[138] He is an empathetic witness ready to represent Job and defend his integrity at the final hearing. Whether this final hearing takes place before or after Job's death is probably secondary to the main argument.[139] This personal witness will not be intimidated by God's violent acts against Job. His friendship will bring redemption, vindication, and peace.[140] Job appeals to the redeemer as someone distinct from God (as in 9:33 where the mediator is between God and Job). This is in contrast to the interpretation of Wilhelm Vischer,

---

J. Gamberoni ("קוּם" *TDOT* 12:589–612) suggests that the word here seems to referring to the "resurrection of the dead" (602–603). However, it is possible that in parallel with the word חַי ("live") the גֹּאֵל will "live on after Job's death and rise to present his case" before God. Thus, the גֹּאֵל should not be understood as rising from the grave (i.e. "in resurrection") as suggested by Gamberoni. Again, contextually the notion of resurrection is absent from the text of Job. Also Habel, *The Book of Job*, 293, 307.

137. The term גֹּאֵל comes from the field of family law. It designates the nearest male relative, who was responsible for protecting a person's interests when that individual was unable to do so. The גֹּאֵל would buy back family property sold in distress (Lev 25:25; Ruth 4:4–6; Jer 32:6–7), recover what had been stolen (Num 5:8), redeem a kinsman sold into slavery (Lev 25:28), or avenge a murdered kinsman's blood (Deut 19:6–12; 2 Sam 14:11). The גֹּאֵל is the embodiment of family solidarity. In Israelite tradition, God is sometimes referred to as the גֹּאֵל of the fatherless and the widow (Prov 23:11; Jer 50:34) and of others who experienced helplessness (Ps 119:154; Lam 3:58). In Psalm 103:4, God is the one who "redeems your life from the pit." In the context of this verse in Job, the גֹּאֵל denotes generally a defender or a protector and more specifically the one who stands up for Job in court. Thus, Job is clearly seeking a גֹּאֵל, a third figure, to defend his case against God. With this notion in mind, it is appropriate also to not capitalize the English translation and render it as "redeemer." See Habel, *Book of Job*, 304; Newsom, *The Book of Job*, NIB, 478; etc.

138. See Habel, "Only the Jackal," 227–236. The present author of this book agrees with Habel and sees the redeemer figure here as a third party. However, from the perspective of biblical theology, specifically the development of the idea of messiah in biblical theology, this ultimate friend is a type that is fulfilled in Christ.

139. Leroy Waterman, "Note on Job 19:23–27: Job's Triumph of Fatih," *JBL* 69 (1950): 379–380. Job's primary argument is the vindication of his case before God.

140. Some commentators (e.g. Mowinckel, Habel, Pope, etc.) disagree with identifying this ultimate friend with *Shadday* for the reason that it seems counter to the tenor of Job's argument and is an illogical reversal of God's character as Job's enemy before the cosmic council. See Habel, "Only the Jackal," 235; Habel, *Book of Job*, 103–105; etc. However, others see that the redeemer figure is God himself. For this latter group of scholars, see, for instance, Waterman, "Note on Job," 379–380; R. A. F. McKenzie, "Job," in *The Jerome Biblical Commentary*, eds. Raymond Edward Brown et al. (Englewood Cliffs, NJ: Prentice-Hall, 1968), 519–533; Th. Meek, "Job 19:25–27," *VT* 6 (1956): 100–103; Andersen, *Job*, 194; and Wilhelm Vischer, "God's Truth and Man's Lie: A Study of the Message of the Book of Job," *Interpretation* 15 (1961): 138–139; Hartley, *Book of Job*, 293–295; etc.

for example, who argues that Job "appeals to God against God."[141] Vicher sees that the witness (16:19) or the redeemer figure (19:25) is God himself. Vicher implicitly raises the question of the relationship within biblical theology of this redeemer and Christ. Within the development of the narrative of the book of Job, Job does not have the ultimate fulfillment of this friend to be in mind. Job is speaking here of somebody who will take his part and defend him before God and argue his case. As God reveals his ultimate plan in Christ, we see that what Job longs for here is fulfilled in Christ. That is, it is fulfilled ultimately by Christ who will plead the part of people before God. But Job is not thinking about this messianic idea here. He does not have it in mind here any more than when Boaz performed his function as a גאל with respect to Ruth. Boaz truly anticipated what Christ will do. Boaz is a type, a figure that points in his very person ahead what God will ultimately do in Christ in human form. But no one reading the book of Ruth understands Boaz to be Christ. In the same way, it is not necessary to say that what Job has in mind here is Christ in the narrow sense of the term, but a type of Christ who is to come.

Another major issue in this redeemer passage should be discussed here is the time of Job's vindication. David J. A. Clines offers a better understanding concerning the textual problem.[142] Clines points out that verses 25–26a and 26b–27 do not refer to the same scene. In verses 25–26a, Job describes his certainty that a redeemer will arise and vindicate him after his death. As important as that certainty is to Job, it is not what he most desires. What he desires is expressed in verses 26b–27, not a postmortem vindication but a vindication that he can experience before he dies, in his flesh and with his own eyes. This interpretation requires no emendation of the MT, only a recognition that the conjunction in verse 26b can be read as "But" (with a capitalized "B") and that the following verbs are not to be translated as simple futures but as modal imperfects expressing a wish. Thus,

> I know that my redeemer lives,
>   and that at the last he will arise upon the earth –

---

141. Vischer, "God's Truth," 138–139.
142. Clines, *Job 1–20*, 461–462; cf. Habel, *Book of Job*, 290–291.

after my skin has been stripped off.
But I would see God from my flesh,
whom I would see[143] for myself;
my eyes would see, and not a stranger. (19:25–27b,
author's translation)

Cline's reading differs from the traditional reading in the following way.[144] First, he takes the verb חזה as a modal imperfect (v. 26b), but more importantly he takes the *waw* in verse 25b, like the traditional reading, as introducing another object of the verb ידע (i.e. "and [I also know that] at the last he will stand on earth"). Second, Clines reads the *waw* in verse 26a differently from the traditional reading by reading it as introducing the circumstantial clause: "after/when my skin has been stripped off."[145] Finally, the *waw* in verse 26b, Clines must take it as adversative *waw*, introducing a completely new idea: "But."[146] Thus, there is no longer connected, and actually draws in contrast that Job wants to vindicate his case to God in this life time. In effect, Job is speaking that somebody will come along later who will take his case. However, Job does not care about that now. What he wants is vindication now. He wants to defend himself before God. And he wants to do it by himself. This is very interesting because this is a contrast with what Job has said before. Previously, he wanted somebody else to help him with his case; now he wants to do it by himself. Thus, the hope for an intermediary has reached its peak. Job no longer longs for this intermediary. He wants a more immediate solution to his case, namely, to defend himself before God (cf. 13:13–16). The texts associating with the idea of the vindicator disappear after 19:25–27.

This understanding of verses 25–27 fits well with the development of Job's thought. As Job has explored the legal metaphor as a model for his confrontation with God, he has imagined the figure of someone who might be a true compassionated friend and side with him: an arbiter (9:33), a

---

143. The Hebrew imperfect verb אֶחֱזֶה, may be rendered either as a modal imperfect (GKC, § 107m–n) or as a cohortative (GKC, § 48b–e), representing a will or desire rather than a simple prediction.

144. The traditional reading is to read the *waw* in verses 25b, and 26 (a, b), as introducing another object of the verb ידע, of what Job knows.

145. See IBHS, § 39.2.3b; § 38.7; also § 11.2.1.

146. IBHS, § 39.2.3c; cf. § 8.3b.

witness (16:19), and a redeemer (19:25). The necessity of this figure has been forced on him by the increasing certainty of his impending death.[147] Yet just as Job's confidence in the presence of such a figure reaches its climax, he realizes that such a solution could not be possible. He desires what he described in 13:13–22, a direct presentation of his case to God and God's reply.[148] Significantly, after chapter 19 Job says no more about heavenly intermediaries; rather, in chapters 23[149] and 31[150] he pursues his strong determination to carry his case to God's presence. However, the tenacity of Job's faith amidst the bleakness of his life leaves him spiritually spent, though hopeful; thus, Job says: "My heart faints within me!" (19:27c).[151]

Job is overwhelmed; there is no doubt about the enormity of what he desires. The fact that Job is facing death does not undermine his faith. What Job knows, over and above the death that he alternatively begs, fears, and resigns himself to, is that his redeemer or advocate lives, with the result that Job, alive or dead (i.e. here and now, or there and beyond), will see God. Surprisingly, at the end of the book Job eventually does see God ("I had heard

---

147. It is noteworthy that Job's impending death is a major obstacle preventing him from defending himself. Thus, Job wishfully thinks of something or someone who would speak for him: the earth (16:18), a heavenly witness (16:19), an inscribed text (19:23), an engraved rock (19:24), and a גֹּאֵל (19:25). Also Newsom, *The Book of Job: A Contest*, 157.

148. Note that throughout the dialogue Job wants God to come to trial with him (9:32), his awareness that no arbiter between him and God (9:33), his desire to speak directly to the *Shadday* (13:3), his ambition to argue his case before God's face (13:15), his wish not to hide himself from God's face (13:20), and his complaint that God hides God's face (13:24). Job's wish to see God face to face is what Habel, *Book of Job*, 64, calls "the unthinkable" of Job in which Job is challenging the ancient wisdom tradition that the invisible God is too holy for the eyes of wise and righteous men to behold. The motifs of "seeing" and the פָּנֶה of God are one of the most significant themes in the book of Job (e.g. in the prologue, chs. 3, 9, 13, 19, 23, 42).

149. In chapter 23, Job expresses more openly about his desire to "see" God, for instance: Job wishes he could find the way to God's "seat" (תְּכוּנָה, 23:3), but at the same time, he realizes that he cannot perceive (בִין, 23:8), behold (חזה, 23:9) or see (ראה, 23:9) God.

150. In chapter 31, Job mentions "a covenant with his eyes" (31:1) where Job denies those sinful crimes (31:7–34). Job gives the oaths of innocence and challenges God to show him openly the charges God brings against Job. He marks: הֶן־תָּוִי שַׁדַּי יַעֲנֵנִי, "Here is my signature, let the *Shadday* answers me!" (31:35).

151. Again, in the context of the vindicator passages, the three texts (i.e. 9:35b; 16:22; 19:27c) give a hint of Job's descents into despair, signaling that this figure is an unreal figure. These closing cries of despair are explicit responses of lamentation following flights of unfulfilled hope. Thus, the friend or redeemer whom Job yearns for is certainly an impossible ideal in his life experience. See Habel, "Only the Jackal," 227–236.

of you by the hearing of the ear; but now my eyes see you," 42:5).[152] On a literary level, this is important, for what Job confesses in 42:5 is exactly what he hopes for here in 19:26b. So, in one sense, God does fulfill Job's hope.[153] Theologically, what Job is looking for is the right relationship, which is not that of divine retribution, not only in the vindication of his case, but also to be with God. In this chapter, Job is moving beyond the retribution principle.

The movement of Job's hope and the effect of the certainty of his imminent death can briefly be seen from the following. In chapter 9 Job states that his own צדק and תם are nullified and irrelevant before God (9:20), and consequently lead Job only to מאס his own life (9:21; cf. 7:16; 10:1). Job realizes that all efforts to be innocent are pointless (הֶבֶל), and he will always be guilty, even if only by God's malicious bullying (9:30–31). There is "no umpire between us," thus, there is no hope for Job to fairly vindicate his case (9:33). In chapter 14, it seems to have hope. Job imagines a time that he could hide himself in Sheol from which he would return to appear in court and defend his integrity (14:13–17). However, immediately afterward Job realizes that his hope is impossible because a hope Job is longing for is not for a man (i.e. only for a tree), and God destroys every hope of man (14:18–22) to live. Also in chapter 16, Job develops more positive picture of his witness and advocate in heaven. That is, Job's wish here is for one who can intervene, for one whose role will be similar to the role of a referee or umpire in 9:33–35, so that Job would no longer fear God's destructive power; thus, Job's hope is that things could be sorted out and life could normalize with God again. As Job senses his imminent death, he begs that a record of his suffering and his cries survive him (16:23–24; the same sentiment is found in 19:23–24). As Job falls into despair, hope finds its way and makes a big leap in 17:8–9. The certainty of his righteousness and his strong desire for vindication lead him to a new stage in his reconciliation with God. As there

---

152. While the word חָזָה ("see") is used in Job 19:26–27, another Hebrew word רָאָה ("see") is employed in Job 42:5. Though these are two different Hebrew words for the term "to see," there are no identifiable bold differences of meaning. The word חָזָה, like רָאָה, refers both to the natural vision of the eyes and to supernatural visions of various kinds. See H. F. Fuhs, "רָאָה," *TDOT* 13:208–242; and A. Jepsen, "חָזָה," *TDOT* 4:280.

153. However, in the OT the phrase "seeing God" gives a sense of theophany (e.g. Exod 24:11; cf. Pss 11:7; 17:15; 27:4; 63:3). In Job 19:26b–27b, the expressions may be understood as meaning a hoped-for theophany (*TDOT* 4:280).

is no hope in Sheol; thus, he must hope for living in order to vindicate his case. Job desires to see his case vindicated in this life. He will not equate hope with Sheol (17:15–16). Now in chapter 19 we explicitly see Job's two faces: While Job is in despair, he is faithfully clinging to God at the same time. The certainty and imminence of death convinces Job that he will not be able to vindicate his case (19:25–26a). But at the same time, Job expresses his determination not to equate his hope with Sheol (17:15–16), and so he strongly wishes for an opportunity for vindication before his death (19:26b–27). Job's desire for death and his hope for vindication in this life time are part of his bigger problem; namely, the problem of divine justice in which Job could not find an answer to the question why the just God allows him, a righteous man, to suffer. The redeemer figure, found in 9:33–35; 16:19–21; and 19:25–27, is also part of Job's seeking of vindication in this life. Although the vindicator theme seems to develop its way toward its peak in a range of mountains (i.e. from an "umpire" in 9:33 to a "heavenly witness" in 16:19, and ultimately to a "redeemer" in 19:25); however, and significantly, once chapter 19 is over, the redeemer theme disappears from the rest of the book. Job comes to the point to realize that this figure is an impossible figure (i.e. 9:35b; 16:22; 19:27c). As Job is also experiencing imminent death, and as the idea of the redeemer figure is not enough to carry him on his own, Job, thus, must turn to God, the source of his problem. He needs the appearance of Yahweh. Therefore, he makes his final plea by lamenting and giving a direct appeal to God in chapters 29–31.

The Third Cycle of the Dialogues (Summarized)

Due to the need to limit the scope of this study, the third cycle of the dialogues will not be examined in detail. To summarize it briefly, in the third and last cycle of the disputations Eliphaz concludes with the same appeal to repentance as in his first speech (Job 5). He further attacks Job directly and explicitly points out that Job is the wicked, who must have done some specific sins. His words signal to Job (and the reader) that there is nothing new from the friends. After Job 19, Zophar does respond to Job in chapter 20. The nature of his speech is the same as what Eliphaz and Bildad have said to Job; namely, emphasizing the horrible destiny of the wicked. Job shows them in return the true horror of the fate of the wicked in chapter 21. Job's point is to respond not only to Zophar but to all of their common view of divine justice. Job is certain that their view is false and tantamount to idolatry. Chapter 21, thus, concludes the second cycle of the dialogues with the friends.

After Bildad's argument in chapter 25 (only five verses), Job can bear no more. He interrupts impatiently and angrily attacks Bildad's inspiration (26:1–4) and finishes Bildad's speech for him (26:5–14). Job makes his own counter-argument in chapter 27 and reconstructs Zophar's third speech by making it for him (27:13–23).[154]

Job 28 is unique in its form and brilliant in its content. The location in the design of the book marks a significant feature of this chapter. The theme in this chapter is wisdom, specifically the inaccessibility of wisdom. Significantly, the thematic connection between 28:28 and 1:1, 8, and 2:3 (cf. 27:5–6) points out that up to this point (28:28) Job has survived the horrendous test and still keeps clinging to his hope in God despite the removal of the hedge. The hymn to wisdom in chapter 28 reflects Job's meditating on wisdom, searching for a new reconciliation with God. As we will see, wisdom takes Job ponders deeper and deeper into the connection with the truths of God, residing in the very core of Job's being. Job is no longer seeking traditional wisdom through his righteousness. He will instead make a direct appeal to God asking that his case can be vindicated. Thus, chapter 28 is Job's last word to his friends. His concluding words in 28:28 also reflect the sense of Job's words in 17:8–9: Despite all the suffering and the accusations of the friends, Job stirs himself up against the godless (i.e. the three friends). He (i.e. Job), who has clean hands become stronger and stronger. The hymn of wisdom in Job 28 teaches us that human cannot find wisdom, whose dwelling place is known only to God. This wisdom is the first principle which governs all other principles of the universe, including the retribution principle in the friends' and Job's worldview. Humans cannot know everything, God does know everything. Job's meditation led him to a conclusion that "the fear of the Lord is wisdom." Therefore, wisdom judges

---

154. See Janzen's analysis on Job 25–27 as he attempts to interpret the text as it stands (*Job*, 171–186).

the counsel of the friends, the wise men, as lacking in wisdom.[155] Job then turns to God in his final speech (chs. 29–31).

Chapters 29–31. Before the start of the dialogue with the three friends, Job opens his lament (Job 3), which gave his heart-felt response to the sufferings that has suddenly come upon him. Structurally, chapters 29–31 represent the corresponding closing lament of Job,[156] which offers a sort of summary of the position Job has now reached.[157] The structure of these chapters is clear and simple. It falls into three main parts: a summary of his "good old days" (ch. 29), an account of his present misery (ch. 30), and a final declaration of innocence and appeal to God (ch. 31).

In chapter 29, Job speaks nostalgically of days of old, the days when things were right between him and God (29:2–5). He recalls the family that surrounded him (v. 5), the care and prosperity of his daily life (v. 6), the respect that all men gave to him (vv. 7–11), the way he was able to help the

---

155. For the wisdom theme in the book of Job, see, for instance, Habel, "Of Things Beyond Me: Wisdom in the Book of Job," *CurTM* 10 (1983): 142–154.

156. This section (Job 29–31) should not be viewed merely as a soliloquy in which Job reflects on his past and present situations. Habel, *Book of Job*, 404, proposes that this section is a formally legal "testimony" (from the term מָשָׁל in 29:1), addressed to a public assembly (also Andersen, *Job*, 230). Newsom, *Job: A Contest*, 185, also uses the term "testimony" for this section of Job, but in a more general sense, referring to the giving of an account of events, of one's experience, or of oneself. In fact, the speeches in this section are not composed according to a specific literary genre, but use a variety of forms of speech. See, for instance, Georg Fohrer, "The Righteous Man in Job 31," in *Essays in Old Testament Ethics* (New York: KTAV, 1974), 1–22; M. Dick, "The Legal Metaphor in Job 31," *CBQ* 41 (1979): 37–50; M. Dick, "Job 31, the Oath of Innocence, and the Sage," *ZAW* 95 (1983): 31–53; John Holbert, "Rehabilitation of the Sinner: The Function of Job 29–31," *ZAW* 95 (1983): 229–237; etc. Job no longer talks to or about the friends, even though the friends are physically there with him. It is possible that Job deliver these speeches before an assembly at the gate (30:28b). Though he does not address directly to God for the whole section, God is the explicit addressee in one brief section (30:20–23). This book agrees with Westermann, "The Literary Genre," 56, and sees that from the perspective of the book as a whole the dialogue is framed by Job laments (Job 3 and 29–31). Moreover, the doctrine of retribution, which becomes rigidified from the friends, stands "over against the burning lament, which arises directly out of an existential anguish. The lament finds no hearing and elicits no consolation; the doctrine ricochets off the reality of pain. Thus the disputation must run its course without resolution; only the higher court can decide [i.e. chs. 38–42]." Therefore, Job 29–31 is a corresponding closing lament of Job. Job must turn exclusively to God for God is not only the heart, but also the resolution of his problem. As the speeches are deliver before an assembly at the gate, they facilitate also the reaction from Elihu, who, like the reader, is a bystander listening to all that have been addressed.

157. As Rowold, "Theology of Creation," 26, observes, the reader sees that Job's "why" questions in chapter 3 have become a sort of "Here I stand" in chapter 31 (31:35–37), where Job challenges God directly.

needy (vv. 12–17), the confidence that God would continue to prosper him (vv. 18–20), and the esteem he enjoyed as a respected teacher and leader (vv. 21–25). Job talks about the image of God's protective presence and the image of household and its well-being. These two images echo life in chapter 1:1–5, presenting a positive relationship in terms of a quid pro quo between God and Job.158 Job's reminiscence of old days is the conviction that his shalomic life was built on relationship under the retribution principle which rooted in righteousness and justice. Therefore, his image of God is strongly shaped by his understanding of his own place in this moral world. Righteousness and justice is the seeds of hope for a meaningful life first with God (29:2–6), and then with community (29:7–11, 21–25). His description of "good life" is portrayed in the sense of moral goodness. As in Eliphaz's description of the life of the righteous person in 5:17–26, Job narrates a good death as the culmination of this kind of a shalomic life. Job states, "I shall die in my nest, and I shall multiply my days as the sand" (29:18).

Under the retribution principle which connected with righteousness and justice, Job locates himself in relation to God, to his children, to his peers, to those who need his protection, to those who need his leadership. This is a world in which persons are not autonomous individuals so much as they are persons in relation, first with God, and then with community. Life in this retributive worldview is a highly healthy life. It includes right relationship with God, peace and serenity of both family's and community's life, even a peaceful death, full of years and in the presence of family. This view of life and death makes no room for an untimely death or bad death. Rather it has only the good death which is in the primetime of life. Like a meaningful life which is not a separation from God, death is meaningfully with and under God.

In chapter 30, the focus shifts completely (וְעַתָּה in 30:1; also in 30:9, 16). Job no longer speaks of the wistful past, when all was right with God and life, but of the brutal present, when God has changed and consequently his life has changed also. Before suffering wrecked Job's life, God was a constant source of blessing and joy. After his life fell apart, God was nowhere to be found, except as the sinister that attacked Job. In Job's upside-down world,

---

158. Note that this quid pro quo relationship is a relationship rooted in justice, not grace or mercy.

the respect he once enjoyed has turned to scorn (vv. 2–8), society's admiration for him has turned to hostile aggression (vv. 9–15), and God, whom Job once knew to be unquestionably just, has become inexplicably "cruel" (vv. 16–19). It appears to Job that God's justice is corrupt. Job knows that he is innocent and now he is still innocent. But God now appears unjustly cruel because he is not maintaining justice. Job's sudden calamities could be understood as divine abandonment or rejection, and as such, an invitation to rejection by the social community. Job describes God's behavior with a series of heavy and accusing verbs: you "persecute me" (v. 21b); you "toss me about" (v. 22b); you "bring me to death" (v. 23a). He concludes God's way as "cruel" to him (v. 21). As Job lives according to the retribution principle, which means that he does not turn against the needy who cry to him for help (v. 24), God appears to follow a different code of conduct. Implicitly, God is guilty of having violated this principle of conduct because God has turned his hand against the defenseless Job. As Job seeks a restoration of his well-being, including his reputation among his community, the attempt cannot be done without reconciliation with God. So Job forms his expectations (cf. 29:18–20), he then appeals for God's mercy: "I cry to you, but you do not answer me" (30:20; also in 30:24, 28). Job states explicitly that God is seeking his death: "For I know that you will bring me to death and to the house appointed for all living" (30:23; cf. 10:8–9). He fears that God will simply end his life as the final ruthless repression of Job (cf. 9:17; 19:10). As death is the finality of all mankind, Job has no hope in death, and no hope for vindication of the one constant in his life, his reputation as blameless and upright, fearing God and shunning evil (1:1). Death is not only Job's final pain, but also his crowning insult. As Job affirms in 30:25–26 that he is an upholder of the moral order, and not God, he speaks of the issue in terms of the failure of the reciprocal bonds that should sustain the social and moral world. Job moves in his discourse from grief to bitter accusation to both God and his community, for both falls short from this principle of moral conduct.[159] Job falls into despair. Only the jackals and ostriches are

---

159. See also Good, *In Turns of Tempest: A Reading of Job with a Translation*, (Stanford: Stanford University Press, 1990), 317, who states that "Job has dropped back to the full retributionist position, has departed the depth of his despair about receiving a fair trial (ch. 23) and the savage redefinition of terms that in chapter 27 portrayed him as the god's moral

his friends (30:29), for they inhabit in the wasteland beyond the bounds of the socially moral order.

In chapter 31 Job links his differing situations in chapters 29–30 and disavows any sin or departure from God that would have led from the bliss of chapter 29 to the reality of chapter 30. The form involved is an oath: "if" (אִם) . . . "then" (expressed in a following verb, but sometimes unexpressed). By means of his oath of clearance, Job avers his blamelessness, and lays the foundation for the face-to-face meeting with God (vv. 35–37) which will provide both exoneration and resolution.[160] His speech has been compared to the process by which an accused person whose opponent refuses to produce evidence compels his accuser to come to court.[161] But note that Job uses the oath in an adapted, rhetorical manner, not as an actual legal proceeding. Job's presumption that innocence guarantees acquittal and restoration suggests that for all his criticisms of the friends, Job still believes in the retribution principle. His innocence means that he deserves better treatment. Job's retreat to conventional understanding of reward and punishment is an indication that "retribution is now the heart on Job's sleeve."[162] Job's moral perspective is that the imposition of evil upon good has no place either in his ethical world or God's. Therefore, in Job's world, there are no exceptions, no contradictions, and no alternatives.[163] Job views that tragedy has no place in his righteous world; therefore, it should have no place in God's. Job wants to improve his view upon God.

At several points, Job refers to God's passion for righteousness and justice as the basis for his own moral seriousness (e.g. 31:13–15). Newsom notes that in this way the reader sees the extent to which Job assumes continuity between his own moral being and that of God.[164] Job's assumption provides the basis for a possible resolution of the conflict between Job and God and a resolution of the issues of the book. Job has a conviction that his complaint

---

superior. Now he trots out the standard terms of reward and punishment to what he so furiously objected when the friends enunciated them."

160. It is noteworthy that these three chapters contain one of the most insightful expressions of the moral life to be found anywhere in the Scripture.

161. Dick, "Legal Metaphor," 42.

162. Good, *In Turn of Tempest*, 315.

163. Balentine, *Job*, 472; cf. Newsom, *The Book of Job: A Contest*, 196.

164. Newsom, *The Book of Job*, NIB, 551.

(רִיב, 31:13) against God can be resolved fairly. Just as God demands justice of him, so also God will show justice to him, despite the difference in power, if Job can gain a hearing (cf. 23:2–7).[165] Therefore, Job culminates his oaths with the demand that God appears:

> Oh, that I had one to hear me!
> > Here is my signature! Let the *Shadday* answer me!
> > Oh, that I had the indictment written by my adversary!
> Surely I would carry it on my shoulder;
> > I would bind it on me as a crown;
> I would give him an account of all my steps;
> > Like a prince I would approach him. (Job 31:35–37)

Job's oath of innocence has to do with what Janzen calls "a primal sympathy," where "conscience function as a sort of internal tribunal or courtroom, examining our behavior against the specific rules and laws by which conscience is informed."[166] It is for moral and ethical relationships that is prior to and generative of the social customs that are codified in legal statues. Job's oath is "preoccupied with the problem of the ethics of power in relationships of inequality."[167] Job has a presumption that an honorable declaration of personal virtues gives God the opportunity to affirm God's own commitment to relationships that are moral and ethical. This commitment is Job's projection viewed under the doctrine of divine retribution. As Job believes in an unassailable claim on God's justice, that is God is a just God, then Job believes that he will be vindicated. While in his opening lament (ch. 3) Job's radical wish is for death as the end of his suffering, he later fears that his death will go unnoticed and unvindicated. Thus, his final desire is no longer death, but vindication.

---

165. Newsom, 552; cf. Janzen, *Job*, 210–212.
166. Janzen, *Job*, 210–212.
167. Newsome, *The Book of Job: A Contest*, 195.

Elihu Speeches: Elihu

The next character will be considered in this chapter is Elihu.[168] He appears from nowhere. His character is different from that of the three friends. He is not presented as Job's friend.[169] He, perhaps, is a bystander who takes up the role of arbiter, whom Job is yearning for in his speeches.[170] Elihu is also presented as a young, hotheaded character, whose words are bombastic. The meaning of his name,[171] the narrator's full introduction of his clan,[172] and the fact that his speeches seem to appear as an interruption between Job's call for a confrontation with God (31:35–37), and Yahweh's speeches in 38:1ff, suggest that Elihu may function literary as a prophet or a forerunner of Yahweh.[173] The angry Elihu (four time אַף, "anger" in 32:2[2x], 3, 5) tries to present himself as an answerer for Job's question about suffering and about God (אַף־אֲנִי אַעֲנֶה, "I will answer; yes, I will!" 32:17, 20; cf. 33:12; also אַף־אֲנִי in 32:10, 17).[174] If Job has been wearied by those good intentions of the friends, he must have been exhausted by the false attempting to

---

168. Although the speeches of Elihu (32:1–37:24) have often been considered as a secondary insertion into the book of Job, the present author sees that their structural and theological issues have no critical problem with this research. His speeches give a significant contribution not only to the issue of death and the retribution principle, but also the issue of suffering which may be an expression of God's mercy, and not of God's wrath. So his speeches will be held as integral to the book.

169. Also in the mouth of Elihu, Job's three friends become the three "men," (not "friends" as they were in 2:11 and in the dialogue; cf. textual note in 32:1).

170. Some scholars see Elihu as Job's mediator, for instance: H. D. Beeby, "Elihu . . . Job's mediator?," *Southeast Asia Journal of Theology* 7 (1965): 33–54; Habel, "The Role of Elihu in the Design of the Book of Job," in *In the Shelter of Elyon: Essays on Ancient Palestinian Life and Literature in Honor of G. W. Ahlström*, JSOTSup 31, eds. W. Boyd Barrick and John S. Spencer (Sheffield: JSOT Press, 1984), 81–98. For suggestion of the role of Elihu as the *alazon* or buffoon, "a comic figure whom the author exposes and ridicules," see J. William Whedbee, "The Comedy of Job," *Semeia* 7 (1977): 1–39.

171. The name Elihu, "אֱלִיהוּא" means "he is my God" (cf. the name Elijah ["Yahweh is my God"], who is a prophet, announcing words from God).

172. He is בֶּן־בַּרַכְאֵל הַבּוּזִי מִמִּשְׁפַּחַת רָם, "the son of Barachel the Buzite, of the family of Ram" (32:2).

173. See Janzen, *Job*, 217; Hartley, *Book of Job*, 429; Balentine, *Job*, 513–516; Good, *In Turns of Tempest*, 320.

174. See a double entendre of the word אַף־אֲנִי ("Yes, I will"), which may be used intentionally by the Joban author to hint a true character of Elihu in Habel, *The Book of Job*, 443–444.

help of this young man. Elihu insists that his words are inspired by God.[175] But he speaks out of anger. His words, thus, appear to Job and the reader as the false prophet claiming to speak God's truth. However, the point is whether God is speaking or not in Job's specific case. If God were speaking, listening to him could lead to life, including restored life; however, if the so-called "prophet" were speaking empty words, listening to him could lead to death. Therefore, the reader will observe later to which voice does Job will respond: Elihu's or God's?[176]

Elihu's Views of Death: Chapters 33:15–18, 19–22, 23–30; and 34:11

Elihu has the same fundamental presupposition of the cause-effect relation between sin and suffering. His lengthy speeches (159 uninterrupted verses within six chs.) present himself not only standing with the friends in rebuke Job, but also an independent voice in rebuke of both the friends and Job (e.g. as a variation of God's reply). His point about the retribution principle is that sometimes it is a balancing mechanism that operates inescapably, and sometimes it is a channel by which God uses to speak to humans. Suffering and dreadful death are not so much a mystery, they are more a testimony, in which God uses them as discipline. This discipline aspect may be not the penalty for sin already committed, but an advanced warning to keep a man back from future sin (33:19–28).

As Elihu addresses Job by name for the first time in 33:1,[177] he does invite Job into a dialogue (33:1–7). He quotes the words of Job's complaints, specifically in chapters 9 and 13 (i.e. God does not answer those who cry out in suffering and encounter dreadful death, 33:8–11). Elihu identifies Job's fault (33:12–13, ריב against God), then he corrects Job's idea of why God is treating Job as God is (33:14–22, 29–30).

Elihu maintains that Job's thought is wrong. Initially, the three friends suggest Job that piety is more important than pain. But Elihu takes a different

---

175. Janzen, *Job*, 218, also suggests that structurally Elihu's similar appeal to inspiration in his speeches (32–37) "may be taken to form an inclusion" with Eliphaz's appeal to inspired words in chapter 4.

176. Southwick, "Job: An Examplar," 375–376.

177. Elihu addresses Job directly by name throughout the speeches (33:1, 31; 34:5, 7, 35, 36; 35:16; 37:14).

approach. He responds to Job's question about suffering and dreadful death by suggesting that pain is one of the means God uses to communicate with human being (v. 14: "in one way and in two;" v. 29: "twice, three times")[178] as a warning. As Job has complained that God does not respond to those sufferers, Elihu maintains that God does but it is Job who fails to respond. In other words, Job is not able to discern what God is trying to communicate to him. Elihu insists that God does speak through "dreams" (חֲלוֹם), "night visions" (לַיְלָה חֶזְיוֹן; cf. 4:13), "deep sleep" (תַּרְדֵּמָה; cf. 4:13), and "slumbers" (תְּנוּמָה; v. 15). He points further that in God's revelatory process of warning (vv. 15–18; 19–22; 23–28), God's purpose is to save life (vv. 18, 22, 28).[179]

Although a man, a sinful man, deserves to see only the face of punishment from God, nevertheless God gives him an opportunity to repent (33:16–18):

In a dream, in a vision of the night, when deep sleep falls on men, while they slumber on their beds,	33:15	בַּחֲלוֹם חֶזְיוֹן לַיְלָה בִּנְפֹל תַּרְדֵּמָה עַל־אֲנָשִׁים בִּתְנוּמוֹת עֲלֵי מִשְׁכָּב׃
then he opens the ears of men and terrifies them with warning,	33:16	אָז יִגְלֶה אֹזֶן אֲנָשִׁים וּבְמֹסָרָם יַחְתֹּם׃
that he may turn man aside from his deed and conceal pride from a man;	33:17	לְהָסִיר אָדָם מַעֲשֶׂה וְגֵוָה מִגֶּבֶר יְכַסֶּה׃
he keeps back his soul from the pit, his life from perishing by the sword.	33:18	יַחְשֹׂךְ נַפְשׁוֹ מִנִּי־שָׁחַת וְחַיָּתוֹ מֵעֲבֹר בַּשָּׁלַח׃

In this first step of God's warning (33:15–18), dreams (v. 15) are used not only to "open their ears," but also to terrify them with warning (v. 16), impelling them, sinners, to change their ways (v. 17). God's purpose is to turn man away from his "deed" (מַעֲשֶׂה), which is not a sin, but a potential sin (according to their pride) that would destine them for death. So if he listens, he will not lose his soul (נֶפֶשׁ) in the pit (שַׁחַת; cf. Sheol, the abode

---

178. Hartley, *Book of Job*, 442–443, suggests that the sequence of number (i.e. one, two) does not indicate the small number of occasions, but God repetitive responses to speak to that person. That is God will keep seeking to communicate with that person.

179. Habel, *Book of Job*, 461, observes that the human mode of experiencing God's revelation or testimony is through "hearing" (vv. 15–18), "feeling" (vv. 19–22), and "seeing" (the face of God) (vv. 23–28).

of the dead).[180] His life (חָיָה) will not experience a sudden and terrified death by the sword (שֶׁלַח). Some scholars see the word שֶׁלַח (parallel to שַׁחַת) as a channel or mythological river of the dead.[181] In either case, the point of this section is to show Job that God will graciously intervene to keep a person who is moving toward sin from encountering the ultimate punishment of sudden and terrified death in the prime of life.

Man is also rebuked with pain on his bed and with continual strife in his bones,	33:19	וְהוּכַח בְּמַכְאוֹב עַל־מִשְׁכָּבוֹ וְרִיב [וְרוֹב] עֲצָמָיו אֵתָן:
so that his life loathes bread, and his appetite the choicest food.	33:20	וְזִהֲמַתּוּ חַיָּתוֹ לָחֶם וְנַפְשׁוֹ מַאֲכַל תַּאֲוָה:
His flesh is so wasted away that it cannot be seen, and his bones that were not seen stick out.	33:21	יִכֶל בְּשָׂרוֹ מֵרֹאִי וּשְׁפִי [וְשֻׁפּוּ] עַצְמוֹתָיו לֹא רֻאּוּ:
His soul draws near the pit, and his life to those who bring death.	33:22	וַתִּקְרַב לַשַּׁחַת נַפְשׁוֹ וְחַיָּתוֹ לַמְמִתִים:

In the second type of warning from God (33:19–22), a message comes to be "felt by the body" (מַכְאוֹב, "[physical] pain," v. 19). This kind of warning may be a more severe discipline than dreams, for it is a person's flesh and bones. This may be a kind of serious illness. His suffering is so intense and continual (v. 19). Food become loathsome to him, he could not enjoy even a piece of bread (v. 20). His flesh wastes away (כלה),[182] even his bones "once hidden, now stick out" (v. 21). His pain is so serious. As "his soul draws near the pit (שַׁחַת), his life to those who bring death (מְמִתִים),"[183] (v.

---

180. The Hebrew word שַׁחַת, "the pit," appears also in verses 22, 24, 28, 30.

181. See, for example, M. Tsevat, "The Canaanite God Šalah," VT 4 (1954): 41–49. Also Habel, Book of Job, 469, who suggests that the titles Šahat and Šelah, Pit and Channel, may be reminiscent of the names of the Canaanite deities: Šahar and Šalim, Dusk and Dawn.

182. The term "waste away" (כלה) has been used already, for example, of the wicked (4:9), of days (7:6), of a cloud (7:9), of eyes (11:20; 17:5), and of the kidneys as denoting the inner being (19:27).

183. Some scholars may understand the terms שַׁחַת, "pit" and מְמִתִים, "death, messengers of death" as underworld powers who receive the dead into their domain. For example, Pope, Job, 251, emends מְמִתִים as lemê māwet-mô, "to the waters of Death," with the enclitic emphatic particle at the end (also Tromp, Primitive, 65). However, as the word שַׁחַת is synonymous with Sheol or grave (cf. 33:18), the term מְמִתִים, as a parallel word, should be

22), it brings the sufferer close to the point of death. Although God afflicts the sinner severely, his intention is to awaken him to the seriousness of his situation. If he repents, then he will be saved from a premature and terrified death.[184] If not, besides his painful experience on his own flesh and bone, he will be brought to the very brink of death, where there is no means to escape.

In the third portrayal of a warning from God (33:23–28), Elihu speaks of a leap of hope when suffering seems to reach its heaviest stroke.

If there be for him an angel, a mediator, one of the thousand to declare to man what is right for him,	33:23	אִם־יֵשׁ עָלָיו מַלְאָךְ מֵלִיץ אֶחָד מִנִּי־אָלֶף לְהַגִּיד לְאָדָם יָשְׁרוֹ:
and he is merciful to him, and says, "Deliver him from going down into the pit; I have found a ransom;	33:24	וַיְחֻנֶּנּוּ וַיֹּאמֶר פְּדָעֵהוּ מֵרֶדֶת שָׁחַת מָצָאתִי כֹפֶר:
let his flesh become fresh with youth; let him return to the days of his youthful vigor";	33:25	רֻטֲפַשׁ בְּשָׂרוֹ מִנֹּעַר יָשׁוּב לִימֵי עֲלוּמָיו:
then man prays to God, and he accepts him; he sees his face with a shout of joy; and he restores to man his righteousness.	33:26	יֶעְתַּר אֶל־אֱלוֹהַּ וַיִּרְצֵהוּ וַיַּרְא פָּנָיו בִּתְרוּעָה וַיָּשֶׁב לֶאֱנוֹשׁ צִדְקָתוֹ:
He sings before men and says: "I sinned and perverted what was right, and it was not repaid to me.	33:27	יָשֹׁר עַל־אֲנָשִׁים וַיֹּאמֶר חָטָאתִי וְיָשָׁר הֶעֱוֵיתִי וְלֹא־שָׁוָה לִי:
He has redeemed my soul from going down into the pit, and my life shall look upon the light."	33:28	פָּדָה נַפְשִׁי [נַפְשׁוֹ] מֵעֲבֹר בַּשָּׁחַת וְחַיָּתִי [וְחַיָּתוֹ] בָּאוֹר תִּרְאֶה:

---

understood literally in the same sense; that is, death or the state of dying permeates the world of the sufferer and threatens his existence. Thus, the MT should be retained.

184. Rhetorically, the Joban poet presents the threatening of death as the intervention of the angel or the messenger of death (מְמִתִים) (cf. 2 Sam 24:16; 1 Chr 21:15; 2 Kgs 19:35; Ps 78:49). Interestingly, the LXX also interprets these destroying angels of death and expanding this idea further in verse 23: "Though there should be a thousand messengers of death, not one of them shall wound him: if he should purpose in his heart to turn to the Lord."

Elihu shifts the focus away from suffering as retributive, seeing it rather as redemptive, a notion expressed in images of redemption "from going down into the pit" and restoration to the light (33:23–28). That is, God will not repay to a sinful man as he deserves it (33:27). These verses (vv. 24–26) are a declaration of God's forgiveness, similar to the assurances given to Job by the friends if Job will repent (e.g. 5:18–26; 11:13–19; 22:21–30). Such a confession is vital in sealing his reconciliation with God. God, then, will redeem him, the sufferer, to be saved from death (מֵעֲבֹר בַּשָּׁחַת, "from going down into the pit," 33:28) and to "look upon the light" (בָּאוֹר תִּרְאֶה; cf. 3:16), which is to be alive and implicitly is contrasted with the darkness of Sheol (10:21–22).

| Behold, God does all these things, twice, three times, with a man, | 33:29 | הֶן־כָּל־אֵלֶּה יִפְעַל־אֵל פַּעֲמַיִם שָׁלוֹשׁ עִם־גָּבֶר׃ |
| to bring back his soul from the pit, that he may be lighted with the light of life. | 33:30 | לְהָשִׁיב נַפְשׁוֹ מִנִּי־שָׁחַת לֵאוֹר בְּאוֹר הַחַיִּים׃ |

Elihu summarizes his positive description of God's communication to human (אֵלֶּה) in 33:29–30 with the recurring theme of God's ultimate purpose (vv. 18, 24, 28). That is, God, a gracious God, uses suffering not to punish arbitrarily the innocent, but to turn him away from pride, deliver him from dying prematurely or being rejected, and restore him to see the light of life (vv. 14, 15, 26, 28). Thus, the redeemed person will be illumined and accepted by God.

In sum, Elihu's speech in chapter 33 is not only about modes of God's communication to human being, but also God's gracious saving act. Elihu affirms to Job that God not only responds to the sufferer, but also has a gracious will to bring the sufferer back from the edge of death to life under him again. Although Elihu's understanding of suffering as divine education (v. 33) is similar to that of Eliphaz (5:17–26), who see suffering only as punishment, Elihu emphasizes God's beneficence, which is attached at the very beginning when he smites and later heals the sufferer. This is a slightly different emphasis in Elihu's speeches to Job. However, in Job's case, Elihu, like the three friends, does not accept Job's claim to be righteous, but speaks only of forgiveness for the repentant sinner. He still affirms the traditional view of retribution principle that "repentance" from sin is necessary in order to be restored.

He emphasizes further that God actively intervenes to exercise retribution:

For according to the work of a man he will repay him, and according to his ways he will make it befall him.	34:11	כִּי פֹעַל אָדָם יְשַׁלֶּם־לוֹ וּכְאֹרַח אִישׁ יַמְצִאֶנּוּ׃

In replying to Job's charge that God is unjust, Elihu emphasizes the principle of justice that God acts justly and pays a person according to what he has done. This same idea is argued by Bildad in chapter 8. Job also asks in 21:31, "who repays him (the wicked) for what he has done?" For Job, the wicked often go unpunished, and God does not perform his just acts. Here, "the work of a man" refers to all that a person does (34:11a). "He" refers to God, as in the preceding two lines. The term "repay" (שלם, in Piel here) means to make suitable return to for a benefit or service or "reward according to one's work."[185] The sense of "repay" here thus refers to receiving what a person deserves. The Hebrew in line b is literally, "and according to the path of a man he causes him to find it." The import of course of conduct here is similar to what Job has said in 17:9 and 21:31. Thus, God causes the person to find his path (i.e. repays him) according to his own conduct. This verse (and the rest of ch. 34) clearly represents Elihu's same traditional wisdom as the three friends. It is also of interest to note that in 34:31–37, Elihu turns directly to Job and concludes that Job's words about his sin are without knowledge. So, Job should be tried to the limit because his answers are wicked, sinful, and rebellious. Interestingly, Elihu is now no longer speaking of discipline, but of punishment. He is also speaking of Job's sinful reaction to God's dealing, not the sin that led to God's punishment in the first place. His words here are thus different from that of the friends.

In his last speech (36:1–37:24), Elihu continues to document God's צֶדֶק. He categorizes the just acts of God and explains to Job the purpose of suffering. What begins as a seeming repetition of the friends' view of God's

---

185. BDB, 1,022.

righteous way of dealing with both the wicked and righteous culminates rather clearly in Elihu's conclusion in 36:8–12:

> And if they are bound in chains
> and caught in the cords of affliction,
> then he declares to them their work and their transgressions,
> that they are behaving arrogantly.
> He opens their ears to instruction
> and commands that they return from iniquity.
> If they listen and serve him,
> they complete their days in prosperity,
> and their years in pleasantness.
> But if they do not listen, they perish by the sword
> and die without knowledge. (Job 36:8–12)

Although God aims to show mercy to those who repent from their sins, under this divine retribution death is the ultimate will of God. As applied to Job, this means Job should give up his rebellion against God (36:16–19) and his iniquity in order to respond to God's way of extending a hand of mercy and life to him.

Chapter 37 expands on the imagery of 36:26–33 and anticipates much of the imagery of Yahweh's first speech. Elihu describes to Job the greatness of God as seen in nature. God is not only above all, but governs all. All depend on God and his will, including the far fringes of the universe. The text of 37:23–24 make a fitting summary of Elihu's speech:

> The Almighty – we cannot find him; he is great in power;
> justice and abundant righteousness he will not violate;
> Therefore men fear him;
> he does not regard any who are wise in their own
> conceit.[186]

---

186. Elihu responds to Job's calling himself as גֶּבֶר many times. For instance, Elihu asks "What גֶּבֶר is like Job, who drinks unscoffing like water?" (34:7), "for he has said, 'It profits a גֶּבֶר nothing that he should take delight in God'" (34:9). "Men of understanding will say to me and the wise גֶּבֶר will hear me" (34:34). "Job speaks without knowledge; his words are without insight" (34:35). As the friends make fun of Job because Job calls himself a priori, a גֶּבֶר (15:7–10), and as such boasts of his wisdom, because wisdom, insight and might (גְּבוּרָה) are with God alone (12:13). For Elihu, Job is not what one would expect in

Elihu stresses the personality of God more than Job's three friends do. But still God has no freedom. God is bound to the retributive concept. As Elihu gradually shifts away from Job's suffering to God's awesome power, his last speeches (chs. 36–37) serves to prepare God's own speech. The concept of retribution is still traditional: God maintains retribution and Job is guilty. Death is viewed as the ultimate recompense from God.

Summary of the Friends' (and Elihu's) Ideas of Death and the Retribution Principle

The three friends primarily come in order to "console and comfort" Job. They (and Elihu) have good intentions and attempt to do their best in applying general principle to Job's specific case. However, they fail in their intention. Instead of helping Job, they add more trouble to Job. What they say will be finally declared invalid by God himself.

In responding to Job's emotional outburst (Job 3), the three friends, led by Eliphaz, recognize the necessity of Job's repentance. As their basic assumption is rooted in the retribution principle, which is a principle of causality, it provides a logical understanding that every action has an appropriate and corresponding result. As God is a just God, he is fairly and actively involved in all events. Thus, God's ways of dealing with human being can be knowable and predictable in terms of the retribution principle.

As we have previously noted, there is some truth in this traditional principle. However, the friends make the mistake of applying the principle backward, and thus regard all suffering as evidence of God's punishment on sin. They hardheadedly view that a man reaps what he sows in this life. Thus, they conclude that suffering, interpreted as punishment, is seen to point back to sinfulness. Job is suffering; therefore, he must be experiencing the judgmental face of God, which is God's punishment. This is a fundamental logical mistake of the three friends in their arguments (also in Elihu's, and Job's sometimes). They directly connect the blessed life, including a restored life of a repentant, with the state of being righteous (e.g. 4:6–7; 5:17–26; 8:6; 11:17–19). They associate suffering and ugly death to the state of being wickedness; namely, the foolish person will come to a tragic end (e.g. 4:8–11,

---

גֵּבַ, Elihu then concludes rightly (and ironically) that the right attitude is the fear of God. God does not regard everyone who is wise in his own conceit (37:24; cf. 42:7).

19–21; 5:2–5; 8:11–13; 11:20; 15:17–35). Specifically, they consider the life of the righteous man in this world, the retribution principle world, as strikingly positive: a righteous man will be only blessed, having a secure family (5:23–24), full of descendants (5:25), and live a long life and die as an old man (5:26). This blessed life is from God and runs to its fulfillment in a peaceful death. Thus, death can find a positive acceptance, in which it ends life that has been fulfilled. Even those righteous whom God has reproved may find this a peaceful and accepted death if they repent or have a right relationship with God again. There is no room for premature, miserable, unfair, or bad death in this view of shalomic life. Only good and full-of-day death will be counted as a peaceful and accepted death.

Death itself (not an unfair or suffering death) can be part of a shalomic life (ch. 1; cf. 5:26; 29:2–5, 18). The point of contention between Job and the friends is that Job is dying a miserable death which would come only to the one rejected by God (i.e. in terms of divine retribution) (4:8–11; 15:22, 30). In one sense, the problem is not death itself as much as the way Job is dying. So when the friends turn to the undeniable reality of Job's dreadful suffering and death, they can only conclude that Job is suffering as divine recompense for his sins. He must have sinned outrageously, because God does not contradict his character by acting capriciously. Therefore, Job's heated denial (cf. 15:2–6) only compounds the sin and hastens the judgment (cf. 15:26–30).

The friends try their best to understand Job's case and to vindicate God's justice at the same time. Their logical explanation reduces God's justice to a moral equation.[187] The judgmental face of Yahweh reflects the negative side of the equation: If a man sins, suffering must be the punishment. In addition, the suggestion of the friends for Job to repent his sin(s) reduces the gracious face of Yahweh, who will show mercy to the repentant, as merely the positive side of this equation. Their one-sided perception of God and his ways binds the freedom of God. Consequently, their applications to Job's specific case lead to the wrong conclusion about both the cause of and

---

187. In other words, their logical explanation makes both faces of Yahweh (judgment/mercy) a function of divine justice. It makes God's goodness part of this moral equation. In effect, their logical explanation does not leave any room for the merciful face of God. It makes God's goodness a function of divine justice: Job deserves this divine justice not because God is gracious but because Job is righteous; thus, Job earns them.

the solution to Job's problem. "Their exhortations for Job to repentance become a temptation by encouraging Job to seek God for reward, not for God himself."[188] The expectation of what the friends say is that all blessings and all sufferings are functions of God's justice, and that the ways of divine justice are predictable by man. Job's friends want to reduce man's relationship with God, and especially God's grace, to a mere moral calculus, which Exodus 33:19 explicitly rules out. This leads to Job's crisis of faith as he faces suffering and imminent death, a crisis that is eventually only resolved by God's own intervention. For Job, the counsel of the friends is wrong. Job cannot accept their counsel, for he knows that he is righteous. Thus, there is no resolution in the dialogues with the friends. Job finally cease to converse with them and turns to lament to God in chapter 29–31, hoping that God will intervene and provide him an answer, the right answer to his specific case.

For Elihu, his speeches aim to teach Job about God's disciplinary use of suffering, and God's just and wise lordship. However, his approach to Job's problem is a bit different from that of the three friends. He tries to direct attention to the purpose of suffering, rather than to try to find its origin, as the friends do. He emphasizes on God's grace by graciously sending a mediating angel to proclaim that a ransom has been found (33:23–28). If the person will pray and accept God's deliverance, God will deliver his life from death. Elihu, like the three friends, does not accept Job's claim to be righteous. He views suffering and dreadful death as explainable result of the sinful acts of a man. The only resolution to be saved is repentance and returning to have a right relationship with God. For Job's specific case, Elihu adds that Job should repent not only for his iniquity but also for his rebellious reaction to God. In this way, Job can receive God's way of giving mercy and life to him. Although God's ultimate will is to grant life, if a sinner rejects him and refuses to repent from his sins, death will become the ultimate recompense from God. He also argues that God governs the world in justice and reveals himself in an awesome way in order to direct people to worship him (36:22–37:13). As Elihu counters Job's complaint by modifying the traditional principle about suffering and by defending

---

188. John E. Hartley, "The Genres and Message of the Book of Job," in *Sitting with Job: Selected Studies on the Book of Job*, ed. Roy B. Zuck (Grand Rapids: Baker, 1992), 65–78.

the idea that God strictly governs the world in justice, Elihu serves as Job's answerer and Yahweh's forerunner, the so-called "prophet," who prepares Job to hear God's speeches.

Summary of Job's Views of Death and the Retribution Principle

In the earlier part of the book, death is a mystery. Job does not question God, but accepts whatever comes from God even his loss and the untimely death of his beloved ones submissively with faith (1:21). When his wife starts to ask a question that reflects a relational problem with God, Job also starts to question God in his mind (2:10). As Job has started to ask "why?" in his opening lament (Job 3), the friends, with good intentions, give him the definite and only answer to the "why" question: Job must have sinned. They further provide a pastoral suggestion that Job must repent in order to flourish again. The position of the friends implies that the ways of God can be comprehended by human reason, as reflected in the retribution principle, and Job accepts their presuppositions. The friends push Job into the direction of expecting to encounter God whose justice is mechanical: if you are good, you are rewarded; if you are bad, you will be punished. This perspective on God is one-sided and predictable. God is then predominantly just. A man can only encounter this face of God primarily in terms of God's wrath. This is what Job is struggling with. This is the nature of his crisis that he is not sinful, and yet he is still encountering the wrathful face of God. What Job is expecting to be predictable, it is not. Job is push into the wilderness of doubt. He does not understand his undeserved suffering. The answer from his friends adds more pain to him. At the same time, Job could not find for himself a satisfied answer. What his friends have said and explained to him, however much he rejects them, becomes at times scarcely distinguishable from his own ponderings. He is experiencing his spiritual chaos.

In the dialogues with the friends, the portrayal of the life of a righteous man from the mouth of the friends is so beautiful and very positive. But it seems for Job that life is not a gift from God to cherish and enjoy, rather it is a burden to suffer the consequences (e.g. 7:1–3). The perspective on life that Eliphaz has described (5:9–27) leads Job to wish for death. Job is a man of faith, he does not end his own life, but he does wish for death. If justice is all there is, and justice becomes perverted, then there is nothing to hope for.

Thus, the reader sees that Job makes many death wishes: 3:10–16, 21–22; 6:8–9; 7:8–10, 15, 20–21; 10:18–19; 14:13. Job wishes for death because there is no graciousness of God to hope for or to trust in, as in Eliphaz's words. There is only divine justice. And Job knows that it goes wrong, so there is nothing to hope for. Job's wishes for death are part of an argument in the confrontation with God. From this perspective, the question that underlines the death question is God question. Job's reaction to the implication of death in divine retribution, thus, vacillates between yearning for life and wishes for death.

In his initial reaction to the onslaught of suffering (1:21), when Job does not question God, he reflects a sense that death is a normal natural event, in the hand of God ("Naked I came from my mother's womb, and naked shall I return"). Death is viewed as submission to God's will, "the Lord gave, and the Lord has taken away." In addition, what Job says of life in more generic terms in 12:10 ("In his hand is the life of every living thing and the breath of all mankind"), Elihu affirms in 34:14–15 in terms of death that "If he [God] should set his heart to it and gather to himself his spirit and his breath, all flesh would perish together, and man would return to dust." Job later on also reflects the reality and normality of death in 30:23: "For I know that you will bring me to death and to the house appointed for all living." Job recognizes the reality of death. It is part of the human condition under the design and lordship of God. Thus, death is in the hand of God and can be accepted as resignation. Significantly, this submissive view of death is accepted in the context of faith where there is no question for the connection between death and the justice of God.

Death may be understood as extinction. However, some of Job's death wishes do not seem to anticipate the notion of extinction. It is envisioned instead as an escape from a suffering life to peaceful rest (Job 3). Furthermore, death at birth is better than to be born to a suffering life. Death is desired as hidden treasures that bring gladness and rejoice to the one who finds it (3:21–22). Job's use of the concept of Sheol in chapter 3 also implies that death is seemingly another form of existence at postmortem, where all are equal and at peace (3:17–19). It is also presumably placed Job with the wicked among others. Thus, death here seems to hold neither threat nor fear for Job (cf. Job 21). As Job alludes to Sheol as a place where a slave is free from his master (3:19; cf. 1:8 and 2:3), he is implying that Sheol is a place of freedom and escape from a just God. Sheol, thus, provides for Job an advantage of separating from God. The idea of death as separation from God can be seen also in Job's lament in chapters 7 and 10: "Leave me alone" (7:16, 19; 10:20). When no one listens to his claim that he is innocent and God keeps silence, Job is in despair and wants to leave this world with the hope that in the realm of death he will be separated from God.

The realm of death seems to be a place where God cannot reach him. If he slips off into the void of death, then God will be the loser for it is seemingly beyond God's retrieval: "you will look for me but I will be no more" (7:8, 21). The sentiment of "I will be no more" reflects also the idea of death as ultimate end of human's life, including Job's empty life. When Job loses all hope for life as he approaching terrified death, the ominous aspect of death fills him with terror, hardly the aspect of escape and peaceful rest that he envisions in chapter 3: "Man wastes away like a rotten thing, like a garment that is moth-eaten" (13:28). Job, thus, at some point views death as an unjust punishment that comes from God. This same place is also recognized as a place of deep darkness and no return (10:21–22; cf. 16:22).

As Job places the responsibility for his suffering on God, he makes an obvious death wish in chapter 6, asking to be "cut off" by God (6:8–9). To terminate his life, the act must be done by God. Job has no idea of committing a suicide. God is the one who is "crushing" Job, so he is willing to die at the hand of God. However, Job is not merely letting go, or viewing death simply as surcease, he wishes too that at least he could have some comfort that he did not die due to recompense for gross sin (6:10; cf. 27:6). Even though he could not find justice of God, he wishes that God will mercifully grant him not only death, but a swift death. The concept of death here thus is outside the realm of the retribution principle. Job wishes for a swift death here is not a punishment, but again a surcease from his suffering life. Job recognizes that death is at the hand of God. Yet, at other times, Job fears that God will simply terminate his life as the final ruthless repression of Job: "For he crushes me with a tempest and multiplies my wounds without cause" (9:17). Job expresses that "he [God] destroys both the blameless and the wicked. When disaster brings sudden death, he mocks at the calamity of the innocent" (9:22–23). God just acts capriciously: "If it is not he, who then is it?" (9:24b). God is the one who "breaks me [Job] down on every side, and I am gone, and my [Job's] hope he pulled up like a tree" (19:10). As Job is subject to such ruthless, destructive power, he has no hope for life, no hope in death, and no hope for vindication his case in this life. Though sometimes Job longs for death as an escape from his suffering life, at another time he views death as an unjust punishment that comes from God. Death from this perspective, thus, is not only Job's final pain, but also his crowning insult. This is death as an undeserved punishment from God. This is part of a problem of death. Sometimes it is seen from one perspective; sometime it is seen from another. Death seen as an unfair punishment makes Job angry or hurt, but death viewed as an escape from God's justice is something that Job occasionally longs for in despair because he knows that he has no any hope.

However, another fascinating perspective on death is yearning for life precisely in the face of what seems an inevitable and unfair death. While mourning the irreversibility of death, Job expresses a hope that God could hide him in Sheol temporarily until God's wrath has passed (14:13). Job is so confused and thinks that his suffering and imminent death is an indicator that God is punishing him. So, he looks for a place where he could hide from God's wrath. Moreover, he desires further that God would call for him, he would answer (14:15), and their relationship could resume normal again. Thus, for Job here death is not a biggest problem. Rather it is the relationship with God which is now not right. The more Job struggles, the more he wants to know the answer from God. Job wants to have a friend who can understand him, and side with him in arguing his case with God. His friends fail from performing their function. But Job finds no one and has no one. He is being pounded and pushed almost beyond endurance.

The answer the friends give to him is not right, and Job also cannot find the answer. Job must turn to God, the only source of his problem, and the only answer that can fulfill his quest. On the one hand, when Job thinks in terms of vindication, he feels stronger and wants to plead his case even by himself (i.e. 9:32; 13:3, 15, 20; 19; 23). Thus, Job has hope for life. But the certainty and immediacy of his death is an obstacle for him. He may not make it in this life time. Thus, death is a problem here. However, this does not mean that death is an enemy. Nowhere else in the book does Job see death as an enemy. Instead it is God who appears to Job to be his enemy because of his apparent injustice. Death cannot be a resolution for his problem. If he dies, he cannot vindicate his case. On the other hands, when Job thinks in terms of relational with God, he is despair and struggling at the same time. What happens to him is not right and cannot be explained according to divine justice in the retribution principle. God seems to be arbitrary, capricious, even diabolical. Job can only lament and wish for death because this suffering life is so painful physically, emotionally, and spiritually. It seems to him that God does not care. Though Job wishes several times for death, he never commits a suicide. During his painful trial, Job still holds fast his faith. Even though he (and the friends) cannot explain his problem, Job never leaves God. He still clings to God by approaching God with lament language. His death wishes, thus, are part of his struggling with the relationship with God, and part of his attempt to find resolution from God.

Job's various reactions or various statements about death seems to conflict with one another because sometimes he is thinking of death as a supreme example of divine justice that becomes corrupt as an unfair punishment. At other times, Job is thinking of death as an escape from this unfair punishment because God's justice is gone awry. Job has no hope and therefore in his despair death is seen as an escape from the fact that his relationship with God does not make any sense because God's justice appears to be corrupt. However, at the end of Job's story we see death as a natural shalomic end of his shalomic life. This view of death re-emerges as a result of the speeches of God and Job's response to them.

CHAPTER 4

Views of Death and the Retribution Principle in the Two Speeches of YHWH and in the Epilogue

During the discourses with the friends (including with Elihu), Eliphaz would have Job believe that his suffering and imminent death are not only insignificant (i.e. Job will be restored if he repents), but also constitute discipline from *Shadday* (5:17). Therefore, Job should accept them. Bildad would also have Job believe that his words of grief and harsh anguish will not be permitted (cf. 8:2). In times of acute suffering, Job, a man of faith, expressed his faith through lament. He has a conviction that God will hear and respond. He has cursed his life and dared to question the justice of God. For the friends, Job's words of complaint are similar to blasphemy; for Job, it is a language of hope, protesting to what it seems to be God's hostile acts. After the disputations with the friends, Job found no comfort and no answer. The friends also had no new ideas to dispute with Job. Their dialogues have been broken down.[1] Job has to turn to appeal to God. Job continues his laments in 29–31, demanding to meet God. As God has inflicted such acute suffering, Job vacillates between life and death. Sometimes he longs for death and seeks escape in Sheol. But

---

1. In the third cycle of the speeches with the friends, Bildad's last speech is disproportionately short (25:2–6). Zophar's third speech also appears to be missing from the dialogues. Thus, a variety of proposals for restoring order to these texts by rearranging them to what might have been their original sequence have been offered. For discussion of these various proposals, see, for example, Driver and Gray, *Critical and Exegetical Commentary*, 215–232; Gordis, *Book of Job*, 276–296; Dhorme, *Commentary on the Book of Job*, 368–398; Pope, *Job*, 180–196; Habel, *Book of Job*, 364–387; Newsom, *The Book of Job*, NIB, 516–526. However, this research agrees with Janzen (*Job*, 171–186) who interprets the text as it stands. For a similar idea, see: Anderson, *Job*, 214–222; Good, *In Turns of Tempest*, 281–290; etc.

other times, he yearns for life. The finality of death provides Job strength and offers him the strong desire to meet with God face to face.

The previous chapters of this book are perspectives of death viewed from the human side. However, when death is viewed from the perspective of God, it is entirely different. Significantly, there is the use of various divine names in the book of Job.[2] When the friends and Job are conversing (including Elihu), God is referred to as *Shadday*, *El*, *Eloah*, or *Elohim*. However, when God appears at the end of the book, it is Yahweh.[3] These terms are used to categorize God in a certain way and signal an important transition in the book.[4] Moreover, Job's rhetorical challenge in 31:35–37, addressing directly to God, also sets up the divine speeches.[5] The dynamics of the story require God to intervene.

Yahweh eventually does appear and reveal his עֵצָה. His appearance "out of the whirlwind" (הַסְּעָרָה) here is outstanding.[6] The storm is used as the divine venue for appearance. This remarkable setting of the divine-human encounter is not only a highly dramatic action of theophany (e.g. 2 Kgs 2:11; cf. Exod 19:16; Pss 18:8–14; 104:3; Hab 3:14; 1 Kgs 19:11–13), but the storm itself also represents a mode of ambiguity, free, unsettling, and mysterious (cf. Ezek 1:4). O'Connor comments that "the storm evokes Job's

---

2. The word *Elohim* occurs fourteen times; *Eloah* forty-one times; *Shadday* thirty-one times; *El* fifty-five times; *Adonai* appears only once in Job 28:28; and YHWH thirty-two times.

3. The name "Yahweh" appears in the prologue and the epilogue. In the poetic section, there is one place in the dialogue, Job 12:9, where "Yahweh" occurs. It is possible that the occurrence of "Yahweh" in 12:9 may be either a scribal error or the verse contains the quotation of a popular proverb.

4. Literary, the appearance of the name "Yahweh" here reaffirms the voice of the narrator as the one who frames the entire book. It recalls the last words of Yahweh, who has given permission to the satan that: "Behold, he is in your hand; only spare his life" (2:6).

5. From this idea some commentators (e.g. Newsom, *The Book of Job: A Contest*, 241) see that Job 29–31 and YHWH speeches are originally juxtaposed, with the result that the Elihu speeches are later addition.

6. The Hebrew term הַסְּעָרָה is a meteorological term used as a motif in theophanic portrayals. See H. J. Fabry, "סָעַר," *TDOT* 10:291–296. Note that although the storm often appears in the context of God's judgment, it also is present in theophanies of God in grace (e.g. 2 Kgs 2:1, 11; Ezek 1:4, Zech 9:14; and here Job 38:1; 40:6). Thus, while the term שְׂעָרָה used in 9:17 is in the context of God's wrath, הַסְּעָרָה in 38:1 and 40:6 are not portraying "Yahweh's onslaught in the terminology of judgment theophanies," as noted by Fabry (*TDOT* 10:295). For further discussion, see T. Hiebert, "Theophany in the Old Testament," in *ABD* 6:505–511.

own stormy life, whipped about within and without by chaotic forces."[7] The storm, thus, represents theological conflict and the resolution of the book. Like other texts typical to the wisdom genre, the form of the two speeches of Yahweh functions as giving an instruction. They use the non-human world to provide knowledge about the human world. Thus they are not destructive or judgmental modes of communication which are used to belittle or put down Job.[8] Rather they are revelatory mode used in order that Job will be moved to discover God and his ways embodied within the world itself. And yet this is special revelation and not general revelation. The nature of the world, its order, and its chaotic elements and complexity are present to Job generally. However, some insights and implications to his dreadful suffering and death are put together and made available for Job.

The Two Speeches of YHWH and Job's Responses

The outline of the divine speeches is quite clear. Each of the two speeches (38:1–39:30; 40:1–41:34[26]) begins with an identical narrative introduction (38:1; 40:6). Challenges to Job follow (38:2–3; 40:7–14), each of which contains the identical demand for Job to gird up his loins and to answer God's questions (38:3; 40:7). These challenges articulate important themes that the body of the speeches are designed to address. In the first speech, the theme is divine עֵצָה ("counsel" or "design" or "plan," 38:2); in the second it is מִשְׁפָּט (40:8), a word that may have legal connotations ("judgment," "justice," "right") or administrative ones ("governance" or "sovereignty").[9] The body of the speech follows (38:4–39:30; 40:15–41:26). Each speech divides into

---

7. Also, O'Connor, "Wild, Raging Creativity," 173, notes in her article that God appears out of the storm implying that he is "wild, beautiful, free, and deeply unsettling."

8. James L. Crenshaw, for example, is one of those scholars who view the God speeches as negative. See Crenshaw, "When Form and Content Clash: The Theology of Job 38:1–40:5," in *Creation in the Biblical Traditions*, eds. Richard J. Clifford and John J. Collins (Washington, DC: Catholic Biblical Association of America, 1992), 70–84. In his words, 84, Crenshaw states: "If anything, the portrayal of deity in the speeches increases the distance between human beings and their maker. This distancing takes place, paradoxically, despite a literary form that emphasizes incredible closeness. Here form and content clash, with the latter gaining supremacy. Must 'the greater glory of God' always require a belittling of human beings?"

9. Scholnick, "The Meaning of *Mišpāt*," 521–529. The present author agrees with Scholnick that in the context of the second divine speech the meaning "governance" or "sovereignty" is appropriate for rendering the word *mišpāt*.

two main parts, according to its content. In the first speech, God talks first about cosmological and meteorological phenomena (38:4–38), then about five pairs of animals (38:39–39:30). The second speech concerns a single pair of animals: Behemoth (40:15–24) and Leviathan (40:25–41:26). After each speech Job responds. Following the first speech, God specifically asks for a response (40:1–2), and Job replies by declining to speak (40:3–5). Following the second speech, Job replies without a specific divine request (42:1–6).

The First Speech of YHWH (38:1–39:30)

In the first speech of Yahweh (38:1–39:30), after the narrative introduction (38:1) the unified theme is announced in verse 2: the design or lordship of God (עֵצָה).[10] Some distinctive features of this speech are the following. First is the constant usage of rhetorical questions: "Who?" "Where?" "How?" "What . . . can you . . . have you . . . do you know . . . ?" The answer to these questions is consistently "No, not you [Job], but I [Yahweh]." Second, following God's acceptance to Job's challenge of confrontation (38:3; cf. 13:22; also 10:2; 23:5; 31:35),[11] the content of the speech concerns with cosmology and meteorology. They are: the structure of the earth (38:4–7); the control of the sea (38:8–11); the functions of the morning and dawn (38:12–15); the place of the spring of the sea and death (38:16–18); the dwelling places of light and darkness (38:19–21); the storehouses of snow, hail, lightning, and wind (38:22–14); the course of rain for the desert (38:25–27); the origin of rain, dew, ice, and frost (38:28–30); the chains of constellations (38:31–33); the control of clouds and rain (38:34–48). After the tour of

---

10. The Hebrew term עֵצָה I can be rendered as "advice," "counsel," "plan," or God's "design." L. Koehler and W. Baumgartner suggest that the term means the "decision" of Yahweh (i.e. "his planning concerning his work of creation") ("עֵצָה" *HALOT* 2:866–867). In the context of the book as a whole, particularly of the speeches of YHWH, the present author prefers to translate this term as "lordship." As already mentioned, the prologue of the book sets the conflict between two truths: the false principle of the retribution principle and the truly divine truth. Thus, rendering the term עֵצָה as "design," or "decision," or to be more specific "lordship," helps the reader to capture the movement of the story that Job's case is under the arbitrary lordship of God disclosed since in the prologue. The two speeches of YHWH serve to enunciate more not only on a marvelous planning of God but also on his absolute and arbitrary lordship.

11. The question in 38:3, "Dress for action like a man (גֶּבֶר); I will question you, and you make it known to me," echoes the divine concern disclosed in the prologue. The intent of this question lies on the same objects as that in the prologue; namely, the concern to find out who Job is in relation to God. See Janzen, *Job*, 232.

cosmology and meteorology come the five pairs of animals: (1) the lions and ravens (38:39–41); (2) the mountain goats and deer (39:1–4); (3) the wild ass and wild ox (39:5–12); (4) the ostrich and the war horse (39:13–25); and (5) the hawk and the vulture (39:26–30).

Chapter 38: The Cosmos. Chapter 38 concerns the cosmos and its non-human inhabitants. God does bring elements of creation forward as witness against Job, but no accusations nor guilty verdict follow.[12] Instead, the morning stars sings together and the heavenly beings shout for joy (38:7). The earth changes like clay under sealing wax (38:24) and the dawn takes its post (38:12). Light disperses, wind scatters (38:24), and the water skins of the heavens tilt to water the earth (38:37). These aspects of creation are exquisitely beautiful, and they exist independently of Job.[13] The rhetorical questions explicitly point to Job's (and the human's) incapacity in the face of God's mighty and marvelous capacity. They are implicit attack on assumed human ability to comprehend the ways of God that is the basis of the retribution principle. For example:

> Where were you when I laid the foundation of the earth? (38:4)
>
> Who determined its measurements . . . and laid its cornerstone? (38:5–6)
>
> Who shut in the sea with doors? (38:8)
>
> Have you commanded the morning since your days began? (38:12)
>
> Have you entered into the springs of the sea? (38:16)
>
> Have the gates of death been revealed to you
> or have you seen the gate of deep darkness? (38:17)
>
> Have you comprehended the expanse of the earth (38:18)
>
> Where is the way to the dwelling of light? (38:19)
>
> Who has cleft a channel for the torrents of rain? (38:25)
>
> Can you bind the chains of the Pleiades? (38:31)

---

12. O'Connor, "Wild, Raging Creation," 173.
13. O'Connor, 173.

To all these questions, as well as to other questions in this speech, Job's answer is definitely "no."[14] That is, Job was not there, does not know, cannot comprehend, cannot bind or loose the constellations, was not the one to do such things, etc. Job has no access. However, these questions are not for intimidating Job. The contents of the speech point to the pride of God over the potent beauty of creation, of God, and of Job himself. The imagery of the cosmos in this speech directs Job to the edges of creation: "The place where the very bases of the earth are sunk, the boundary between the sea and land, the place of dawn at the edge of the earth, the springs of the sea, the gates of the underworld, the paths that terminate at the houses of light and darkness at the edge of cosmos."[15] These images distinguish the boundaries between "formlessness and structure, order and disorder, life and death, the darkness that harbors violence and the light that dispels it."[16] They highlight not only Yahweh's design for the cosmos as a meticulously controlled network of structures and processes, but also the limitation of human being to understand God's treatment of this world and cosmos. As Newsom points out "the very oppositions that simultaneously make life possible and threaten it are thus manifested even as they are declared to be unknowable and uncontrollable by human understanding and will."[17] Thus, the objective of these rhetorical questions is not to put down Job for failed understanding. Rather, it is to summon forth new affirmation that invites Job (and the reader) "to adopt a new position on, and indeed a new mode of participation in, the realities of creatureliness and creativity, light and darkness."[18] In fact, the whole section of the first speech of Yahweh is a kind of an implicit attack. It is not to put down Job of his misunderstanding, but to demonstrate to Job the limit of human

---

14. In his dissertation, Rowold, "Theology of Creation," points out that the typical challenge question consists of a pronominal subject (e.g. I, you, who), a verb delineating Yahweh's lordship in action (e.g. create, measure, command), and an object describing the extent of that lordship (e.g. earth, sea, stars). Thus, the answer to these questions are not "Who knows?" or "I did not," but "You [Yahweh] alone did."

15. Newsom, *The Book of Job: A Contest*, 242.

16. Newsom, 242.

17. Newsom, 242.

18. Janzen, *Job*, 226. Also Balentine, *Job*, 633–634. Job has accused God of injustice and improperly punishing him, and has despaired about this because he has accepted the presupposition that human reason can understand the way of God. Here God is undermining that presupposition by these questions, and therefore forcing Job to reassess his understanding of his relationship with God, which cannot be based on what human reason said.

reason. In other words, it is an attack on the presupposition of the retribution principle; namely, that human reason can understand the ways of God and the justice of God. The questions that God asked here force Job to recognize the limitation of human reason, and the inability of human reason to judge the way of God and the justice of God. It undermines the presupposition of the retribution principle and forces Job to see that having adopted it as the friends' operating principle here, Job has adopted the presupposition about what human reason can know that God has now shown to be false.

Though Job gropes with the crisis of faith in his heart and the accusations of his friends, in his enunciation of God's majesty in chapter 26 he recognizes that "*Sheol* is naked before God, and *Abaddon* has no covering" (26:6). He understands that while death is at "the outskirts" of God's ways (26:14), it is within the lordship of Yahweh.[19] Likewise, as Yahweh takes Job on a breath-taking tour of his universe, not only challenging Job's limited and self-rooted stance before God but also illustrating the wonders and expanse of his עֵצָה, he asks Job:

Have you entered into the springs of the sea,[20] or walked in the recesses of the deep?[21]	38:16	הֲבָאתָ עַד־נִבְכֵי־יָם וּבְחֵקֶר תְּהוֹם הִתְהַלָּכְתָּ׃
Have the gates of death been revealed to you, Or have you seen the gates of deep darkness?	38:17	הֲנִגְלוּ לְךָ שַׁעֲרֵי־מָוֶת וְשַׁעֲרֵי צַלְמָוֶת תִּרְאֶה׃
Have you comprehended the expanse of the earth? Declare, if you know all this.	38:18	הִתְבֹּנַנְתָּ עַד־רַחֲבֵי־אָרֶץ הַגֵּד אִם־יָדַעְתָּ כֻלָּהּ׃

---

19. See Janzen's interpretation, *Job*, 177–178, for the connection between 26:14 and 12:13 in which the four terms: "wisdom," "counsel," "power," and "understanding," in 12:13 are used in relation to God's "thunderous power" (26:14), pointing to "the voice of God speaking publicly in and through Job's suffering and other similar human calamities.

20. The springs of the sea refers to the underground sources of water thought to supply the oceans. The Hebrew word rendered as "spring, source" (נֵבֶךְ) appears only here, but another variant form of the word (בְּכִי) is found in 28:11 and is rendered as "streams." The term used here in 38:16 may be compared with "roots of the sea" in 36:30. The evidence is from a Ugaritic text describing the distant abode of the Canaanite deity El at the extremity of the subterranean waters that בְּכִי is a noun meaning "watery source" or "spring" (see Habel, *Book of Job*, 390, 522).

21. The Hebrew term "recess" (חֵקֶר) is used in 11:7 as "deep things" of God. The term has the sense of "something to be explored, researched, discovered, investigated," and, thus, it

Although Job has not died yet, he has portrayed the realm of death with imaginative vividness (e.g. 3:17–19; 10:21–22; 12:22; etc.). He has described his physical and spiritual suffering in such a way that he is experiencing the realm of death (e.g. 7:5; 16:12–15; 30:23, 27–30; etc.). He expresses his emotional closeness to Sheol by describing it in terms that evoke the image of a home, depicting death with the family terms like "bed," "father," "mother," "sister" (17:13–14). Yahweh, thus, now takes Job to the edge of the waters of the underworld and the region of death. The Hebrew term הִתְהַלָּכְתָּ ("have you walked")[22] in verse 16 is in the Hitpael as in 1:7, where the adversary answered Yahweh that he is from purposefully inspecting by "walking up and down" on earth. Yahweh's question here is ironically echoing Job's self-involving language he used for death and Sheol in the dialogues. As view from Job's language, it is true that the gates of death (v. 17) has been revealed (הֲנִגְלוּ) to him (i.e. he has been "purposefully inspecting" there with his imagination and feeling). The verbs "reveal" (גלה) and "see" (ראה; 38:17) suggest that Job not only knows how to uncover the hidden mystery of death but recognizes also that it is Yahweh who "reveals" (גלה; 12:22) the deep things of darkness and brings deep shadow into light (צַלְמָוֶת, 12:22; cf. 10:22; 16:16). The phrase "gates of death" (שַׁעֲרֵי מָוֶת; 38:17) marks the seemingly physical entrance to the world of the dead.[23] The parallel phrase is "gates of deep darkness" (שַׁעֲרֵי צַלְמָוֶת). In 3:5 the term "deep darkness" (צַלְמָוֶת) refers to the darkness of Sheol, emphasizing the idea that the land of the dead is thought of as a dark place (cf. 10:21–22). Job has consigned the day of his birth to the deep shadow, and at times spoken of death as his only escape (3:21; 7:15). However, here the realm of deep darkness is portrayed as if it is not outside but distinctly inside the world; namely it is inside the domain of the עֵצָה of Yahweh.[24] In 38:18 the term "expanse" (רֹחַב) denotes

---

22. Cf. Gen 13:17; Job 1:7; 2:2; Zech 1:10–11.

23. This phrase is found also in Pss 9:13; 107:18. A similar phrase "gates of Sheol" (שַׁעֲרֵי שְׁאוֹל) is found in Isaiah 38:10. However, the gates of death/Sheol in these three passages are used symbolically to portray the closeness of death to the speaker, rather than the physical realm of death as in Job 38:17 to find out what is hidden (as in Ps 95:4). The phrase "the recesses of the deep" (מֶחְקְרֵי תְהוֹם) connotes the unknowable mysteries of depths of the ocean.

24. Brown, *Theology of Creation*, 83.

the idea of width or more generally the dimensions.²⁵ The Hebrew term אֶרֶץ in verse 18 here should be translated "earth."²⁶ Although verse 16 may refer to the underworld as well as verse 17, verse 18 could possibly shift to the related theme of the "earth's expansive breadth."²⁷ The phrase "the expanse of the earth," thus, shifts the idea ironically from the land of the dead to the earth. Yahweh is asking Job if he comprehends how large the earth is. The shift gives a contrast of depth (i.e. of the underworld) and breadth (i.e. of the earth) in verses 16–18.²⁸ Again, the rhetorical question is not intended to have a reply, but to emphasize Job's ignorance of the size of the earth. The challenge to Job's lack of knowledge heightens "the distance between Job and both the extremities of earth and Yahweh's עֵצָה which stands behind them."²⁹ The tone of the text of chapter 38 provides a sense of sole lordship of Yahweh over the created world. This lordship covers all including the mysterious and forbidden realm (death included) of the world.

In sum, as Alter notes, God's speech in Job 38 constitutes "a brilliantly pointed reversal, in structure, image, and theme," of Job's opening lament (Job 3).³⁰ God's imagination of the world, thus, transcends the limitations of creaturely modes of perception. God's speech here affirms that creation is becoming filled to overflowing with life and vitality. Those life forces fulfill their appointed roles by aggressively challenging the boundaries God imposes on them. For instance, the chaotic sea, a traditional symbol of chaos with threatening nature, is under the attention of God. It is portrayed as a cosmic baby bursting from the womb, yet coddled and swaddled in clothes of clouds by its loving guarding Yahweh, becoming an infant bursting into

---

25. The term "expanse" also serves to conclude this section (38:4–18) on the extremities of the earth.

26. Some commentators interpret the term אֶרֶץ here as "underworld," with the reason that it is like various terms in the previous verses (i.e. sea, deep, in v. 16; death, deep darkness, in v. 17), indicating the underworld, the land of the dead. See this interpretation, for instance, in Dahood, *Psalms 1–50*, 111; Tromp, *Primitive*, 50; Andersen, *Job*, 276; Habel, *Book of Job*, 517, 541 (Habel translates the word as "earth," but understand it as "underworld"); Janzen, *Job*, 236. Hartley, *Book of Job*, 498.

27. Johnston, *Shades of Sheol*, 101. Also Dhorme, *Commentary on the Book of Job*, 584; Pope, *Job*, 289; Gordis, *Book of Job*, 436; Fohrer, *Das Buch Hiob*, 505.

28. Johnston, *Shades of Sheol*, 101. The same sentiment of contrast is like light and darkness in verse 19.

29. Rowold, "Theology of Creation," 84.

30. Alter, *Biblical Poetry*, 96–110.

life, nurtured and protected (38:8–11).[31] This vision of creation, as Alter comments, is "a virtual oxymoron, expressing a paradoxical feeling that God's creation involves a necessary holding in check of destructive forces and a sustaining of those same forces because they are also forces of life."[32] God is teaching Job that his purpose is not to eliminate forces of opposition but to preserve and direct them, "because they are vital elements in the architecture of life."[33] At the same time, not all are destructive forces. There are also examples of aspects of creation that is beyond human reason. In other words, God is also teaching Job the limitation of his understanding of God's ways.

Chapter 39: The Realm of Wild Animals. From the creation of the habitat, now Yahweh moves to its animal inhabitants: the world of wild animals (38:39–39:30). Yahweh's use of these animals gives new meaning to Job's words in 12:7–9. What Job has said to the friends now is turned on him: "But ask the beasts, and they will teach you; the birds of the heavens, and they will tell you; or the bushes of the earth, and they will teach you; and the fish of the sea will declare to you. Who among all these does not know that the hand of Yahweh has done this?" Like the chaotic sea which is restrained and protected, these wild and untamed animals are presented as chaotic forces that are part of the world but limited by divine power. The descriptions of these animals (five pairs of them) show that each of them is unbounded, fearless, and beautiful.

---

31. The image of "womb/tomb," or "life/death" in Job 3 is transformed positively in the first speech of Yahweh. Alter, *Biblical Poetry*, 99, gives a beautiful and graphical insight of these two chapters, saying, "Job's first speech (ch. 3) begins with birth and conception and circles back on the belly or womb where he would like to be enclosed, where he imagines the fate of the dead fetus as the happiest of human lots. Against those doors of the belly (3:10) that Job wanted shut on him forever, the Voice from the Whirlwind invokes a cosmic womb and cosmic doors to a very different purpose: "[He] hedged in the sea with doors/ when it gushed forth from the womb" (v. 8). The figuration of setting limits to the primal sea as closing doors on a gushing womb produces a high tension of meaning absent from Job's unequivocal death wish. The doors are closed and bolted (v. 10) so that the flood will not engulf the earth, but nevertheless the waves surge, the womb of all things pulsates, something is born." As Job perceives the womb as to be shut for death, Yahweh encourages that the womb is a place in bringing life to birth.

32. Alter, 100.

33. Balentine, "What Are Human Beings," 267.

The first pair is lions and ravens (38:39–41). The lions, who lie in ambush, hunt for their young; the ravens seek prey to feed its starvelings.[34] The specific imagery of this pericope points to Yahweh as protector and provider. No man would hunt prey for a lioness. Yet Yahweh listens, understands their cries, and supplies them food.

The second pair is the mountain goats and wild deer (39:1–4). They give birth, in home totally inaccessible to man and thus beyond observation of man. The imagery here is marvelous, illustrating the mystery of instinct by which mother gives birth and kid quickly learns self-preservation.[35] How easy is birth and growth under the עֵצָה of Yahweh.

The third pair is the wild ass and the wild ox presented in 39:5–12. The wild ass (39:5–8) roams far from civilization, free to search steppe, salt land, and mountain for greenery. The section emphasizes on the freedom of the wild ass. Notice that in Job's opening lament (Job 3), he wishes that only "there" (שָׁם) an afflicted person like him would be truly free (חָפְשִׁי; 3:19). That is, to be free means to be apart from God in which the realm of death could provide him the ultimate freedom.[36] While Job's freedom is in death, the wild ass's freedom is joyous and enervate in its wild life. Ironically, for the wild ass to be free is not to be apart from God, but from man (cf. 3:19).[37] The wild ox (39:9–12) is portrayed more on its untamable will and strength.[38] This enormous animal is self-reliance, dependent on no one, subject to no one, knowing no lord. However, even its massive strength, the wild ox is part of a larger עֵצָה of Yahweh.[39]

---

34. In 4:10–11, Eliphaz draws a general moral rule from the world of the lion, asserting his confidence that God will constantly destroy the wicked. His point is that in God's just world even the fiercest of beasts (i.e. lion) can be disabled, as powerful evildoers in the human world will get their deserved penalty. Here (38:39–41) in his just world, God evokes the image of the lion, along with other beasts of prey, as the strong that devour the weak, representing God's harsh truth in his providential governance of the world.

35. Andersen, *Job*, 280.

36. See this insight in Rowold, "Theology of Creation," 100–101.

37. Andersen, *Job*, 281, gives an insightful note that "there is no rebuke of man as a hard taskmaster, as if God is accusing Job of abusing the trust of Genesis 1:26ff. It is God who has set this beast free, forgoing the legitimate claims He might have on its service."

38. The wild ox is mentioned totally nine times in the Old Testament as the standard symbol of strength (Num 23:22; 24:8; Deut 33:17; Job 39:9, 10; Pss 22:22; 29:6; 92:11; Isa 34:7).

39. Rowold, "Theology of Creation," 102.

The forth pair is the ostrich and the war horse (39:13–25). The silly ostrich, possessing no wisdom and understanding, enjoys its laugh at the fastest horse with the outstanding rider. Yahweh's עֵצָה has space even for this senseless bird. In other words, among other animals some are created to be useful to men, but some are there just for God's entertainment (and ours).[40] The war horse fills with his uncanny lust for battle. He is portrayed as "the epitome of the vibrant, positive joy of life, which characterizes the עֵצָה of Yahweh."[41]

The fifth and the last pair of animals is the hawk and eagle (39:26–30). They soar high, build their nest, and sight their prey from afar for their young. The question to Job is whether the birds do this by Job's discernment or whether Job comprehends how they fly so gracefully and build their nests so high. Like lions, they are the beasts of prey. The imagery of their fierceness, as well as that of the lions, serves to frame the wildness of the whole catalogue of these wild animals' in these sections.

In summary, the imagery of this untamed world of animals provokes the real principle of the animal kingdom that the strong devour the weak in order to sustain their own lives and those of their young. It is an uncompromising, even harsh, truth that God specifically chooses to reveal to Job his providential lordship of the world. These wild animals look to Yahweh as their protector and provider. They live their lives in trust in Yahweh's עֵצָה. Even the weird and senseless bird, the ostrich, can live her live happily in God's lordship. God is pleased in creating a bird deficient in wisdom.[42] The relationship is carried on completely without reference to man. "None owe man anything; the ways of none are comprehended by him."[43] The עֵצָה of Yahweh provides not only the animal's protection and provision, "but also the mutual relationship of trust and care which binds the animals to Yahweh, who listens to and understands their cries."[44] The vision of a harmonious

---

40. Also Andersen, *Job*, 281.

41. Rowold, "Theology of Creation," 105.

42. Andersen, *Job*, 282, points to a connection between this senseless bird and Job that "the essential point is made in verse 17. If God is pleased to create a bird deficient in wisdom, so what? Is Job being reminded that some of his behavior might be equally lacking in *understanding* unless he receives it as God's gift? Cf. Psalm 49:12, 20."

43. Greenberg, "Job," 298.

44. Rowold, "Theology of Creation," 98.

order to which violence is intrinsic and where destruction is part of creation is meant to affront and affirm Job with the limits of his moral imagination. Job's moral imagination has been shaken by the retribution principle. And by forcing him to confront the limit of that imagination, God is forcing Job to acknowledge the limits of the human understanding of the ways of God. The implication for Job's situation is the recognition that the retribution principle (built, as it is, upon human reason) is not an adequate way of judging everything that God is doing. So, these examples demonstrate the limits of human knowledge, not only Job's personal knowledge but what is knowable by man and by human reason. Therefore, they point out the failure of the retribution principle. The retribution principle cannot factor in everything that God is doing. It cannot even comprehend everything that God has done in creation. Death is one of those aspects of creation under God's design. It is not an evil force, nor something that is threatening, but serves to sustain the splendor and vastness of life (e.g. the lions and ravens, 38:39–41; the hawk and eagle, 39:27–30). Through the world of the wild animals, Job is implicitly invited to accept not only God's lordship, which includes the realm and reality of death, but also his own limitation to comprehend God's ways.

The first speech of Yahweh (38–39) elaborately points to Job the sphere of creation, not the real court of justice as Job has asked for. It is, moreover, "a creation that barely reflects the presence of man,"[45] a creation where human concepts of justice have no place. However, as Job is the addressee to whom Yahweh offers the descriptions of creativity and creatureliness, he is "not so insignificant a creature as to be overlooked in the general cosmic picture. Rather, humankind is that part of creation whom God addresses with questions concerning the rest of creation."[46] Janzen rightly points out that the omission of humankind, together with the questions "Who are you?," "Where were you?," and "Can you?" serve to open Job's question to

---

45. Alter, *Biblical Poetry*, 104. Also, Janzen, *Job*, 229.

46. Janzen, *Job*, 229. Also, in his "The Yahweh Speeches and Job's Responses," *Review and Expositor* 68 (1971): 497–509, Samuel Terrien notices that "the architect of the cosmos, occupied as he [God] is with bringing about smoothly the sequences of spatial and temporal phenomena, offers to Job alone, a simple mortal and indeed an individual who has lost all historical significance, the wonders of a personal encounter."

a possibility for transformed self-understanding.[47] The whole presentation of cosmological and especially zoological poem aims to inform Job that it is not God's justice, but God's tender mercies are over all his creatures. God's rhetorical questions invite Job to acknowledge his limited wisdom. The intent of God's questions to Job is not to answer the problem of why the innocent suffer generally, nor even why Job has suffered. Instead, they portray both a constant of life, renewing and nurturing life, and a constant clash of vigorous conflict. As Job has adopted the view of divine justice based upon the retribution principle that the friends have imposed on him; God's questions lead Job to see the limits of his own moral imagination, a moral imagination far more honest but only somewhat less conventional than that of the friends.[48] While the friends (and Job sometimes) see life of the one who fears God as perfect without any harm, the first speech of Yahweh presents life in this created world with a possibility of violence and destruction. The friends view and interpret all incidents that happen to man rigidly from the perspective of God's justice according to the retribution principle. In this speech God shows Job the reality in which life and chaos, even unfair death (i.e. of the prey) are inseparable. However, this reality is purposefully gracious, for it aims ultimately to sustain life. Job may not know how to apply this purposeful administration in the universe to his case. At least, he may not see how his case is aimed to give or sustain life. However, Job is learning from the first divine speech that Yahweh is the Lord of the universe and the Sovereign. The following is how Job actually responds to this divine speech.

Job's First Response (40:4–5)

God's first words to Job in 38:2–3 has stated his intention to ask Job and receive an answer: "Who is this that darkens counsel by words without knowledge? Dress for action like a man; I will question you, and you make it known to me." He asks Job מִי זֶה ("Who is this?" 38:2) and calls him גֶּבֶר ("a strong man," 38:3; cf. 3:3; 40:7). During the discourses, Job has uttered as if he is a prince (31:37; cf. he speaks of kings and princes in 3:14; 12:18; 29:9–10), and likened his life before his calamity as to that of a king (29:25).

---

47. Janzen, *Job*, 230.
48. Alter, *Biblical Poetry*, 106.

Thus, Job has spoken presumably as if he is a kingly rival god, who not only dares to meet God face to face but also passes judgment on God for not fulfilling his duties as a just ruler of the world (i.e. divine retribution according to man's behavior). For the term גֶּבֶר, as noted previously, designates not an ordinary man, like אָדָם, אֱנוֹשׁ, or even אִישׁ, but the sexually exceptional man, the athlete, the battle brave, and the royal chief.[49] Thus, it is an ironic picture to see Job, sitting on the ash heap and still in revolt, encountering the great God, who appears in a grandiose manner out of the whirlwind. And now after all the questions of the first speech, Yahweh demands that answer, by challenging Job in 40:1–2:[50]

> And YHWH said to Job,
>
> "Shall a faultfinder contend with the Almighty?
> He who argues with God, let him answer it."

During the disputations with the friends, Job repeatedly requests a trial with God, so that he might directly present his case (רִיב) as an innocent sufferer, and eventually hear from God himself the charges which might be laid against him and thus be able to refute them (9:3, 14–20, 28–35; 13:22, 23; 23:3–17; 31:35–37). Job has reproached God publicly (e.g. 6:4; 9:17; 12:9; 13:21; 16:7–13; 19:6–12, 21; 23:15–16; 30:19, 21–22); God has responded and called him as the הָרֹב ("the faultfinder"), who has dared to engage the *Shadday* in a court. God has also addressed Job as the מוֹכִיחַ ("he who argues [with God]," 40:2; cf. 9:33). Even though Job's language

---

49. The term גֶּבֶר is akin to the גִּבּוֹר, the "hero" of legend. See Terrien, "The Yahweh Speeches," 501; H. Kosmala, "The Term גֶּבֶר in the Old Testament and in the Scroll," *SVT* 17 (1969), 159–169. It is noteworthy that the reference to Job as a "warrior" or a "mighty man" may be viewed positively as a "summons to make the right preparation for a valiant encounter that God intends and desires" (see Balentine, "What Are Human Beings," 266; also Janzen, *Job*, 232–233). It is true that Job uses a language of self-deification and alludes to himself the social responsibility, and the kingly leadership throughout the poetic discourses. Yet the speeches of Yahweh intend not to rebuke but to confront and confirm Job, by calling Job as a mighty man, whom God is proud.

50. Janzen, *Job*, 241–242, observes that God's challenging Job in 40:2 is similar to the divine response to Jeremiah (Jer 12:5). For the case of the prophet Jeremiah, Janzen notes that "the point of this divine response [Jer 12:5] is not to put the prophet down with an impossible question, but to express surprise over the quickness with which the prophet succumbs to discouragement and disillusionment and to challenge the prophet to a deeper loyalty and vocational endurance." In the case of Job, thus, God's challenge is for Job to ponder deeper on his vocation.

during the discourse seems to be presumptuous, God does not "crush" Job. God's unanswerable questions are to remind Job the inequalities between him and God. God is God, and Job is a creature. Thus, in the review of creation in 38–39 and the tone of God's challenging Job here, they are to invite him to respond. That is, God calls Job to go beyond the limit of his own understanding.[51] Job, thus, now must answer God.[52] However, he says,

> Behold, I am of small account; what shall I answer you?
> I lay my hand on my mouth.
> I have spoken once, and I will not answer;
> twice, but I will proceed no further. (Job 40:4–5)

In 31:35–37, Job has demanded the intervention of God, declaring that he would approach God "like a prince." He has been expecting to defend himself in the presence according to the rules of his nobility. However, when Yahweh appears out of the whirlwind, the royal figure Job is stunned (40:4–5). Job says קַלֹּתִי ("I am small," 40:4).[53] Job starts to acknowledge failure of human reason to know the ways of God. However, instead of confessing his ignorance and, by implication, his presumptuousness, in judging God, Job responds that "if" he is so little, so how can he possibly give any response that will matter to God; thus, he will say no more.[54] In addition, the opening word הֵן carries two meanings: "behold," calling attention to some fact upon which action is to be made; or "if," introducing a hypothetical possibility as a ground on which a question is based.[55] When this particle introduces a question, as here, it typically introduces a

---

51. Terrien, "Yahweh Speeches," 502, states, "Job is invited to liberate himself from the microcosm of his egocentricity, and to discover that broad horizons of the macrocosm of life on the grand scale."

52. It is a dramatic irony that Job once has promised to "answer" if summoned (13:22). Now Yahweh has responded as he requested, so Job must answer.

53. The verb קלל is in Qal, connoting the idea of shame and contempt, often in the context of those who complain that they have been belittled by others (cf. Gen 16:4–5; 1 Sam 2:30; 2 Sam 6:22) or by God (e.g. Nah 1:14). See C. A. Keller, "*qll* to be light," *TLOT* 3:1141–1145. Cf. Tsevat, "The Meaning of the Book of Job," 205–206, draws an attention to the fact that the root קלל is antonymous to כבד which yields the noun כָּבוֹד (i.e. Job concerns himself with כָּבוֹד in 19:9; 29:20). So Job is responding here that he is now the opposite of כָּבוֹד.

54. Also Greenberg, "Job," 298.

55. BDB, 243.

conditional statement (e.g. Hag 2:12; Prov 11:13); thus, the text reads: "If I am of small account, what shall I answer you?" Janzen directs the attention to the possibility of the latter meaning. He points out that what Job is saying here is ambiguous.[56] It can "indicate either that Job gives up what he formerly said, or that, continuing in his former state of mind, he gives up on the attempt to make his point to such a one as God, resigned to harbor his convictions in the solitariness of his silence."[57] Job also adds a gesture to his words-placing his hand over his mouth. Some scholars view Job's words and his accompanying gesture as from the discourse of honor.[58] However, this gesture may convey something else (e.g. Job's disapproval; or Job's futile effort to silence his anguish; or Job is making a temporary pause; etc.).[59] Contextually, it is possible that the gesture of being silent here denotes that Job no longer protests his innocence, nor does he claim for his undeserved sufferings. However, he is not yet ready to surrender his pride, nor can he

---

56. Janzen, *Job*, 243. Also Greenberg, "Job," 298, quotes the observation of Saadya Gaon in the tenth century that this response is ambiguous: "When one interlocutor says to his partner, 'I can't answer you,' it may mean that he acquiesces in the other's position, equivalent to 'I can't gainsay the truth'; or it may mean he feels overborne by his partner, equivalent to 'How can I answer you when you have the upper hand?'" J. Miles, in his *God: A Biography* (New York: Alfred A. Knopf, 1995), 317–318, also says that in Job's first response to Yahweh here, "a refusal to speak can be wondrously inscrutable"; see Balentine, *Job*, 667–669.

57. Janzen, *Job*, 243. In this way, Job is using again his strategy which he used in his second response in the prologue (2:10), "offering words behind which he may keep his own counsel."

58. Charles Muenchow, "Dust and Dirt in Job 42:6," *JBL* 108 (1989): 597–611. Muenchow views that Job is silenced here in 40:3–5. This silence is the silence of one who has just been shamed (29:9–10, and cf. 11:3). Muenchow comments (608) that "because Job's questioning of Yahweh's ways has touched on a point of honor, Job's reaction to Yahweh's overwhelming demonstration of his lordly priority can only be one in which Job admits his own lowly status over against this Yahweh. At this culminating point in the contest, Job must acknowledge Yahweh's precedence. This he quickly proceeds to do in both word and gesture." However, as noted already, the tone of the first divine speech is not to put down Job, but to invite him with a didactic purpose. In addition, as the book unfolds, we see that Yahweh continues to speak to Job in the second divine speech, and draws on more specific features of two beasts: Behemoth and Leviathan. The presentation of the second divine speech affirms that Yahweh is not satisfied with Job's silence in 40:3–5. Contextually, it seems that Job does not totally "admit his own lowly status," as Muenchow points out.

59. See the analysis of placing the hand on the mouth by Gregory Yuri Glazov, "The Significance of the 'Hand on the Mouth' Gesture in Job XL 4," *VT* 52 (2002): 30–41. Glazov proposes, 40–41, a number of connotations (five connotations) for Job's gestures at 40:4. There are: (1) a gesture of discretion, (2) a gesture of disapproval, (3) a gesture of reflecting his strenuous effort to contain his anguish, (4) a gesture that taking place in the ensuing dialogue with YHWH, and (5) a gesture of Job's breaking through to a new understanding.

express a confessional affirmation on faith in words. Thus, the Joban author emphasizes a kind of negative response, or, at least, an ambiguous response of Job to the first divine speech here. As already noted, every response from Job needs to be considered. As Alter points out the silence in the narrative serves to signal that there is something about to happen next.[60] In addition, the presentation of the following second divine speech affirms to Job (and the reader) that God demands something more than his act of silence here.[61] The encounter must continue.

The Second Speech of YHWH (40:6–41:26 [41:34])

The second divine speech may be divided into three parts: (a) the introduction (40:6–14); (b) the Behemoth pericope (40:15–24); and (c) the Leviathan pericope (40:25–41:26 [Eng 41:34]). Starting from 40:6 God appears out of the whirlwind, as in 38:1, and begins his charges against Job in verses 7–8 and his challenge to Job in verses 9–14. God accuses Job of questioning the nature of divine justice to put God in the wrong in order to justify himself: "Will you even put me in the wrong? Will you condemn me that you may be in the right?" (v. 8). If Job had only defended his own integrity, he would have been in the right, but he has accused God of being unjust (i.e. according to the view of divine justice in the retribution principle) and challenged God's moral right to rule the world.[62] Thus, God wants Job to reconsider what constitutes justice (מִשְׁפָּטִי, lit., "my justice," v. 8).[63] As Job has attributed the prosperity of the wicked to divine indifference or cruelty, God invites Job to assume the divine arm: "Have you an arm like God, and can you thunder with a voice like his?" (40:9). The implication to these questions is that since Job lacks God's power, he has no right to question his justice. The answer to both questions in verse 9 is "no." God continues to challenge Job to execute justice and righteousness in the world:

---

60. Alter, *Biblical Narrative*, 114–130.

61. Also Greenberg, "Job," 298, observes that "in order to elicit an unequivocal response, God speaks again."

62. Bildad has asserted that God does not pervert justice (מִשְׁפָּט, 8:3). But Job argues repeatedly that God in fact does so. Also in his first oath, Job swears by the God who has taken away his right (מִשְׁפָּט, 27:2). Up to this point, Job is still trapped in the system of divine justice in the retribution principle. Ironically, in his accusations against God "Job may be doing to God what he accuses God of doing to him" (Janzen, *Job*, 243).

63. See Scholnick, "Meaning of *Mišpāṭ*," 522–523.

Unleash the fury of your wrath,
> look at every proud man and bring him low,
look at every proud man and humble him,
> crush the wicked where they stand.
Bury them all in the dust together;
> shroud their faces in the grave. (Job 40:11–13 NIV)

It is the anger of Job that is emphasized here (אַף). Since Job supposes that the moral governing of the world calls for swift punishment of the wicked, he is now given a chance to perform it that he will "humble" all the proud and "crush the wicked where they stand." Thus, God, who has been considered unjust by Job, challenges Job to govern the world and to show that he has the integrity and power to control the wicked.[64] If Job can do that, God will honor him (40:14). To demonstrate to Job his ignorance and impotence, God singles out two primordial forces of chaos for Job's special consideration: Behemoth (40:15–24) and Leviathan (40:25–41:26 [Eng 41:1–34]).

Chapter 40–41: The Sixth Pair of Animals and Pre-eminent Animals[65] – Behemoth (40:15–24)

¹⁵Behold, Behemoth,[66]
> which I made as I made you;
> he eats grass like an ox.

---

64. In the light of 40:8, it is possible to see that because Job's defense has placed God in the wrong, Job would now appear to be included in the classification of the wicked. In addition, in the light of 40:12, the wicked here may be understood not to be human being but the two forces of evil – Behemoth and Leviathan. "These brutish creatures are not only caricatures in themselves; they are also caricatures of human endeavor." See Terrien, *Job*, 246, 261–267; idem. *Job: Poet of Existence*, 237; also, Gammie, "Behemoth and Leviathan," 218.

65. Because of the length of these passages the present author will omit the Hebrew texts. Where it is necessary to comment on aspects of the Hebrew texts the study will provide the Hebrew texts in the footnote(s).

66. Unlike the name Leviathan in which its name attested in several other biblical and non-biblical passages, there are no earlier instances of the name "Behemoth." Another passage in the book of Job that contains the exact Hebrew pointing is in Job 12:7 (cf. Deut 32:24; Pss 50:10; 73:22; Jer 12:4; Hab 2:17). However, the term with its explanation in 40:15–24 is the only passage in the OT where בְּהֵמוֹת has the meaning "giant beast," sea monster," or "hippopotamus." The plural form of this word is used here as an "intensive plural" for a specific beast of great size and strength ("the beast *par excellence*"). In this plural form, the term is never used with the definite article, suggesting that it is also a proper name (i.e. "Behemoth," as it is usually rendered here). The term בְּהֵמוֹת has been understood, for example, as an elephant, hippopotamus, crocodile, or water buffalo. For a further discussion

¹⁶Behold, his strength in his loins,
  and his power in the muscles of his belly.
¹⁷He makes his tail stiff like a cedar;
  the sinews of his thighs are knit together.
¹⁸His bones are tubes of bronze,
  his limbs like bars of iron.
¹⁹He is the first of the works of God;
  let him who made him bring near his sword!
²⁰For the mountains yield food for him
  where all the wild beasts play.
²¹Under the lotus plants he lies,
  in the shelter of the reeds and in the marsh.
²²For his shade the lotus trees cover him;
  the willows of the brook surround him.
²³Behold, if the river is turbulent he is not frightened;
  he is confident though Jordan rushes against his mouth.
²⁴Can one take him by his eyes,
  or pierce his nose with a snare?

Unlike the preceding animals, Behemoth is introduced with affirmation, not rhetorical challenge question. Job is not asked to do anything except to look, listen, and learn.[67] Significantly, Behemoth, unlike all others, is a

---

on בְּהֵמוֹת and בְּהֵמָה, see Botterweck, "בְּהֵמָה," *TDOT* 2:6–20. With respect to the hyperbolic description of this beast, conclusive arguments cannot be given exclusively to support the view that Behemoth is a zoological designation for a literal animal (i.e. hippopotamus, or water buffalo) or to deny the mythical connotation of the term, particularly with the use of those terms like Yam, Leviathan, Tannin, etc. in the book of Job. However, as the present author approaches the text of Job with a literary reading, it is appropriate to discover the original intention of the Joban poet in creating or using this specific term in the specific section of the book (i.e. in the second divine speech). The term Behemoth, thus, connotes also a figurative meaning and is used to mirror Job's own characteristics.

In addition, the term בְּהֵמוֹת does appear previously in 12:7–8 (with precisely this Hebrew pointing) as a simple plural of the common noun. "But ask the beasts [בְּהֵמוֹת] and they will teach you" (12:7). In the context of chapter 12, it develops the theme of how the hand of God is responsible for Job's calamity (12:9), and of how "He [God] pours contempt on princes and loosens the belt of the strong" (12:21). The use of the intensive plural here in 40:15–24 is a development of that earlier usage. Behemoth is identified with the quintessential animal of the natural world, which God has made "with Job" (40:15)," and is used like the common plural of chapter 12 to teach a lesson to Job.

  67. Habel, *Book of Job*, 558.

creature in which God made as "I made along with you" (אֲשֶׁר־עָשִׂיתִי עִמָּךְ, 40:15).⁶⁸ Both Behemoth and Job have a common origin and their destinies are bound up together in some way. That is the Joban poet uses the Behemoth figure as a creature like Job himself.⁶⁹ Thus, God who subjugates Behemoth can control Job's anger and boasting (i.e. "his nose/anger" and "his mouth," v. 24). In the light of comparison between Behemoth and Job, the following will briefly draw some characteristics of Behemoth that can provide some clues for Job to see his own identity and his relation to God.⁷⁰

The first characteristic is its extra-physical strength and power (vv. 16–18).⁷¹ The poet highlights this extraordinary strength with the descriptions of its bones like "tubes of bronze," and his limbs like "rods of iron," v. 18). This means Behemoth is a creature with great strength, which has the ability to protect itself from life threatening forces. This extraordinary strength also includes the regenerative power to give life again (v. 17).⁷² In comparison with Job, the reader is invited to reflect upon the way that, even though Job has been pounded and lost his children, with regenerative powers and extraordinary strength he could regain his energy and acquire a new set of children, as he indeed does at the end of the story.

The next characteristic of Behemoth is in verse 19a, where he is described as the "first (רֵאשִׁית) of the works of God." In the light of verse 20, this description may be expressing pre-eminence, excellence or superiority. However, Balentine points out that the word רֵאשִׁית recalls not only the creation narrative

---

68. Balentine, "What Are Human Beings," 270, observes that this is the only direct reference to the creation of humans in the divine speeches, thus suggesting that "Behemoth represents the one true analogue for humankind that God has placed in the created order."

69. Though Habel, *Book of Job*, 557–561, views that Behemoth and Leviathan have a mythic nuance, he also agrees with Gammie that Behemoth and Leviathan invite comparison with Job.

70. The analysis of Behemoth and Leviathan sections offered here rests mainly on the study of Gammie, "Behemoth and Leviathan;" and Balentine, "What Are Human Beings."

71. The focus on Behemoth's extraordinary strength suggests that its superiority is praised. This same understanding is found also in the presentation of Leviathan as a creature "without equal," a king over all the proud (41:25–26 [Eng 41:33–34]). The force of the description of Behemoth, as well as of Leviathan, is not containment of their power but the intense representation of their extraordinary ability. See also Newsom, *The Book of Job*, NIB, 619.

72. It is generally recognized that the description of Behemoth's "tail" (זָנָב) which "sways like a cedar" (NIV) in verse 17 is a playful piece of poetry, functioning as a euphemism for the Beast's penis. See Habel, *Book of Job*, 565–566; Alter, *Biblical Poetry*, 108.

in Genesis 1:1, which presents God's design for the cosmos, but also the description of Wisdom in Proverbs 8:22, who celebrates its role as a co-creator at the beginning of the master plan for creation.[73] In addition, the following verses 20–22 present Behemoth as a king in its own domain. That is the mountains pay tribute and the wild animals sport as its happy subjects. As Behemoth seems to stand supreme among all animals of the field and the mountains, the description as the "first" of creation's works here presents him as a "model of royalty" that invites from Job the very self-understanding that he has a special royal status as a near equal to God (vv. 20–22; cf. 15:7).[74]

The third revealing character is found in verse 23. Behemoth belongs in the turbulent chaotic waters of the river and is at home in the raging floods. The text presents his distinctive response to those raging and violence waters. The beast may be subject to attack (i.e. by aggressive waters), even by God (cf. vv. 19b, 24),[75] but he responds with "confident resistance."[76] The beast, when oppressed, neither flees in fear nor abandons trust. Furthermore,

---

73. Balentine, "What Are Human Beings," 270–271.

74. Balentine, 270–271. Another well-known alternative interpretation of verse 19a is, for instance, from Habel, *Book of Job*, 566, who points out that "wisdom is the first eternal principle, Behemoth the first created design. Thus, the world apparently began with the chaos God created, personified here, as in other mythic traditions, by a monster, he then overcame and controlled." It is true that the text acknowledges that only God can approach Behemoth with a sword (40:19), but there is no indication that God really does that. Instead of expressing the hostility, the tone of the presentation of Behemoth (as well as of Leviathan) as a whole presents God's proud of him. Thus, "if the ancient combat myth of creation lurks here, it has been seriously defanged" (O'Connor, "Wild, Raging Creativity," 76).

75. Note that the Hebrew text in verse 19b is ambiguous (הָעֹשׂוֹ יַגֵּשׁ חַרְבּוֹ:). H. Rowley, *Book of Job*, 257, suggests positively that the term "his sword" refers to Behemoth's sword that Yahweh brings to him as a token of his lordship over other animals (v. 20). Others (e.g. Gammie) see the term refers to God's sword that is used, in implication to Job, as an attack to Job. However, the force of the description in the Behemoth pericope presents no violence associating with Behemoth here. In addition, as Newsom, *The Book of Job*, NIB, 617, 619, rightly observes, there is no hostility between God and these two beasts (i.e. Behemoth and Leviathan). The context of the Behemoth and Leviathan as a whole does not point to the ancient battle between the creator god and the chaos monster(s); rather God boasts and praises these two beings as if proud of them. For the former understanding, see, for instance, Tryggve Mettinger, "God the Victor," in *The Voice from the Whirlwind: Interpreting the Book of Job*, eds. Leo G. Perdue and W. Clark Gilpin (Nashville: Abingdon, 1992), 45–46; John C. L. Gibson, "On Evil in the Book of Job," in *Ascribe to the Lord: Biblical and Other Studies in Memory of P. C. Craigie*, JSOTSup 67, eds. Lyle M. Eslinger and J. Glen Taylor (Sheffield: JSOT Press, 1988), 399–419.

76. Balentine, "What Are Human Beings," 271; also Gammie, "Behemoth and Leviathan," 220.

Behemoth is made to dwell in the river's shades (vv. 21–22). The darkness of the shades may be compared with darkness of suffering and imminent death of Job. Job, therefore, even under the attack (i.e. from his friends and God) has never abandoned his faith and responded with trust and "could take heart even there in his dark valleys there is a protective covering and covert."[77]

As God says: "Behold, Behemoth, which I made as I made you" (40:15), the command invites Job to compare himself to the beast. The strong Behemoth ranks first among the works of God, only his master can approach it with sword (40:19). However, the master, God, does not really do such battle.[78] We see the picture of contentment instead in the following verses. The beast eats, plays, rests under the lotus, and finds the shade among the willows. If the river is turbulent, Behemoth is not alarmed; he is secure, facing the raging waters with confidence. According to these distinguished characteristics of Behemoth, Job has fierce kinship with the beast. Job is fearless before his friends and before God. As Behemoth is the closest to Job, it is presented as the prime object lesson to which Job is invited by God to see himself as similar threat. That is, he, like Behemoth, has: (a) extraordinary strength, with regenerative power; (b) special position (i.e. the first of the works of God); and (c) fierce trust (i.e. fearless and confidence when oppressed). God demonstrates to Job how even though Behemoth possesses a place of pre-eminence with God (40:19a), God does bring his sword against him (40:19b); even though Behemoth has a high standing among his equals (40:20), God in the end pierces even his "anger/nose," thus bringing him low (40:12–13). If God pierces the wrath of such a wondrous monster as Behemoth, then he will do the same to the wrath of Job. Even the greatest of God's creations is subject to God; by the same token, Job needs to learn to accept in peace what comes from the hand of God.

Leviathan (40:25–41:26 [Eng 41:1–34])

¹Can you draw out Leviathan[79] with a fishhook
    or press down his tongue with a cord?

---

77. Gammie, "Behemoth and Leviathan," 222.
78. This observation is from O'Connor, "Wild, Raging Creativity," 176.
79. The name "Leviathan," unlike Behemoth, carries with it a well-developed idea of symbolic associations. In Canaanite mythology, Leviathan (or Lotan) is well known as the name of a seven-headed sea-serpent, which was defeated by Baal at the "creation," a defeat

> ² Can you put a rope in his nose
>   or pierce his jaw with a hook?
> ³ Will he make many pleas to you?
>   Will he speak to you soft words?
> ⁴ Will he make a covenant with you
>   to take him for your servant forever?
> ⁵ Will you play with him as with a bird,
>   or will you put him on a leash for your girls?
> ⁶ Will traders bargain over him?
>   Will they divide him up among the merchants?
> ⁷ Can you fill his skin with harpoons
>   or his head with fishing spears?

---

which must annually be repeated ritually if creation is not to revert to chaos. However, the Leviathan of Job 40:25–41:26 has only a single head (i.e. the poet speaks of the head only in the singular [40:31; Eng 41:7]). Both are called "Leviathan." With demythologized import, it is used in Isa 27:1 and Ps 104:26 as a picturesque description of the monstrous forces of evil which Yahweh has defeated and neutralized. Apparently, the term "Rahab" (i.e. the dragon; (Job 9:13; 26:12; Ps 89:10[11]; Isa 51:9; cf. the term "Tannin" [sea monster] in Job 7:12; Ps 74:13; Isa 27:1; Ezek 29:3; 32:2) is an epithet for the same monster, and is used in the Bible in the same way, with special reference to Egypt (i.e. Isa 30:7; 51:9; Pss 87:4; 89:11). For a review of the meaning of the term, see, for instance, John Day, "Leviathan," *ABC* 4:295–296; Lipins, "לִוְיָתָן" *TDOT* 7:504–509.

In the book of Job the term Leviathan is mentioned earlier already in 3:8. Job uses the mythic image of Leviathan, a creature of chaos, in his calling forth creation's antithesis. As day and night are cursed, so Leviathan is awakened from the watery depths of its habitation. Whoever is skilled enough to rouse this monster is one who is well versed in the science of cursing, of defying both creation and Creator. Leviathan is chaos personified; Job, the master of malediction, is the executor/perpetrator of chaos. Cf. Brown, *The Ethos of the Cosmos*, 322–323.

This Leviathan reappears with a lengthy description in 40:25–41:26 [Eng 41:1–34]. It is interesting that the boundary between the mythical and the non-mythical connotations, as well as the uncertainty status of the chaotic element in relation to creation, is founded in biblical texts to the extent that the term "Leviathan" and "Tannin" are creatures formed by God and not at all hostile. For example, in Genesis 1:21, the term הַתַּנִּינִם refers to sea animals created as part of the work of the fifth day of creation in which God said that "it was good." In Psalm 148:7, the word תַּנִּינִים are called upon to praise God as part of universal praise. In the same manner, in Psalm 104:26, Leviathan is an animal that God has formed to play in the sea. Newsom, *The Book of Job*, NIB, 621–622, points out that the presentation of Leviathan in the second divine speech in the book of Job "draws associations from both the mythic tradition and the tradition represented in Genesis and the book of Psalms." These exemplified passages attest that the polytheistic element of the term's original myths was removed from the Hebrew Bible usage. Leviathan, like Behemoth, carries at the same time a naturalistic and mythical meaning, as well as a figurative connotation, which is aimed to point to Job his own characteristic and his place in God's design.

⁸ Lay your hands on him;
   remember the battle— you will not do it again!
⁹ Behold, the hope of a man is false;
   he is laid low even at the sight of him.
¹⁰ No one is so fierce that he dares to stir him up.
   Who then is he who can stand before me?
¹¹ Who has first given to me, that I should repay him?
   Whatever is under the whole heaven is mine.
¹² "I will not keep silence concerning his limbs,
   or his mighty strength, or his goodly frame.
¹³ Who can strip off his outer garment?
   Who would come near him with a bridle?
¹⁴ Who can open the doors of his face?
   Around his teeth is terror.
¹⁵ His back is made of rows of shields,
   shut up closely as with a seal.
¹⁶ One is so near to another
   that no air can come between them.
¹⁷ They are joined one to another;
   they clasp each other and cannot be separated.
¹⁸ His sneezings flash forth light,
   and his eyes are like the eyelids of the dawn.
¹⁹ Out of his mouth go flaming torches;
   sparks of fire leap forth.
²⁰ Out of his nostrils comes forth smoke,
   as from a boiling pot and burning rushes.
²¹ His breath kindles coals,
   and a flame comes forth from his mouth.
²² In his neck abides strength,
   and terror dances before him.
²³ The folds of his flesh stick together,
   firmly cast on him and immovable.
²⁴ His heart is hard as a stone,
   hard as the lower millstone.

²⁵ When he raises himself up the mighty are afraid;
   at the crashing they are beside themselves.
²⁶ Though the sword reaches him,
   it does not avail, nor the spear, the dart, or the javelin.
²⁷ He counts iron as straw,
   and bronze as rotten wood.
²⁸ The arrow cannot make him flee;
   for him sling stones are turned to stubble.
²⁹ Clubs are counted as stubble;
   he laughs at the rattle of javelins.
³⁰ His underparts are like sharp potsherds;
   he spreads himself like a threshing sledge on the mire.
³¹ He makes the deep boil like a pot;
   he makes the sea like a pot of ointment.
³² Behind him he leaves a shining wake;
   one would think the deep to be white-haired.
³³ On earth there is not his like,
   a creature without fear.
³⁴ He sees everything that is high;
   he is king over all the sons of pride.

In contrast to the Behemoth pericope, this poem contains a number of rhetorical questions that serve to challenge Job in a manner similar to the interrogations of the first divine speech. For example, a series of questions introduced by the interrogative *he* in 40:25–41:1 [Eng 41:1–9] ask generally: "Can you, Job, draw out Leviathan?" The expected answer is then "no." The questions with the interrogative pronoun *mi* in 41:2–6 [Eng 41:10–14] ask generally in the sense that: "If you, Job, cannot confront and control this monstrous beast, who can?" The logic of the question is that Job should answer: "No one can. Only you, God, can control Leviathan." The latter half of the poem (41:10–26 [Eng 41:18–34] contains descriptive statements, describing the distinctive features of Leviathan. Like Behemoth poem, there is no hostility between God and this fearsome and dreadful Leviathan. The major subject of the poem concerning this monstrous beast is its לְשֹׁנוֹ ("his tongue," 41:25 [Eng 41:1]), and what comes forth from its mouth (40:27; 41:5, 10–13 [Eng 41:3, 13, 18–21]).⁸⁰

First, Leviathan, like Behemoth, is a creature *par excellence*. It cannot be domesticated by man (40:28 [Eng 41:4]). That is, it is not subject to human but is controlled by God (41:3 [Eng 41:11]). Its extraordinary power is described in 41:4–24 [Eng 41:12–32]). The specific description of Leviathan's proud withstanding of oppression in 40:17–21, 22–26 [Eng 41:25–29, 30–34] presents his ability and nature that though under attack (cf. 6:4; 16:13–14; 19:11–12; etc.) he could defend against all assault (i.e. sword, arrows, slings and club). The tone of these descriptions, like Behemoth poem, conveys the idea that "God is not in conflict with this symbol of chaos and terror. God is simply and eloquently proud."⁸¹ Leviathan is praised as if he is not only a king but a victorious king (cf. 41:26 [Eng 41:34]) whom God is proud to brag about.

Second, the motif of Leviathan's speech has been emphasized here. Leviathan would not speak "soft words" (40:27–28 [Eng 41:3–4]). Instead what comes forth from his mouth is emphasized as fire and light, smoke and flames (41:10–13 [Eng 41:18–21]).⁸² The Joban author employs the poetic hyperbole language to reflect Job's very fierce words of public defiance. Leviathan's presence with an awesome fierceness calls for attention and defies coercion. The emphasis on these remarkable and mighty defenses of Leviathan intends to mirror Job's own verbal defenses and at the same time to affirm his protests.⁸³ God's admiration and praise on this fierce beast also implies that Job's words of defenses and protests are not without merit in the sight of God. That is, what God says about Leviathan is more didactic, intending to mirror Job and his own defiant speeches.

---

80. Structurally, the Hebrew final words are often key words, signaling subject matter to be discussed (i.e. "his tongue," in 40:25 [Eng 41:1]), and final lines in strophes often anticipate subject matter of following strophes (i.e. a boasting of the strength of the armor of Leviathan). Gammie, "Behemoth and Leviathan," 222–223.

81. O'Connor, "Wild, Raging Creativity," 177; also Janzen, *Job*, 244.

82. Alter, *Biblical Poetry*, 109–110, comments that the imagery here may be compared to the cosmic imagery of light in the first divine speech (Job 38), which functions rhetorically to counter Job's opening curse of creation in Job 3.

83. For the details of some textual indicators that support this alternative interpretation, see Gammie, "Behemoth and Leviathan," especially 224–225.

Last, Leviathan, like Behemoth, is portrayed as the king (מֶלֶךְ) in its own domain (41:26 [Eng 41:34]). As noted already, Behemoth's royal status derives from its status as the "first" of the work of God, the one whom all creation offers respectful tribute (40:19–22). Leviathan's kingship is portrayed through images of governance – Leviathan "looks on everyone who is high (כָּל־גָּבֹהַּ יִרְאֶה)" (41:26 [Eng 41:34]).[84] Likewise, Job, throughout the story, is portrayed as one of regal proportions (i.e. in his prosperity described in the prologue, in Job 29 and in the epilogue; 29:25; 31:37). He is summoned, like a king, to put on the regalia of "glory and splendor" (40:10).[85] From Job's royal status, Yahweh has challenged him if Job could "look on everyone who is proud (רְאֵה כָל־גֵּאֶה)" (40:11–12) and deal with them justly. The implication is that the Leviathan in the Leviathan poem is intended, in part at least, as a figure of Job. In addition, the status of Leviathan as "king," invites reflection on Job's own identity and his vocational role (i.e. a creature, who is near God and in the image of God [cf. Ps 8]). To be more specific, during the discourses, Job's understanding of his royal image has placed him a dangerous position between being the merely human and the supremely divine.[86] Thus, the two speeches of Yahweh, particularly the second divine speech, lead Job to realize his self-understanding and bring him to a new understanding of his place as a creature (i.e. whose understanding is limited), and show him his creatureliness (i.e. his proud of himself in holding on his moral conduct, and consequently his judging God as wrong). Job is invited to recognize his participation in the mystery and wild freedom of creation and its creator.

Both Behemoth and Leviathan are part of God's creation. They are the final pair and biggest examples of animals. They teach Job something like

---

84. As Newsom points out the conclusion of the Leviathan pericope (41:26 [Eng 41:34]) forms an *inclusio* with 40:11b.

85. The term "glory and splendor," echoing Psalm 8, suggests that God is reminding Job the role that God has specially created for human beings (see Balentine, "What Are Human Beings," 268). For the royal imagery that is used as reference to Job in 40:10-13, see Janzen, *Job*, 243–244. Janzen and Balentine are in the same line of thought here about the royal image in the character Job. In the context of Job's suffering, Job is invited to acknowledge his own place in God's creation. He is a creature, who is "a little lower than God." The way that God is delight in the two beasts' uncanny power implicitly applies to Job's.

86. Note also that in Hebrew, Job is given his position as "on the dust" (2:8; 30:19; 42:6). The same feature is stressed on Leviathan who has no equal "on the dust" (41:25a).

the other animals. What all they teach Job is part of the limit of human to understand the way of God, including everything that goes on the world. There are things in God's creation that beyond the scope of human reason to comprehend. Both Behemoth and Leviathan can be destructive and violent and they also illustrated that they are the destructive forces within nature, within creation, that are not comprehensible in terms of human reason. They do not fit the paradigm of the retribution principle. Their actions cannot be comprehended by human reason. They cannot be wholly understood by man. Yet they still are embraced as part of God's creation and subject to God. They are part of the "goods" of God's creation, and yet we have to acknowledge that we do not know their way.

Job's Second Response (42:2–6)

In the second speech of Yahweh, Job has been charged particularly on accusing God of wrongdoing (מִשְׁפָּט). Yahweh says: "Will you even put me in the wrong? Will you condemn me that you may be in the right?" (40:8). By adopting the retribution principle for judging God's justice, Job has been found guilty of condemning and putting God in a wrong. It was as if he were a rival god, who not only dare to meet God face to face but also put himself on at least equal to or better than God in performing justice in this world. As Yahweh challenges Job to perform the administration of justice in this world, it is clearly that Job could not do that. Many things are too wonderful and mysterious beyond the boundary of human reason. Humans, including Job, have limitation and cannot understand everything in God's creation. The Behemoth and Leviathan poems are presented to show Job Yahweh's lordship, his power, authority, and control over these chaos forces. At the same time, both are mirrors of Job himself, whom Yahweh has been proud in their wild and beauty. Job is invited to ponder upon his anger, and his fierce words of protests against God. No man can claim against God that God must pay (41:11). However, Yahweh comes and speaks to Job. God's revelation is not to punish Job or put him down, but to summon, to teach, and to correct him. This divine-human encounter is from God's own initiative, not because of Job's claim, but a grace, a loving revelation.

Job responds,

I know that you can do all things, and that no purpose of yours can be thwarted.	42:2	יָדַעְתָּ [יָדַעְתִּי] כִּי־כֹל תּוּכָל וְלֹא־יִבָּצֵר מִמְּךָ מְזִמָּה׃
"Who is this that hides counsel without knowledge?"[87] Therefore I have uttered what I did not understand, things too wonderful for me, which I did not know.	42:3	מִי זֶה מַעְלִים עֵצָה בְּלִי דָעַת לָכֵן הִגַּדְתִּי וְלֹא אָבִין נִפְלָאוֹת מִמֶּנִּי וְלֹא אֵדָע׃
"Hear, and I will speak; I will question you, and you make it known to me."	42:4	שְׁמַע־נָא וְאָנֹכִי אֲדַבֵּר אֶשְׁאָלְךָ וְהוֹדִיעֵנִי׃
I had heard of you by the hearing of the ear, but now my eye sees you;	42:5	לְשֵׁמַע־אֹזֶן שְׁמַעְתִּיךָ וְעַתָּה עֵינִי רָאָתְךָ׃
therefore I retract [my words][88] and change my mind[89] concerning dust and ashes.	42:6	עַל־כֵּן אֶמְאַס וְנִחַמְתִּי עַל־עָפָר וָאֵפֶר׃ פ

---

87. It is generally accepted that 42:3a and 42:4 are virtual quotations of Yahweh's challenges to Job in 38:2–3 and 40:7. See Robert Gordis, "Virtual Quotations in Job, Sumer and Qumran," *VT* 31 (1981): 410–427; Andersen, *Job*, 291–292; Habel, *Book of Job*, 576; Janzen, *Job*, 251. However, some scholars suggest that these two quotations as being misplaced. See this latter group of scholars, for instance, in Dhorme, *Commentary on the Book of Job*, 645–646; Rowley, *Book of Job*, 265; Pope, *Job*, 348; etc.

88. In Hebrew there is no direct object after the word מאס, "retract." The term אֶמְאַס is in the first-person common singular imperfect Qal form of the root מאס I ("to despise, reject"). William S. Morrow points out that out of sixty-six occurrences in the Hebrew Bible, the object is always indicated with four exceptions (Job 7:16; 34:33; 36:5; 42:6) ("Consolation, Rejection, and Repentance in Job 42:6," *JBL* 105 [1986], 214). Some English versions (e.g. ESV, NIV, "therefore, I despise myself and repent in dust and ashes") see that the term may have a reflexive nuance as in the Niphal form; thus, "I despise myself" (cf. LXX and 11 QtgJob). However, this researcher sees that the MT should be retained. It is possible to assume, from the context of the usages in the book of Job, either that מאס I demand an implicit object, or that the Joban author may have deliberately set up a double entendre based on the rare verb מאס II ("to dissolve, melt") or the more common מאס I. See the number of possibilities of the assumed direct object in Morrow's article, "Consolation," 211–225.

89. Structurally, the word נחם is a *hendiadys* of מאס, in which one adverbially modifies the other; thus, for example, Job "utterly changes his mind." The Hebrew term נחם means "to regret, have a change of heart, relent, turn from a former attitude, and hence repent; to allow oneself to be sorry; to comfort or console oneself" (*Holladay's Lexicon*, 234; also BDB, 636–637). The term וְנִחַמְתִּי may be construed either in the Niphal or the Piel. The meaning

Job not only acknowledges God's power (v. 2a), but also confesses the inaccessibility of God's ultimate lordship (v. 2b). Job cannot know or fully comprehend the divine marvels (vv. 2–3). Job takes the very words of God's speech (38:2) on his own lips – the very words in which God has charged Job's accusations as "without knowledge." In repeating God's words (v. 3a), Job is speaking in agreement with God, accepting his lack of knowledge about God and his ways of dealing with human and the world. "Therefore" (v. 3b) Job cries out as a liberated man, not being broken or humiliated, announcing that wonderful things are beyond him to understand. Job quotes again in verse 4 what Yahweh has said in 40:7. The import of this quotation may serve to set the stage of the following verse 5. That is, Job is to hear while Yahweh is speaking. Thus, when Yahweh questions Job, then Job is to make him known (i.e. to give Yahweh a response). The Hebrew term ידע, "to know," opens verse 2 and closes verse 4, suggesting an inclusion before the climatic statements of Job in verses 5–6.[90]

During the dialogue, Job has sought to see God face to face. But God is silent. Job has said in 9:11, "Behold, he passed by me, and I see him not; he moves on, but I do not perceive him." And "If I summoned him and he answered me, I would not believe that he was listening to my voice" (9:16). Job also states with his bold faith, "Though he slay me, I will hope in him; yet I will argue my ways to his face (13:15). Job has wished not to hide himself from God's face (13:20), and complained that God hides his face (13:24). Similarly, Job states, "I would know what he would answer me and understand what he would say to me" (23:5). Job continues that "Behold, I go forward, but he is not there, and backward, but I do not perceive him; on the left hand when he is working, I do not behold him; he turns to the right hand, but I do not see him" (23:8–9).

---

of Piel ("comfort, console") does not appear to fit the context here. When the Niphal form of נחם, followed by the preposition על, the meaning is to change one's mind about something one had planned to do (e.g. Exod 32:12, 14; Jer 18:8, 10; Amos 7:3, 6; Joel 2:13; Jonah 3:10, 4:2). That is, Job "repents" or "changes his mind" "concerning" dust and ashes. For a discussion of this rendering on the idiom נחם על, see, for instance, Morrow, "Consolation," 215–216; D. Patrick, "Short Notes: The Translation of Job 42:6," *VT* 26 (1976): 369–371; B. Lynne Newell, "Job: Repentant or Rebellious?," *WTJ* 46 (1984): 298–316.

90. Janzen, *Job*, 252–253.

However, these sentiments appear in stark contrast to the fleeting conviction that Job once has yearned for: "But I would see God from my fresh, whom I would see for myself; my eyes would see, and not a stranger" (19:26b–27b). What Job longs for in chapter 19, namely to see God, is repeated here in 42:5. The hope of 19:26b–27b has found its fulfillment. What God has addressed, Job responds, "I have heard of you by the hearing of the ears" (42:5a). How God has appeared, Job reacts, "now my eye sees you" (42:5b). God, who once was silence, speaks to Job; God, who once was absent, now appears so Job may see him. God's words and his appearance, thus, fulfill what Job has been asking for during the course of the dialogue. God reveals to Job something of his ways and his purposes and cares in the administration of the world. These are things beyond what Job can comprehend. God's justice includes not only the justice in terms of human understanding but also his authoritative lordship. Consequently, the fact that God does not crush Job affirms that God is not angry with Job. The appearance of God is, thus, a grace, a loving revelation of God. The portrayal of the Behemoth and Leviathan directly leads Job to acknowledge God's mystery and love in dealing with even the impertinent one like Job.

The nearness of Yahweh, including his gracious words, leads Job to the revolution of his thought. The message of Yahweh's second speech brings him to repentance, rather than a simple submission (cf. 40:4–5). Job responds: "Therefore I retract [my words] and change my mind concerning dust and ashes" (42:6). The Hebrew term עַל־כֵּן ("therefore") introduces verse 6 as a consequence of verse 5: "because I have seen you." The verb מאס is rendered here as "retract." If it is מאס I, an active form of the word takes an object. But there is no identified object in the Hebrew.[91] Contextually, it is possible that "my words" (i.e. Job's words of presumptuousness during the discourses) is an assumed direct object.[92] Job, then, "repents" or "changes

---

91. On the contrary, John B. Curtis proposes that the usage of מאס here is similar to the one used in 7:16; thus, has an intransitive connotation (i.e. "to feel loathing contempt"), suggesting that God who has revealed himself is utterly disgusting to Job ("On Job's Response to Yahweh," *JBL* 98 (1979): 497–511. Curtis argues that Job did not repent, but totally and unequivocally rejects God. Contextually Curtis' radically different translation does not fit and is irrelevant to the epilogue that follows. See a counter-argument to his position in, for instance, Morrow, "Consolation," 211–225; Newell, "Job: Repentant," 299, 301, 307–316.

92. Another possible and interesting alternative is proposed by Scholnick, who sees that Job's words of response in 42:6 signify his retraction of the lawsuit. He suggests that the

his mind" (נִחַמְתִּי) "concerning"⁹³ dust and ashes. Job recognizes that he has sinned, so he repents of that sin. However, this sin is not committed prior to his suffering. It is also not the cause of his suffering. Rather, his sin is in the words he has spoken, accusing and condemning God during the dialogues with the friends, as he justifies himself according to the rule of the retribution principle. He also sins in exalting himself as a "rival god."⁹⁴ As the meaning of נחם, "repentance," implies sorrow and regret because of that sin, it also connotes the idea in which that regret produces a change of mind which is followed by a change of plan(s).

The following phrase in 42:6b gives an important clue, affirming that Job's response is no longer a merely negative acceptance of silence. The phrase "dust and ashes" (cf. עָפָר וָאֵפֶר; its occurrences only three times in Gen 18:27; Job 30:19; 42:6)⁹⁵ is traditionally used in the context of mourning or self-abasement (e.g. 2 Sam 13:19; Isa 58:5; Jer 6:26). In Job 2:8, Job is described as sitting among the ashes (בְּתוֹךְ־הָאֵפֶר). In Job 2:12, Job's friends see his terrible condition, and to express their grief and sympathy they sprinkle dust on their heads. The use of dust and ashes, thus, implies in acts of mourning or self-abasement. In Job 30:19, Job compares his misery to dust and ashes. His personal experience leads him to conclude that he is consigned to live in a world where he cries out to God, and God does not answer (30:20). Dust and ashes, thus, are symbols of human finitude and mortality as creature coming from and returning to the dust of the earth. From the usage in the context of the book, Job acknowledges his own finitude and mortality. As the phrase refers also to the rite of mourning in the ceremony of the dead, Job finds himself as dying to his old self;⁹⁶ namely, he is transformed in

---

direct object of מאס should be מִשְׁפָּט, and the term נחם, with forensic connotation, should be rendered "retract." He draws support from Job's last major speech in 31:13, where the object of this same verb is מִשְׁפָּט. He views the term מאס as a shortened form of מאס מִשְׁפָּט (cf. a comparable idiom, סוּר מִשְׁפָּט, in 27:2). Thus, his translation of 42:6 is: "Therefore, being but dust and ashes, I withdraw and retract [my case]" (Scholnick, "Meaning of *Mišpāṭ*," 356–357). This translation helps answer the question of the resolution of Job's lawsuit against God.

93. With נחם, the force of the preposition עַל is relational; thus, it is appropriate to render it as "concerning." Cf. Job 2:8, where Job is said to sit "in/among" the ashes (בְּתוֹךְ־הָאֵפֶר), connoting spatial-locative idea in its reference. See Janzen, *Job*, 255.

94. Newell, "Job: Repentant," 315; Newell, "Job, Repentant or Rebellious?"

95. The phrase is rare also in post-biblical literatures: Sir 10:9; 40:3; and 1QH 10:5.

96. Also Terrien, "The Yahweh Speeches," 505.

his self-understanding after the second divine speech. Literally, the phrase "dust and ashes" here functions partly in linking Job's state in 2:7, which has introduced Job's posture, with here where Job is about to be resumed in the epilogue (42:7ff). Up to this point, Job is now intending to abandon the posture of mourning.[97]

Moreover, in the context of Genesis 18:27, God, the "judge of all the earth," stands waiting to hear what "dust and ashes" (i.e. Abraham) will say on the subject of divine justice. Thus, the appearance before Yahweh as "dust and ashes" confirms Job's heritage as a faithful descendant of Abraham, who dares to protest God with the standards by which God is assumed to judge the world (i.e. according to the retribution principle). Like Behemoth and Leviathan, who are fierce, unbridled contenders for justice, sometimes with God and sometimes against God, God provides human beings freely with power and responsibility for their domains. By implication, Job's transformed understanding of "dust and ashes" here in Job 42:6 teaches Job that a human being (i.e. being dust and ashes) may image God "not by acquiescing to innocent suffering but rather by protesting it, contending with the powers that occasion it, and, when necessary, taking the fight directly to God. It is just such power, courage, and fierce trust that God seems to commend to Job in the figures of Behemoth and Leviathan."[98] Theologically, Job, therefore, retracts his seemingly blasphemous words and changes his mind concerning all that he has previously protested to God.

---

97. See also Patrick, "Translation of Job 42:6," 369–371. Patrick interprets 42:6 as: "Therefore I repudiate and repent of dust and ashes." He views 42:2–6 as Job declaring that, because of the wonder of God's ways, Job will change his speech from lament and accusation of God to praise. Although Patrick does not see Job as repentant in the usual sense, his view does agree that Job changes his attitude, action, and finally he can praise God.

98. The analysis on this section partly rests on the investigation of Balentine, "What Are Human Beings," 276–277, and Janzen, *Job*, 254–259. Note that Balentine's interpretation is similar to that of Janzen. However, the major difference is that while Janzen views that the innocent suffering of Job, resembling the suffering servant in Second Isaiah, can be accepted and embraced, Balentine sees from the context of the book of Job itself that Job's suffering does not on behalf of others, but "for no reason." In addition, the immediate context of Job's final response (i.e. after the Behemoth and Leviathan's poems), Job's new understanding of "dust and ashes," thus, means that his protesting to God concerning his innocent suffering is significant or justified in the sight of God.

Summary of Two Divine Speeches and Job's Responses

Structurally, in the prologue, Job's responses to the divine dialogues (i.e. in the heavenly court) correspondingly appears in two stages (i.e. 1:21 and 2:10). In the end of the book, the Joban author also put in Job's mouth two responses (i.e. 40:4–5 and 42:2–6) to the divine speeches. In the prologue, while Job's first response (1:21) remarks his confessional submissive faith in God, his second response (2:10) is ambiguous. In the end of the book, Job's first response to the first divine speech (40:4–5) continues the tone of ambiguity, whereas his second and final response (42:2–6) expresses the tone of his confessional affirmation of faith in God, the same position as he did in 1:21 but with a deeper conviction and understanding.

Contextually, the revelation from Yahweh and Job's personal terrible experience lead Job to a new position. In the dialogues Job's speeches and attitudes present a mixture of features: doubt, questioning, emotional outburst, faith, hope, hopelessness, confidence, perplexing, wishes for death and yearns for life. He, arguing with the friends on their own ground, has uttered many things presumptuously. He defends himself against the accusations of his friends and maintaining his own righteousness. He also addresses God and speaks about him. When he struggles to reconcile the friends' (and his) theology of the retribution principle and past experience of God with his present agony, Job sees only the capricious and evil side of God. Job can only conclude that God has changed from being his friend who cares for him (e.g. 1:1–5; 29:2–5a) to his enemy who pursues and treats him cruelly (e.g. 10:8–12; 13:24–27; 30:21). As Job has tried to reconcile divine justice in the retribution principle with his own experience and to refute the accusations of his friends at the same time, he accuses God for so many things. Job mocks God in his speeches: God oppresses him without telling him the cause (10:2–3), attacks him in anger, and shatters him and makes him his target (16:9–12), wrongs him and counts him as his enemy (19:6–11), denies him justice (27:1), and with his mighty hand God attacks him cruelly (30:19–20). His words in referring to God as abusive and horrible do not appear anywhere else in the Bible. These references (also in 6:4; 9:17; 12:9; 13:21; 16:12–14; 19:21; 23:15–16; 30:19, 21–22; etc.) reflect a false picture of God that reveals the bankruptcy of the retribution principle, which has led Job to view God as arbitrary, capricious, and evil during the dialogues with the friends.

To the extent of what Job has said in the dialogues, he is, at the same time, either consciously or unconsciously, passing judgment on God by accusing him,[99] specifically a judgment on God for not performing his divine justice as a ruler of the world (e.g. God does not intervene to help those who are oppressed by the wicked, 24:1–12; also his case – an innocent sufferer). Therefore, in judging God, Job is claiming of self-deification and implying that he would be a better ruler according to the rule of the retribution principle.

However, Job never lost his faith. All that he has uttered (i.e. either as blasphemy in the eyes of the friends, or as a direct and fierce appeal to God in Job's own eyes) must be heard in the context of Job's struggles to reconcile his real and painful innocent suffering with his beliefs about God and to reject the accusations of the friends at the same time. Significantly, Job also expresses his bold faith in God and in his righteousness and justice (e.g. 12:13; 13:15; 14:15–17; 17:3, 8–9; 19:25; 23:6–7, 10–12). Although what Job has stated seemingly appears to be scorning God, in fact it affirms that Job is seeking God and his answer as he has a bold faith and hope in the gracious face of God.

After the two revelations from Yahweh, Job now (42:2–6) leaves no doubt of his position as he confesses his ignorance and his presumptuousness in speaking of matters beyond his knowledge. This confession is a radical change of Job's viewpoint. At this point, the reader learns that the accuser has lost his wager. Job has proved that he has neither rejected God (i.e. he has clung to God even in the time of despair) nor stated any regret for having lived piously. Job's utter faith is now justified. It is not because of Job's own merit, but because Job is dear to God that Yahweh comes to him (cf. Job had expected he would in 14:15). The two speeches of Yahweh move Job beyond the constricted view of himself, of divine justice in terms of the retribution principle, of the world, and of God and his ways. Job is finally enlightened and humbled, accepting that as a mere human being he could not comprehend and explain God and his ways. There are many mysterious

---

99. Also Newell, "Job: Repentant," 315.

and wondrous things that beyond the boundary of human reason. The retribution principle is not enough to explain events in this life, including his innocent suffering. God is God, who is the sole ruler of the universe. His administering of the world supersedes and is outside the sphere of justice in the retribution principle. As a mere human being, Job has been granted understanding of the inscrutability of God; this, in effect, has freed him from the false expectation heightened by the view of divine justice contained in the retribution principle, which misguided him, his wife, and his friends during the discourses. Job repents and changes his mind. Through God's questions to Job, he has come to realize the limit of his reason and his ability. Job comes to the point where he is willing to accept whatever comes from God's hand in faith and to rest in whatever comes from God by trusting that God is not his enemy, even though he may be suffering along the way.

What happened to Job does not mean that God is unjust or God is his enemy. In fact, Job cannot know the reason of his suffering. But what he can do is continue to rest in trust that he has in God and in his relationship to God, even in the face of suffering. In the presence of God, Job is content. The divine mystery cannot thoroughly be made clear in human language and concepts. God's justice, as a man conceives it, is not the absolute explanation of his dealing with men. Job does not receive or know the answer. Of things beyond him, Job could not understand. And Job just accepts that truth. He is not able to know all the answers. The relationship between God and man, and specifically the relationship between Yahweh and Job, transcends divine justice as expressed by the retribution principle. The major issue of the story of Job is that suffering and death cannot always be interpreted in terms of the retribution principle. Through God's revelation, Job is brought to finally return to his right position as in the prologue (1:21). And his return to the right position of the prologue is the resolution of the rhetorical tension of the book. That resolution is still submission. Job's willingness to accept in faith whatever comes his ways without losing his trust in God that brings him back to the position in which he began, and at the same time, resolves the issue of the book. This is the message of the book: *not all the suffering is a result of reward or a punishment, and humans should not speculate about it since we do not know enough about God's ways.* Whatever comes, it does not shake Job's faith and trust in God, and it should not shake ours. Job is willing to trust in God's graciousness, even if it seems to be suffering unjustly because Job does not know whether it is God's punishment or whether some other that causes his suffering (e.g. the destructive forces in nature or the way of the fallen world).

Job comes to realize that his relationship with God must be based entirely on trust and faith in God – in the language of the accuser: "fearing God for nothing" (1:9). It is not so much that Job has passed the test, but that he comes to recognize that the retribution principle has failed. So he returns to trust in God without having to judge God's actions, which is his position at the beginning of the book. This is the resolution of the crisis of the book, which makes what follows into a true epilogue. The issues of the book are resolved now before the epilogue. The major issue of the book is now completed, and the epilogue is an afterword. It is not that Job is being rewarded in terms of the retribution principle in the epilogue. In one sense he is not rewarded, he is blessed.

The Epilogue

The epilogue of the book of Job contains only eleven verses (42:7–17). It is the voice of the narrator who gives a prose report that appears to some to reinforce what the friends have been saying all along in the dialogues, namely that piety brings major prosperity. However, it does not.

> After the Lord had spoken these words to Job, the Lord said to Eliphaz the Temanite: "My anger burns against you and against your two friends, for you have not spoken of me what is right, as my servant Job has. Now therefore take seven bulls and seven rams and go to my servant Job and offer up a burnt offering for yourselves. And my servant Job shall pray for you, for I will accept his prayer not to deal with you according to your folly. For you have not spoken of me what is right, as my servant Job has." So Eliphaz the Temanite and Bildad the Shuhite and Zophar the Naamathite went and did what the Lord had told them, and the Lord accepted Job's prayer.
>
> And the Lord restored the fortunes of Job, when he had prayed for his friends. And the Lord gave Job twice as much

as he had before. Then came to him all his brothers and sisters and all who had known him before, and ate bread with him in his house. And they showed him sympathy and comforted him for all the evil that the Lord had brought upon him. And each of them gave him a piece of money and a ring of gold.

And the Lord blessed the latter days of Job more than his beginning. And he had 14,000 sheep, 6,000 camels, 1,000 yoke of oxen, and 1,000 female donkeys. He had also seven sons and three daughters. And he called the name of the first daughter Jemimah, and the name of the second Keziah, and the name of the third Keren-happuch. And in all the land there were no women so beautiful as Job's daughters. And their father gave them an inheritance among their brothers. And after this Job lived 140 years, and saw his sons, and his son's sons, four generations. And Job died, an old man, and full of days. (Job 42:7–17)

The narrator starts a particular concluding story of Job with God's reproaching Eliphaz, the representative of the friends, for not speaking what is right (נְכוֹנָה, 42:7, 8)[100] about him as Job did. The friends think they honor God in their exhorting and condemning Job. Job once condemns the friends that they speak deceitfully for God, and so God will "surely rebuke" them (13:7–10). In God's announcement in 42:7, God, thus, condemns them and requires sacrifices for them (42:8).[101] God publicly rejects the misconception about himself that the friends have promoted, namely that Job's terrified suffering and imminent death is a result of divine punishment. God orders the friends to seek Job's prayer of intercession on their behalf. This act of Job recalls Job's role (i.e. of priest) and what he had always done for his children in the prologue (1:5). By recalling the prologue's description of Job's piety,

---

100. Koch, *TDOT* 7:89–101, suggests that the Niphal participle feminine singular form of נְכוֹנָה denotes the trustworthiness of someone's words (Ps 5:10[9]). However, Good, *In Turns of Tempest*, 381, notes more that the term does not signify "truth" in the merely intellectual sense but bears on the satisfaction of what has been established. The friends, thus, for all their certainty about traditional principle, have failed to speak satisfactorily of God, whereas Job has done so.

101. Ironic at best, Eliphaz once suggests Job that "he [God] delivers even the one who is not innocent, who will be delivered through the cleanness of your hands" (22:30).

the narrator invites the reader to see the true definition of what God now validates as "right." Before Job's prayer, God is angry, and intent on doing נְבָלָה with the friends (42:8).[102] After Job's intervention the hidden conflict between God and the friends is resolved.[103]

The restoration of Job follows. Job's full restoration (שׁוּב שְׁבוּת) (42:10) is established on several levels: "in relation to God, society, and the natural order."[104] After Job has abandoned his posture sitting on the ash heap, he is now receiving a new, restored life from the Lord. Job's material possessions are doubled.[105] This is not to highlight materialism or Job's virtue but to emphasize the magnitude of the "reward of grace."[106] At the beginning of the narrative Job was a man blessed by God. So he is again at the end of the book. This blessing is an act of grace, not a reward for Job's repentance in terms of the retribution principle, because "Yahweh's greatest gift had already been given, his fellowship, which had given Job a resolution already while still in the midst of his suffering."[107] Job's brothers and sisters came and ate in his house in order to comfort Job (42:11), fulfilling the role that the friends have intended but failed to do (2:11). Their coming happens before Job's fortunes are restored. Their communal meal marks his welcome return to social life. All the misfortunes are described as כָּל־הָרָעָה ("all the evil," 42:11) that Yahweh had brought upon him. The text underscores the agency of the satan, the accuser, as irrelevant.[108] Job is correct in his understanding that the רָעָה (i.e. "evil, harm") is indeed from Yahweh (2:10; cf. 30:26). God is the cause of his suffering, which is a part of his lordship.

---

102. For further discussion on the Hebrew text of 42:8 where God is described to be the one doing נְבָלָה, see Balentine, "My Servant Job Shall Pray for You," *ThTo* 58 (2002): 502–518.

103. The report of the fate of the friends in 42:7–9 serves as a chiastic balance of the narrative text of 2:11–13 which introduces the coming of the three friends.

104. Habel, *Book of Job*, 580.

105. Andersen, *Job*, 293, sees a connection of this text with the legislation in Exodus 22:4 and comments that "It is a wry touch that the Lord, like any thief who has been found out (Exod 22:4), repays Job double what he took from him" (also Murphy, *Book of Job*, 102).

106. Horace D. Hummel, *The Word Becoming Flesh* (St Louis, MO: CPH, 1979), 488–489.

107. Rowold, "Theology of Creation," 29, n. 22; also Fischer, "How God Pays Back," 40–41.

108. Also Habel, *Book of Job*, 585.

Job may not understand this, but he knows that all things are under God's control, and Job is content.

Significantly, the text mentions Job giving his other three daughters an inheritance among his other seven sons (42:15).[109] Like God, Job is moving beyond justice. He is being generous when he did not have to be. In terms of moral and social practice of that time, Job is not unjust, but he is being gracious. In this way Job is modeling God's behavior. God has not changed, but Job's understanding of God has changed. Job now understands that God is beyond justice. God is merciful, gracious, kind, and good. So, in some way of modeling God, Job goes beyond justice. It would have been just, as justice was understood within the cultural context of his own day, for Job to have given an inheritance to his sons but not to his daughters. That was the conventional social practice of that day. No one would have thought Job unjust, if he had not given an inheritance to his daughters. But Job acts graciously, as God has acted toward him. Having received undeserved blessings from God, Job now gives undeserved blessings to others. It is not that Job has a new understanding of God's justice, but Job's understanding that God's action cannot be explained (it cannot always be explained) in terms of justice.[110] Job now is a transformed Job. He has a new understanding about God; namely that God's ways transcend justice, especially justice as understood by the retribution principle. Job demonstrates, like God, that he is gracious and kind where he does not have to be. God is gracious and kind, and goes beyond justice. Job goes beyond justice in social conventional practice with his treatment of his daughters. His suffering and dreadful death have transformed Job to a new understanding of God that transcend justice. Justice is what Job thought he wanted from God during

---

109. Some scholars understand the ambiguous Hebrew numeral שִׁבְעָנָה in 42:13 as "twice seven," that is fourteen sons (see e.g. the Targum; Dhorme, *Commentary on the Book of Job*, 651–652; Mitchell, "Job," 170–171; Newsom, *The Book of Job*, NIB, 635; etc). This interpretation leads to the resurrection idea that Job would have fourteen sons, twice the original number (cf. 1 Chr 25:5). However, the text does explicitly confirm the double of his wealth, but not of his beloved children (i.e. not the total of twenty whom the original ten children were still there with Job). This speculative extremity should be avoided.

110. For this insight, I am indebted to Habel (*Book of Job*, 585), and Balentine (*Job*, 717). However, while Balentine sees that Job has a new understanding of what constitutes justice, the present author would see that Job goes beyond justice. It is not justice, but a generous act of Job that Job is imitating God in moving beyond justice, especially justice as comprehended by the retribution principle.

the discourses, but what Job learns in the end is that what he actually wants is something beyond justice. He wants mercy, and compassion. Eventually, Job mirrors God's action in his own action. He goes beyond justice and social convention as the way that he understands that God goes beyond justice. What Job learns is that God does not treat man solely on the basis of justice, especially justice as comprehended by the retribution principle. It is not that the retribution principle is completely wrong, for God does punish the wicked and reward the righteous, but the retribution principle is not by itself a sufficient paradigm to understand all that God does. God is certainly beyond justice in the retribution principle. Therefore, Job does not have to interpret suffering and death solely in terms of the paradigm of the retribution principle. The retribution principle has shown to be an inadequate understanding of the way of God. The retribution principle is not wholly wrong, but just not wholly right. By reporting this unusual state of affairs, the narrator masterfully gives a hint that Job now abandons and moves beyond his understanding of justice, the law of reward, and cause-effect nexus in the retribution principle.

Yahweh "blesses" (ברך; 42:12) Job. The narrator does affirm that God restores his fortune. The seventh and last appearance of the term ברך here in the epilogue highlights the full restoration of fellowship with God as Job had experienced before in the prologue (1:1–5). So this is the blessing of God. It is not divine justice, not מִשְׁפָּט. If it is the retribution principle, Job would be rewarded just because of his good deed. But the text emphasizes that Job is not being rewarded, he is being blessed. This is beyond מִשְׁפָּט. That is, not all suffering and death are tied up with מִשְׁפָּט, and not all reward or all blessing are tied up with מִשְׁפָּט. Some suffering and death happen because of destructive forces of the world, and some happen for other reasons. In the case of Job it could not know about, it could not understand. So it is not always simply a matter of מִשְׁפָּט. Here the use of the word ברך, "bless," underscores this fact. Job is granted to live twice the normal life span after his affliction – the additional 140 years (42:16). As a result, he can see four generations of his descendants. Consequently, the "happy ending" of the book of Job is that "Job died, an old man, and full of days" (וַיָּמָת אִיּוֹב זָקֵן וּשְׂבַע יָמִים; 42:17). The phrase "old and full of days" recalls the accounts of the patriarchs. Like Abraham (Gen 25:8), Isaac (Gen 35:29), and David

(1 Chr 29:28), Job's death is reported in the same manner, reflecting a grand *inclusio* with the patriarchs' accounts.[111] With Job's full restoration, long life, with a presence of a full family, the Joban author closes the story of Job with a final beautiful touch. Job's story ends with his happy death (cf. 5:26; 29:18). This peaceful death from the narrator's perspective indicates that death can be part of shalom. It is still something under God's control. It is not something to be resisted. Implicitly, it does not remove a person from God. Death here is not that important as Job has mentioned several times during the discourses with the friends. It is secondary subject to God. The resolution from God finally concludes death. The relationship between God and Job is there in such a way of Job's full days.

The freely gifted restoration in the epilogue seems to return to the truth in the retribution principle. However, the limitation of that truth is seen in the rest of the book of Job. So what is presented in 42:7–17 is not in the form of the retribution principle as appeared in the explanation of the friends. It is a form of God's authoritative freedom. And it happens only after Job has passed through his great suffering and found a greater faith in God. Thus, far from nonexistence or separation from God, death for "my servant Job" is affirmed to be what Job understood at the beginning, the natural and shalomic conclusion of a shalomic life.[112]

Job radically abandons the retribution principle (i.e. after the revelation from Yahweh) and dramatically replaces it entirely with faith and trust in Yahweh at the end of the book. Eventually, Job rests in trust of God. The death and suffering of this righteous man, which is presented as a terrible, frightening, and horrible problem in terms of the theology of retribution, at the end does not appear in that way when seen from the perspective of

---

111. In his commentary, Balentine, *Job*, 718, comments that the expression of Job's death not only links Job's death with that of Israel's revered ancestors, but also invites speculation on particular connection. He points out that "in Abraham's *insistence* that the "Judge of all the earth do what is just" (Gen 18:25), in Isaac's *trust* in his father's wisdom, even as he offers him for sacrifice on the altar (Gen 22:1–19), in David's *flawed fitness* to serve as God's king (e.g. 2 Sam 7:14–17), and also in Job, whose life embodies all their legacies in important ways, the expression "full of days" becomes an invitation to a larger understanding of what it means to live in relationship with God" (italics original).

112. For some insight of this section, I am indebted to Dr Henry Rowold's presentation on "Life and Death, Death and Life: Echoes from the Book of Job," addressed at the 17th Symposium of Concordia Seminary on 20 September 2006.

faith. Suffering and death remain a mystery in the hands of Yahweh. But when viewed through the lens of faith in a gracious God they are a mystery which is much more open and inviting. Death is no longer something to be afraid of, but a thing to be received in hope in the goodness, love, mercy, and compassion of Yahweh. At the end God remains *deus absconditus*, and by faith that is enough for Job.

CHAPTER 5

Conclusion

In the preceding chapters we have shown how Job's complex and sometimes apparently conflicting statements about death and the tension inherent in Job's encounter with the "two faces of God" are seen as connected to the theology of the retribution principle and to the claim that its view of divine justice allows human to know the hidden God. The resolution of the rhetorical tension for Job is to move from the debate about God's justice to the recognition that God transcends justice as being understood in human terms. Job is moving beyond justice to grace and compassion. As the story unfolds, Job in effect also has two faces. The struggling and despair Job views death either as a supreme example of divine justice that becomes corrupt as an unfair punishment for sin or as an escape from this unfair suffering or unjust Judge. However, the faith-filled Job views death as a shalomic end of his life before God. This view of death is peaceful and is the right position (42:2–6; cf. 1:21). This right position will occur only when Job rests in faith and trust in God, accepting whatever comes from God's hand without any question. This chapter will summarize findings and implications of the study.

Job 1

The story of Job starts with Job's faith and his pious life. The narrative stipulates that Job is the perfect man, religiously and morally. The Joban author subtly introduces the problem of the book (i.e. the right relationship between God and man) and the question of understanding of divine justice in terms of the retribution principle by the challenge that the satan put before God (1:9). As a result of the satan's questioning Job's integrity or Job's motivation, God has allowed Job to become cruelly afflicted by the lost of his property and his health. The answer of the problem is found in the divine speeches at the end of the book.

The narrative flow of the story of Job presents several stages in the development of the position of Job. In Job 1, Job's initial response is in 1:21. Job accepts submissively all bad things that happened to him. He did not ask God "why?" Here in his first response to God and his lost in the prologue, Job refuses to see any connection between his own behavior and his subsequent suffering. His confessional of faith in 1:21 indicates that Job spontaneously acknowledged that God owed him nothing, and therefore has no just cause for complaint. The question for the justice of God simply does not arise. This is vital. So Job can maintain his righteousness and loyalty to God. His first response (1:21) not only justifies God's confidence in him, but also refutes the accuser's false claim on his disinterested righteousness. Job has proved himself already in 1:21 that he will not curse God, and he can praise God even the removal of God's blessings. This response is significant. The reader sees later that Job will return to this right position again at the end of the book (42:5–6). This right response in the prologue is affirmed and appears to be the resolution of the rhetorical tension of the book. Before he returns to this correct position (i.e. trust in the truly divine truth), Job will undergo horrendous suffering and doubt about God's justice through the process of the dialogues with the friends.

Job 2

Unlike his initial response (1:21), where Job responds to no one but God, Job's second response (2:10) in the prologue is a reaction to a human being, namely to his wife. His wife functions as the first foil of the story. What she said (2:9) has the effect to interpret Job's suffering that God now does not operate his divine justice and becomes for Job an enemy. Her words are similar to what the accuser has asked God (1:9) but in a reversing direction: if God is not faithful to his divine justice, then Job should not continue to praise him; therefore, Job should "curse God, and die" (2:9). Though Job does not curse God as his wife has suggested and as the accuser has predicted two times (1:11; 2:5), he does not bless God in his second response (2:10). This response with questioning reticence signals his contradictory understanding of God's grace. Though Job has demonstrated his disinterested piety (1:5, 21) that he has not served God for the sake of only "good," he does experience a paradox in his faith in God. The visibility of his painful body anguish and dreadful death are so real.

Compounding to his wife's suggestion and his own reflection during the seven days of silence, Job has been pushed into the wilderness of doubt. In responding to "curse God, and die," Job does none of them. He does not curse God or committing a suicide. Instead of cursing God, he curses the day of his birth (Job 3) and approaches God with lament language. Instead of committing suicide, Job makes several death wishes as part of his struggle to understand his suffering as an act that comes from God and God's justice in allowing him, a righteous man, to suffer.

Job 3

In his outburst cry in chapter 3, Job begins to ask the fatal question "why?" His questioning reflects Job's acknowledgement that there is something wrong in his relationship with God. It is a lament. It is not strictly a death wish per se, but a forlorn and futile wish that God would press the delete button on his life, so that he would never have to deal with, and try to make sense of, his unbearable suffering.

What Job has uttered here in chapter 3 is outside the explanation of divine justice in the retribution principle. It is in his heart that he wants to make sense out of it. Job curses the day of his birth and the night he was conceived as he cries out in anguish. His emotional expressions appear in its deepest form. They identify the domain of life and his terrible experience in which Job deeply agonizes over what has happened to him (3:11–20). Thus, death is viewed as an escape from his suffering life. Job imagines that the land of the dead could provide him a quiet place where he could have peace, rest, and be separated from God. As Brueggemann points out, Job's lament draws God into the fray of human pain and trouble.[1] Job's deepest grievance and the most profound basis of his hope here lay in the domain of life and experience, namely, the domain of the relationship between God and man.

---

1. As Brueggemann notes, this means that God must do or be something new. Walter Brueggemann, "A Shape for the Old Testament Theology: II, Embrace of Pain," *CBQ* 47 (1985): 28–46.

The Friends and Their Views of Death and the Two Faces of YHWH

When the retribution principle is introduced from the mouth of the friends (4:6), Job's view of death then changes significantly. To Job it suddenly appears that, if the concept of divine justice articulated by his friends is true, then Job is being treated improperly by God. The friends, like Job's wife, function as a foil to Job. They offer to Job an alternative interpretation of his suffering, that God is punishing him publicly. It is Job who is wicked. It is Job who has become God's enemy and is experiencing God's wrath. Instead of putting hope in the domain of the relationship between God and man, the friends offer the claim that Job can put his hope in the domain of justice. For them this is very serious, for Job's visible suffering and his ugly imminent death are the proof that Job must be guilty of some sin(s). To be specific, they signal that Job is experiencing God's judgmental face. So what God is teaching through his suffering is important. The only resolution they try to offer to Job is that Job needs to repent his sin(s) in order to receive God's mercy once again; otherwise, Job will experience the ultimate recompense from God – death.

The point of contention between the friends and Job is the way that Job is dying. It is an ugly, terrified, and untimely death of Job that is interpreted as experiencing God's wrath. The friends' basic assumption is based primarily on the understanding of divine justice promoted by the retribution principle. Job himself also has this basic assumption in mind (cf. 19:29; 29:1–18), but he has never applied it to his own case. Thus the reader sees two different attempts to understand the faces of God, namely the friends' and Job's. It is in this context that death becomes an important issue.

In light of the retribution principle God is encountered as either punishing or rewarding, based on the unrighteousness or righteousness of the person. The friends' understanding makes both "faces of God" into behavior predictable by the moral calculus of the retribution principle. It reduces blessing to mere reward and thus eliminates gracious face of God entirely. They directly connect the life of the righteous man with a healthy and prosperous life. Their understanding of life of the righteous is very positive in the sense that the righteous will be only blessed and there will be no harm in his righteous life. The idea of blessed-only life is applied also to those who repent their sin and regain their right relationship with God. Death in this view of blessed life will be at the ripe old ages. The person will live old and be full of family. A full-of-days death is viewed as a fulfillment of a shalomic life. This projected view of life and death reduces God's mercy and his mystery to the extent that it can be predictable.

In addition, the friends interpret suffering and death, specifically a terrified or untimely death, as a consequence of sinful deeds in this life time. This is one of the fundamental problems about the friends. Their view of the relationship between God and man in general is almost exclusively in terms of justice, conditioned by the retribution principle. Death becomes the ultimate conclusion of suffering in this life. Thus, the understanding of life and death in this retributive framework is mechanical, a moral calculus. It not only reduces God's mercy to a reward for good behavior, but also constrains God within the limits of human reason. While the friends view God's treatment in light of this belief as just, Job perceives it as unjust. This is because Job does not receive what he is expecting based on the retribution principle; namely, the suffering of his righteous life is not in accord with this traditional theology. Job knows that he is not sinful, and yet he is still experiencing the judgmental face of God. By adopting the retribution principle as an explanation of the relationship between man and God, Job has lost sight of the fact that God does not deal with people solely in terms of justice, but God's relationship with man is beyond justice. It is his mercy and graciousness and his mystery that are beyond our understanding of his ways. The retribution principle by itself is not wrong, but is not wholly right, especially in the case of Job. So while the friends affirm the punishing/rewarding face of God promoted by divine justice in the retribution principle, Job rejects it. But in denying this principle, Job is left with what appears to be a diabolic, arbitrary, and capricious face of God (e.g. 6:4; 9:17; 12:9; 13:21; 16:7–13; 19:6–12, 21; 23:15–16; 30:19–22). Job characterizes God as abusive because, if the retribution principle is right, God must be unjust since he permits the righteous Job to suffer as unrighteous. What Job says about death in the disputations with the friends reflects his struggle to understand his relationship with God in terms of this principle. In fact this portrayal of God as abusive and horrible is a false picture of God that reveals the bankruptcy of the retribution principle. The retribution principle in effect eliminates the merciful face of God by making "mercy" a function of "justice." When divine justice appears (to Job) to fail, he is left with nothing for which to hope and comes to the point of despair.

Job, Death Wishes, and His View of the Two Faces of YHWH

Job's complex and sometimes apparently conflicting statements about death and the tension inherent in his encounter with these two faces of Yahweh (i.e. the punishing/rewarding and the gracious/hidden faces) are, therefore, connected to divine justice in the retribution principle and to the claim that its view of divine justice allows human to know the hidden God. To that extent, it is significant to understand that Job's many wishes for death are part of his argumentation with God. They are part of his own inner struggle of trying to know what is wrong in his relationship with God. Job cannot bear for this judgmental face of God to look upon him and thus longs for death as escape, from suffering and/or from God. Every time that Job wishes for death, the plea is addressed either directly or indirectly to God. For example, Job's opening lament (Job 3) is his emotional outburst: "why" God creates him for such a fearful fate. He, embittered by such fate, wishes for the grave with the hope that it could provide him a place separated from God. After the friends have accused him of sin on the basis of their counsel shaped by the retribution principle (4:6), his problem becomes more complex by their accusation. Job argues that they are not true to their function. Their defense of God on the basis of human reason leads Job away from the *deus absconditus* that alone preserves the gracious face of God. The struggling Job, thus, begs God to mercifully grant him a swift death (6:8–10). He is willing to be "cut off" by God's hand, not by a gross sin. As death appears to be an inevitable result of his inexplicable sufferings, he prefers to have a swift death from God. At all times, Job recognizes the reality of death. The expressions like "I shall be no more" (7:21), "the land of deep darkness," and "the land of no return" (10:21–22; cf. 7:9; 16:22) are examples of his cries in despair, reflecting the relational symbiosis between God and man. These expressions also specify not only Job's view of life as cruel but also his view of God as cruel. As death is the land of no return, God seemingly could not retrieve him back; so then God will lose him, his worshipper, forever. Death is seen as an escape from his terrible situation. Death itself, which is under the control of God and for which Job yearns for several times in the dialogues, becomes in the dynamic movement of the text a source of despair for Job.

However, when Job thinks in terms of his integrity, the increasing certainty of his imminent death forces him to seek help from someone or something who would speak for him: the earth (16:18), a heavenly witness (16:19), an inscribed text (19:23), an engraved rock (19:24), and a redeemer (19:25). Sometimes it grants him strength and he does not want to die (17:8–9). Other times he wishes to "see" God either through "an umpire" (9:33) or by himself (13:3, 20; 19:26b–27; 23:3; 31:35). Job cries out, sometimes in hope, sometimes in despair, sometimes for an intermediary who could plead his case before God and seek justice on his behalf. These cries, including his wishes for death, are part of his struggle to understand his suffering as an act that comes from God, and especially with God's justice in dealing with him (i.e. in allowing him, a righteous, to suffer). The two faces of Job (i.e. the despairing Job and the faithful Job) reflect his own psychological conflict, a cognitive dissonance, as he struggles with the difference between what he has faith in (divine justice) and the actual experience in his life. Job and his friends could not find any resolution to the question "why?" There is no escape from the contradiction because the retribution principle in Job's specific case is fundamentally wrong. The workings of divine justice are not comprehensible to human logic. By implication, death (i.e. the ugly and untimely death) is fearful, threatening, and mysterious within divine governance. The fundamental problem of Job's friends (and later of Job himself) is that they view the whole of the relationship between God and man in terms of justice. This is compounded by their attempt to understand divine justice in terms of the retribution principle. Since there is no answer from the disputations with the friends, Job must turn to God, the primary source of his conflict.

Job's concluding speeches, chapters 29–31, also present Job in defiance against the theology of divine justice as presented by the friends, but in view of hope. As already mentioned about chapter 29, where Job reminisces on his previous shalomic life, death is viewed as natural, and a culmination of life (i.e. "full of days"), not an enemy that separates a child of God from

God (29:2–4, 18; cf. life in 1:1–5). In chapter 30, Job describes his present situation in an inversion of his past (ch. 29). As a result of the misguided influence of his friends, Job can only perceive the judgmental face of God through the system of divine retribution. Significantly, even though the judgment includes a blessing for obedience it has no room for the gracious and merciful face of God. Job's words in the second half of this chapter (30:20–31) make clear that one thing remains constant, that is, Job still "holds fast in his integrity" (cf. 2:3), with the faint hope that God will respond to his cry with the friendship he desperately expects ("I cry to you for help," 30:20, 24, 28; cf. 29:4). Job's last speech (ch. 31) sets the stage for Job to move beyond the retribution principle and find hope in the graciousness of God. Job is preparing the first movement or the first step in coming to understand that God does not always function in terms of divine justice, that his only source of comfort lies in the fact that God is gracious, not in the fact that God is just. As Job makes his request to plead his case before God (31:35), his oath presents his own inner transformation.[2]

Job's last speeches (29–31), thus, are not to utter an indictment, but to invite an embrace. They represent Job starting to move beyond the retribution principle, not just an appeal for justice within it.[3] They also move the struggling Job to look for a peaceful death in face of his imminent and dreadful death. As Job reminisces about the gracious and passionate aspect of God in chapter 29 and expresses the "cruel" aspect of God in chapter 30, Job is struggling with these two aspects of God, which is inexplicable and in conflict with divine retribution. So to move from the judgmental face of God to the gracious face of God, one has to leave the retribution principle behind. As Job struggles with these two aspects of God, he approaches God by submitting his conscience to the judgment of God (i.e. submitting his oath)[4] with the hope that the imminent death that Job fears in chapter 30 will become a desirable and peaceful death as Job predicts in chapter 29.

---

2. Janzen, "Job's Oath," *RevExp* 99 (2000): 597–603, comments that "this [chapter 31] is not an act of moral bitterness. It is an act in which he [Job] reaches beyond his bitterness, beyond his own self-knowledge, to God. And the oath that bridges the abyss between his inner self and God becomes the avenue along which God's response can come to him."

3. The details of Job's oath of innocence or self-glorification possibly are one of the inevitable results of the doctrine of individual retribution of the Old Testament.

4. This is what Janzen calls Job's "self-imprecating language" (*Job*, 210–212).

Job will find out later that the encounter with God collides to recognize that God in his freedom will act as he acts. What Job is called to do is to rest in faith and to trust in God's mercy, in his grace and compassion, even in the midst of suffering; rather than trying to explain it. By approaching his own struggling from the perspective of faith, Job's view of his suffering, of God and his ways, and of death are all changed to what we have at the end of the book. Job accepts in faith whatever comes from God.

The YHWH Speeches – The Resolution of the Book

At the end of the book, God calls Job to trust in his care for Job without demanding (or expecting) an answer to the question of his suffering (which, by the way, Job never receives). Only when Job does so can he return to his peaceful view of death. The hidden face of God is presented and is not the punishing/rewarding face of God as the friends have explained. God's revelation and speeches make clear to Job that there is no "answer" to the "why?" (cf. the reader does know "why"). Significantly, Yahweh is not coerced by Job's oath of innocence, but rather he has come out of concern for his servant Job. He appears when he wants to (i.e. in his freedom). The two speeches of Yahweh are corresponding to the two heavenly scenes in the prologue. Likewise, God's freedom has been presented in the frame narrative of the story. God's appearance here after the speeches of Elihu is a delay after chapter 31, where Job wants to see God.

More significantly, the moment that Yahweh begins to address Job, Job already receive his answer. However, the answer is beyond expectation and not what Job has been inquired. It is that God cares enough about Job to reveal himself to him, a human,[5] and to give him "some intimation of the order and direction of his creation."[6] The two speeches of Yahweh, thus, present the mystery and unknowable of the truly divine truth. They also implicitly reject the false foundation of the retribution principle. They present instead God's nurture and care of the world which is mysterious and

---

5. Janzen, *Job*, 229, insightfully notes that humankind is present is chapters 38–41 as the addressee to whom Yahweh offers the descriptions. This means Job is not insignificant. God is giving Job a new dimension of considering himself: "To be a human being is to be a creature who is yet God's addressee and whom God confronts with the rest of creation vocationally."

6. Alter, *Biblical Poetry*, 87.

no divine justice in retributive terms. It is life, not death that is portrayed in these two speeches.

In the two speeches of Yahweh (38:1—41:26 [41:34]), Job (and the reader) are presented with images of the boundaries and laws and rules of a well-ordered and coherent world. The images of care and tenderness, and images of wildness and strangeness are present: wild seas, wild animals, and wild weather, the uncertainties of the night, and Behemoth and Leviathan. While the proponents of mythological readings understand these images as, for example, "evil powers active in both the natural and supernatural world,"[7] a more literary reading of these images reflects the fact that at the heart of God's lordship there remains a mystery. These wonders are revealed to Job in order to show him how inadequate his understanding of the ways of God has been. On a literary level, these two speeches do not voice much about death.[8] Rather, the loving but hidden face of Yahweh and the hiddenness of his way are revealed. The content in these speeches has evidently no direct concern on Job's personal suffering or his whishes for death. Significantly, they speak highly of the sustaining of life and the mystery of God's lordship. More significantly, they are keys to Job's acceptance of God's care without having to understand, which transforms Job's view of death. The rhetorical and challenging questions aim not to merely display God's mighty lordship, but also for the purpose of revealing the nature of God's relationship with man. Job is called to accept the limitations of human understanding of Yahweh and his ways and to subject his understanding of all things, including death, to the mysterious and arbitrary lordship of God.

The first speech (38:1—39:30) focuses on the issue of the "design" or "lordship" (עֵצָה) of God (38:2). God asks Job rhetorical questions because Job has interpreted his undeserved suffering and terrified death in terms of a wrong and hardheaded understanding of the way in which God performs in this world. Job, like his friends, has believed in a strict retributive principle that every cause has its logical and appropriate consequence and that all suffering is rooted in sinful behaviors. With a strong belief in his own righteousness, the problem lies with God, who has designed this world with

---

7. Fyall, *My Eyes*, 73–81.

8. The only explicit place that mentions death is in the first speech of Yahweh: Job 38:16–18.

chaotic elements. God reveals his design of this world and presents to Job his lordship over the world of nature and animals. The images of the cosmos and of the wild animals portray God as not cruel or capricious, but as who cares, protects, and provides abundantly to all under his lordship. Moreover, the mysterious ways of God in his creation reveal that creation is not subject to human reason. It is what it is. Man cannot explain it. Job is right when he states to his friends that this world does not function in a strictly ordered way (12:1–25); however, his interpretation is wrong for it is precisely this kind of world God designed for a specified purpose which humans cannot fully understand. Human suffering and those dreadful deaths "may indeed occur in a good, well-ordered, and reliable creation, for that world is not a risk-free world! Indeed, being a part of such a world means that suffering can take place quite apart from sin and evil,"[9] that is, for reasons that are not part of the moral calculus of the retribution principle. So, in that sense, the speech is not so much of God's gracious face, but is more of his hidden face. What God has said reaffirms the hiddenness of God, that Job has to trust in faith that the hidden God is the gracious God. God's call for Job, a גֶּבֶר, to "gird up his loins" (38:3; 40:7) is a call for him to probe his experience of suffering more deeply in terms of God's complex and hidden design of the creation and man's limited place within it.

In the second speech of Yahweh, Job has been charged particularly on accusing God of his justice (מִשְׁפָּט).[10] Yahweh says: "Will you even put me in the wrong? Will you condemn me that you may be in the right?" (40:8). As a model of moral virtue, Job has expected to receive what he deserves.

---

9. Fretheim, *God and World*, 235. Fretheim's point is that suffering can occur in God's not-a-risk-free world. He sees that suffering can take place apart from sin and evil by pointing that the primary cause of Job's suffering in Job 1–2 is natural evil/harm. However, Freitheim misses the fundamental problem of Job's suffering. It is true that Job's tragedies are from moral evil (i.e. the wicked men-Sabeans and Chaldeans) and natural evil (i.e. fire and lightning, windstorm, and disease). However, these are means that God uses to inflict Job. Therefore, God and his decision that he allows these means to befall on Job are in fact Job's fundamental problem. Job does not understand why God does not act justly according to what he has believed in the divine justice. Thus, Job's suffering cannot be explained plainly by natural evil/harm in the not-a-risk-free world. The resolution of Job's problem must be found only from God himself. However, from the perspective of wisdom and creation theme, Fretheim's contribution to the book of Job and other books in the whole bible is very useful indeed.

10. Note that Newsom, *The Book of Job: A Contest*, 248, thinks differently that the second speech of Yahweh "says nothing new. Since Job appears to be hard of hearing, God simply repeats the message, louder and more slowly."

With this kind of expectation, he is reflecting that he should not have served God for nothing. Like his friends, he has accepted divine justice and put his trust in the individual retribution based on a logical account between deeds and rewards. As Job attempts to apply the rule of the retribution principle to his life, he not only concludes that he could do better than God but also that God is wrong in not performing divine justice. Job, thus, is guilty of this kind of attitude toward God because by implication it was as if he were a rival god. Yahweh, thus, challenges Job to take over the administration of justice over this world if he could (40:9–14). Obviously, Job could not do that. As Job and the friends assume the divine principle as the operative dynamic of divine lordship, and as Job also performs that principle, "there would be certain and comprehensive death for the wicked,"[11] which is not necessarily to be known to us.

Yahweh confronts Job with Behemoth and Leviathan, creatures *par excellence*. The scholarly interpretation of these two monsters varies from literal animals (e.g. hippopotamus or water buffalo, and sea-serpent) to mythic forces of evil (i.e. Mot, a god of death, its subordinate, and the so-called "Satan"). Though they have some mythic tonal connotation, the study views them as figurative. On a literary level, they serve as literal animals which are employed by the Joban author as part of God's diverse and beautiful world. Any relations they may have to ancient Near Eastern reputations are "literary not substantive."[12] Behemoth is not a figure of the Canaanite Mot, a god of death. Leviathan is not the power of evil, the so-called "Satan," as understood by those who approach the book of Job with mythological reading. Rather they function literarily as exemplars of God's pride in his creation. God is not engaged in a battle with these two beasts.[13] God celebrates and praises these wonderful creatures with pride, and even in awe of them. The text seems to present God's delight in their power, beauty, and independent fearlessness.[14] This contrasts with how a man would view

---

11. Rowold, "Life and Death," 11.

12. Newsom, *The Book of Job: A Contest*, 248.

13. Contrary to Perdue, *Wisdom and Creation*, 179.

14. Newsom, *The Book of Job: A Contest*, 243–244, 248–252, rightly observes that there "is a little or no reference to enmity or hostility between God and these creatures" (cf. O'Connor, "Wild, Raging Creativity," 176–177).

these terrifying beasts, thus illustrating the gap between man's understanding and God's. As Behemoth's anger and his special status in God's creation are the emphasis of the text, they do also represent Job's anger and his special status of a man created in the image of God. Likewise, Leviathan's tongue is figuratively portrayed to mirror Job's own fierce, rebellious words and his protests during the discourses. Both of them, as Gammie proposes, are mirrors of Job's self, his own beauty and fearlessness in protesting to God.[15] As they are chaos forces, Yahweh reveals also his power, and authority over these chaos forces (cf. לִי־הוּא, "he is mine," 41:3 [Eng 41:11]). More importantly, these pre-eminent creatures do not question God's justice but simply accept what comes from God's hand. They are what Job should learn from and be like. God is God, and Job is a creature, belonging to God – this simple but fundamental relationship is the primary effect of this encounter.

Significantly, God's perspective on Behemoth and Leviathan signify the truth that God is not bound by or to the operative retribution principle, but is the Sovereign, who is free and unbounded by human logic. God invites Job to step beyond the constricted view of himself, of God, of the world that is offered by the theology of retribution. God's justice and the problem of human suffering and death cannot be reduced to a formula that allows man to predict what God will do. The two speeches of Yahweh invite Job to acknowledge the limits of his own understanding and to accept God's authoritative freedom and hiddenness in this world. They are not condemnation – God accepts all those complaints and the accusations that Job made on him. They function as a mean to help Job to understand his smallness. They also invite Job to take his place along with the mountain goat, the wild ass and the wild ox, the wild horse and even the silly ostrich, and all of that other things, even Behemoth and Leviathan, in the עֵצָה of Yahweh. They trust in God's care for them and submissively receive whatever comes from God's hand. God preserves his own freedom in the lordship of this world. Suffering and death are part of his mysterious lordship. They are far beyond the reach of human reason. God's way of dealing with humanity is to grant life, so that Job can respond to Yahweh's implicit invitation to return to a relationship of love and trust in him. Thus, death is not the final end or the

---

15. Gammie, "Behemoth and Leviathan," 217–231.

ultimate will of God. While death is threatening, unwelcome, and viewed as a punishment matter under the divine retribution, it serves instead to sustain life. Death itself, then, is a positive matter under the lordship of God. It becomes a secondary subject to God. Suffering and death still remain, but they do not destroy the relationship with God. Job cannot understand them, but by trusting in God's graciousness he need not fear them.

Job's Restoration from Death to Life

In response to Yahweh's implicit invitation, and over and above Job's reluctant submission in 40:4–5, Job responds in faith to Yahweh (42:5–6). He repents of what he ended up making of himself (i.e. a rival god), and, in the process, what he ended up making of God (i.e. an abusive, capricious Judge). In fulfillment of the vision in chapter 19, Job says that "My ears had heard of you, but now my eyes have seen you" (NIV, 42:5).[16] Already before death, while still on the way to death (42:17), but fundamentally unthreatened by death, Job has already seen God, which by extension allows him to see himself in his presumptiveness which leads to repentance, but also see himself standing before a gracious, accepting God. Job receives a full restoration to life in the epilogue (42:7–17). Job's acceptance by God is affirmed by God's call that Job serve as intercessor for the friends (42:8, 10), so that even they whose words are deemed folly by God (42:8) are brought into a right relationship with God.

In addition, Job's struggling with a judgmental God against a merciful God, with hope in despair, with sight in darkness, and with life under threat of death; in this place God declares that Job has spoken of him "what is right" (נְכוֹנָה, 42:7). Job may have spoken with despair and anger, but Job was closer to God in his struggling with God than were the friends in their defending their ability to understand the way that God works. The friends in all their certainty about the dogma of retribution have erred by assuming that Job must have sinned since God, the righteous, must have a good reason

---

16. In his article, "Life and Death," 15, Rowold rightly comments that "what Job means when he talks about the time that my ears had heard of you is likely, not his time of dispute and accusation, but his time before all this began (e.g. 1:1–5), when he, like the friends (4:3–4), knew much about God, which after all that God has led him through, is only hearsay compared with "seeing" God in his own life and on God's terms."

for letting him suffer. Job also has erred by assuming that God must be unfair to let him, a righteous man, suffer. However, unlike the friends, Job does not believe that God is only just. He merely could not see how God has been being gracious to him at the moment. Though Job has mocked God in his speeches, he has never lost his faith. Job approached God and hoped in the gracious face of God. As a consequence, the "happy ending" of the book of Job is that "Job died, an old man, and full of days" (42:17). Thus, far from nonexistence or separation from God, death for "my servant Job" is on one level the natural and shalomic conclusion of a shalomic life. Significantly it is the mark of the continued blessing of God, the God whose lordship includes death, the God who calls Job to himself where there is no death.[17]

Job demands liberation from the explanation of suffering in terms of divine justice, and later death in despair at the failure of divine justice. In the end he receives restoration of his fortunes, not as divine justice but as a divine gift. It is not a reward, but a blessing from God. For the outsider it might seem that the concept of retribution still functions: Retribution may be delayed, but it still works. God's final words to Job's friends are an explicit rejection of this position. For the knowledgeable insider it is evident that it has changed.[18] Job never learns the reason for his suffering, and stops seeking it. The friends, perhaps, continue to think Job must have sinned. Job is at peace, however, because he has learned to accept in faith all that come from God's hand. In this way Job has moved beyond justice. What Job gets is not a retributive payment from God for being falsely accused but a gift from God, who is free and not constrained by human thought. Wisdom comes not in understanding the way God and the cosmos work, but in a proper "fear of Yahweh" (28:28) that recognizes that man cannot understand God's way. The phrase "the fear of the Lord" almost always means to understand one's place before God rightly, to understand one's relationship with God as creature. This means that one must know one's limitation rather than to question God. This is also a conclusion of the whole book, that the retribution principle represents a form of human wisdom, a way of trying to figuring it out the way the world works by some observations.

---

17. For part of this section, I am indebted to Rowold, "Life and Death."
18. Fischer, "How God Pays Back," 39.

This effort, the experiences of Job reveal, does not work. It might work if we knew everything that God knows, but we do not. Human understanding has limits, and so trust in Yahweh alone can find peace, even in death. Job, therefore, comes to recognize that God's ways transcend the retribution principle, and this extends even to death. Rather than trying to understand death in terms of what man can know (i.e. in terms of human wisdom), Job accepts death however it comes from the hand of God. This is the view of death in terms of the fear of the Lord. Contrary to his wife, who denies God as not keeping divine retribution at the outset, Job's final response (42:2–6) is to simply trust in Yahweh: trust in God's goodness, grace and love, and not assume knowledge of divine justice. It is the right response which Job started out since in the prologue (1:21). It is this position where Job rests in faith and trust in God accepting whatever comes from God's hand without any question.

In summary, Job turns against the view of God that would be required by the theology of retribution, and which was advanced by the friends in the dialogues, and consequently questions the concept of retribution. At the end of the book, Yahweh does speak to Job. The simple fact that Yahweh's speeches do not answer all of Job's questions means that suffering and death remain mysterious. They remain a part of God's unknowable ways. By implication, we simply do not know and we do not need to know in every case why there is suffering and why there is terrified and untimely death. The divine speeches enable Job not only to realize that his understanding of divine retribution is wrong, but also his attempt to impose a limited human understanding of justice upon God is fundamentally offensive to God. Yahweh has introduced the whole new perspective for the world and for the mystery of the world. The world of animals, for example, shows that justice is not "a rule" for their existence. Questions of God's "good" and "justice" cannot be answered by Job and are thus irrelevant. The ways of God transcend "morality," and "justice," as these terms may be understood by man. Under his lordship, divine justice is God's sovereignty over his universe.[19] The portrayal of the dynamics of the world points to the authoritative

---

19. Cf. Sylvia Huberman Scholnick, "Poetry in the Courtroom: Job 38–41," in *Sitting with Job: Selected Studies on the Book of Job*, ed. Roy B. Zuck (Grand Rapids: Baker, 1992), 421–439.

freedom of God and the limitations of Job's understanding of God and his way. Though God's system of justice is far more complex, God's grace and mercy transcend his justice. God does not operate the world under the concept of retribution. Job learns to trust in the gracious face of God even when all he can see is the judgmental face of God. God does have his own authoritative freedom. "God has a committed relationship to that world to let it be what it was created to be (Gen 8:22). Such a commitment means divine constraint and restraint in the exercise of power in the life of the world."[20] When Yahweh reveals to Job the mystery of suffering and death – when the mystery is part of Yahweh's gracious lordship, including Job's life – Job has no need to understand everything. He must simply trust in Yahweh. The appearance of Yahweh (i.e. the theophanic mode in that God's speaking is accompanied by meteorological phenomena [e.g. Ezek 1:4, "stormy" wind]), his revelation to Job (i.e. Yahweh reveals creation order which is all under his lordship), and the acceptance of Job from Yahweh (i.e. Yahweh does not condemn, nor kill, nor reject, but accept Job) are things Job does not have in the earlier part of the book. Through these gracious revelations from God, Job comes to a new understanding not only of the failure of retribution principle but also of the necessity for faith. Job discerns that God is not simply the keeper of retribution principle, but is free. While Job's wife denies God and urges Job to curse God and die, Job overcomes those wrong ideas and gains a new understanding of his relationship to God. Job cannot understand the way God is. He simply trusts in God. Job radically abandons the retribution principle (i.e. after the revelation from Yahweh) and dramatically replaces it entirely with his faith and trust in Yahweh at the end of the book.

Likewise his understanding of death is radically changed at the end of the book. When all is right, death is natural and accepted, even welcome. It becomes a culmination of life, and not an enemy that separates a child of God from God. When all is not right, death is viewed as threatening and disruptive, even punitive. Because life and death are under the lordship of God, a yearning and a conviction of life that is not destroyed by death is also one of the unique perspective on life and death in the book of Job. Thus,

---

20. Fretheim, "God in the Book of Job," *CurTM* 26 (1999): 87–91.

death is not the final end or the ultimate will of God. It becomes a secondary, unimportant thought. The ultimate insignificance of death is also part of a significance of death in the book of Job. Death, which begins as a terrible, frightening, and horrible problem, at the end does not appear in that way when seen from the perspective of faith. After Job receives a new understanding about God and the world, and his own place in God's creation, suffering and death not only remain, but also become a positive mystery in the hand of Yahweh. When viewed through the lens of faith in a gracious God they are a mystery which is much more open and inviting. Death in the face of this grace may be reality but not disruption. Death is no longer something to be afraid of, but must be embraced in hope in the goodness, love, mercy, and compassion of Yahweh. At the end God remains *deus absconditus*, and by faith that is enough for Job (42:5; cf. Jer 15:20; Hab 2:3–4).

Some Theological Reflections

This understanding of Job's struggle to understand his suffering and its result has implications for a number of other secondary issues related to Job and his experiences.

Job's Wife

The prologue does not focus on the character of Job's wife or the motivation behind her words. So she is not the Satan's subordinate, as understood by those who approach the book of Job with mythological reading. Interestingly, she is the only character who is vocal in the book, but has no name. She plays a role of a literary foil in the story of Job. Her words, like the three friends', are deemed folly. She suggests to Job that "Do you still hold fast your integrity? Curse God and die" (Job 2:9). For her, there is no retribution for being faithful. She denies God, not in an atheistic sense, but as not keeping the doctrine of retribution in this world. It seems that for her a God, who does not keep divine retribution, is not reliable for man.[21] Thus, she suggests that Job "curse God." Her last advice for Job is "to die." However, in a literary movement, she, like the satan, is a marginal person. She is not mentioned anywhere else, except in the prologue and in the epilogue.

---

21. Also Fischer, "How God Pays Back," 37–38.

Therefore, her appearances are to emphasize the preciousness of Job's faith. In the story, she is the most surprising character. She, like Job, is brought out of the retribution principle, and has a new life with Job. And therefore she has a new life with God. At the end, both Job and his wife are blessed with all the children. Job's wife, therefore, shares with Job the blessings that God has given to Job.

Job and the Afterlife

There is certainly a sense of life after death in which Job hopes. However, the main point within the book of Job is that Job is not willing to accept the answer that the theology of retribution will balance itself out in the afterlife (e.g. Ps 73 and Hab 2, where the scale of divine justice will be balanced in the eschaton). Job contemplates this position, but sets it aside in favor of seeking an answer to the problem of divine justice in the here and now; that is why the resurrection and the afterlife are not emphasized in the story of Job. Ultimately what God reveals to Job is that in the here and now Job must simply trust in the graciousness and mercy of a God whose purposes and ways are hidden from the reason of man (i.e. a hidden God who finally reveals himself in Christ). So in the end, the answer that God gives Job is much like the answer that he gives to Habakkuk 2 and in Psalm 73 – Today the righteous must walk in faith and trust, and not by sight. Unlike Habakkuk 2 and Psalm 73, the difference in the book of Job is that there is no affirmation that the scale of divine justice will be balanced in the afterlife; the emphasis is on trusting in the graciousness of God without demanding an answer, even when God's graciousness and mercy seem to be hidden. This is not a rejection of the view that God will balance the scale of justice in the eschaton, it is a positive assertion of the nature of the life of the believer in the here and now.

Job and Christian Theology

In understanding Christian typology, it is important to distinguish the role of the type in its historical and literary context from the ultimate fulfillment in Christ to which the type points. In this way one may affirm both the reality and importance of the type in its own context and the way in which the type points forward to God's fuller revelation in Christ. This approach shapes our understanding of both the redeemer figure and the roles of Behemoth and Leviathan in the book of Job.

For the redeemer figure in Job 19, it is important to understand this figure in the context of the unfolding narrative of the story. At this point Job is looking for someone who will defend his case. Job thinks of redeemer figure primarily in terms of defense and vindication. And the point which God calls him ultimately is repentance and trust. When viewed from the perspective of the revelation of God in Christ, however, the redeemer figure in Job anticipates the full revelation of biblical understanding of Redeemer, and thus may be understood as a type of Christ. That is not, however, the main point here. Within the context of the book of Job, Job is looking for a vindication in here and now, not eschatologically before God. He is looking for somebody who can side with him now. And within the context of the book of Job, the question that Job tries to get an answer to, the ultimate answer is not found in the redeemer figure, who plays no part in the concluding chapters of the book. The ultimate answer is found in Job's acceptance of the need to move away from the retribution principle as a way to understand the relationship to God and simply trusting in God's graciousness and mercy. So while the redeemer figure is an important step in the revelation of Christ as Redeemer, it is clearly secondary to the resolution of Job's struggle. It appears rarely and is entirely omitted in God's speeches and in Job's responses to them. This is really part of Job's seeking of vindication in here and now within the book of Job itself.

Ultimately it is true that Yahweh's rule over the Behemoth and Leviathan are a type of God's victory over the "Satan." However, that is not the point of the book of Job. Ultimately seen from the perspective of reading this from the New Testament Christian, it is a type of the victory of Yahweh over the "Satan." Whenever Yahweh defeats those who are opposed him, it is ultimately a type of Christ's victory over on the cross. So in one sense, it is a type of Christ's victory over the "Satan."

However, that is not the main point within the book of Job itself. Both Behemoth and Leviathan are more as a critique of Job's trust in human reason and his arrogance and pride in questioning God (i.e. in his presumptiveness). Job's reaction to divine speech in chapter 41 is the recognition of the need to his own repentance (42:2–6). So the conclusion of that is Job's repentance.

The reader sees, at least in the book of Job, that Job responds to what God said about Leviathan by repenting. This is the chief part of his response. So clearly, within the context of the book of Job, God's comments about the Leviathan are taking by Job as an indication that Job needs to repent. This understanding is presented within the text itself. God's comments about Leviathan are understood by Job as a critique of himself.

This study has de-emphasized the Leviathan-Satan connection. This is because those who take a mythological approach have tended to elevate Behemoth and Leviathan to being equals with Yahweh, reading the text in the light of the dualistic/polytheistic religion of Ugarit. To counter their errors, this study has demonstrated that it is possible to understand Behemoth and Leviathan (who play a relatively small role in the overall book) within the literary framework of the book itself. Certainly, within the book, Behemoth and Leviathan are connected with disorder and chaos, and so in some sense are opposed to God. But they are never seen as equals with Yahweh. They serve as exemplars to Job of the mystery of God's creation, and the limits of Job's ability to comprehend God's ways. Certainly the present author would agree that Yahweh's rule over Behemoth and Leviathan is a type of God's ultimate victory over the Satan on the cross, but that is not the main point within the book of Job itself. Within the book itself, the primary role of these figures is to represent the arrogance of Job's trust in human reason as he questions God. So, for instance, Job's reaction to God's speech about Leviathan in Job 41 is the recognition of the need of his own repentance (42:2–6). In other words, God's comment about Leviathan is understood by Job as a critique of Job.

By implication, the book of Job presents a coherent gospel message on its own terms: the hidden God is gracious and merciful (Exod 34:5–7), and those who live by faith trust in God's graciousness and do not understand their relationship with God to be governed by the moral calculus of divine justice in the retribution principle (i.e. expecting reward and punishment based on their good works), but trust in the graciousness and mercy of God alone.

Death in the Mythological and Literary Readings of Job

It is true that there is the presence of mythological allusion in the book of Job. However, as McKenzie points out, the Old Testament often revised existing myths for its own usage.[22] The Joban author does put a highly international character in his work. Those mythological allusions of death are used as lively pictorial figurative, or poetic language. For example, in Job 3, the references to those who dwell in Sheol (3:13–19): kings, prisoners, slaves, the wicked, are recalling a passage in the "Epic of Gilgamesh" telling that the underworld (the house of dust) comprises of kings and commoners.[23] The point of our text in Job 3 is to show that Job is looking for a place where all men are equal in death, a place providing to all a peaceful rest. The text uses those references merely to highlight the contrast between Job's present troubled life and the peace in the land of the dead. Likewise, the description of the realm of the death as deep darkness in 10:21–22 gives the reader the tension between the land of life and light, where Job yearns for, and the chaotic and gloomy atmosphere of the land of the dead, where he will finally descend. Other references to the personified Death are employed, for example, in a hymn to wisdom (28:22). Job meditates in verse 12 where wisdom should be found. It is not in the land of the living (v. 13), nor in the deep (v. 14). In addition, Abaddon and Death, powers of underworld, declare that they have heard a rumor of it (v. 22). Thus, the land of the dead here is described as in the depths of the ocean.[24] These expressions or motifs employ terms and phrases that may be part of the fund of religious language common throughout the ancient Near East, but this does constitute the adoption of the worldview of Israel's neighbors. They are simply part of the rhetoric of the book of Job.

The forgoing studies have affirmed that the mythological reading of the text of Job is not only a false approach to understanding the concept of death in the book of Job, but leads to a mistaken conclusion that death is a competing power or god (i.e. Mot, the god of death, in the Canaanite culture). The tendency of this group of scholars to see mythology everywhere "results in

---

22. John L. McKenzie, *Myths and Realities: Studies in Biblical Theology* (Milwaukee: Bruce Publishing, 1963), 182.

23. See Pritchard, ed., *Ancient Near Eastern Text*, 72.

24. The studies of the mythological allusions of death in the book of Job are out of the scope of this study. However, there are many scholarly works on this specific topic, see, for instance, John Barclay Burns, "The Mythology of Death in the Old Testament," 327–340; James Barr, "The Meaning of Mythology in Relation to the Old Testament," *VT* 9 (1959): 1–10; Elmer B. Smick, "Mythology and the Book," 221–229; Smick, "Another Look," 231–244; etc.

more misinterpretation than the well-meant but misdirected attempt to rule out all mythological expression. Reading primitive meaning into a piece of monotheistic literature where the idiom can be viewed as a result of simple observation or the use of quaint expressions is poor methodology."[25] Such interpreters tend not to treat Job's understanding of the concept of death contextually within a literary framework of the book, and as a result they misinterpret the theological meaning of the concept of death. By reading Job as an exemplar of the broader ancient Near Eastern religious context, rather than as an exemplar of the Israelite wisdom tradition, they impose a dualistic worldview upon the text of Job. They misdirect the reader from seeing Job as a monotheistic person who views death as under the lordship of Yahweh. Their interpretation concerning death, hence, is false and anachronistic in the context of Old Testament wisdom literature.

This study has anticipated the affirmation that Job's reflection on the subject of life and death are part of the broader issue within the book (i.e. the relationship between God and man, and not, as is sometimes suggested, between God and Satan). Job's understanding of death grows from his struggle to conceive whether the retribution principle is right or not. If it is right, then the three friends are right: Job must have sinned and must be under God's judgmental face. Job, therefore, might see death alternately as an escape, a punishment, a warning (cf. Elihu), or an ultimate recompense from the wrathful God, because he has done something wrong, something he does not understand. But if the theology of divine retribution is wrong, then there may be some other explanation for Job's suffering and imminent death. Job can be right in affirming his innocence and righteousness, and still suffer because there is no connection between suffering and punishment. His suffering is not necessarily the proof that God is wrathful toward him. Thus, despite suffering Job can conceive death as a rest or as a peaceful death which fulfills his life.

Job's argument is that, assuming God is just, the theology of divine retribution can not be right because he is innocent. Job tries to justify himself in a variety of ways using his own reason. Job, sometimes like the friends and his wife, calls upon the retribution principle as a way of explaining how

---

25. Smick, "Mythology and the Book," 222.

God works in this world. The three friends attempt to impose the retribution principle on Job's suffering. Their conclusion would be that either God is unjust or Job has sinned. But since God can not be unjust, the only reasonable cause of Job's affliction is to be found in Job himself and not in God: Job must, therefore, have sinned; there is no other explanation. There is truth in the retribution principle; namely, that God blesses the righteous and punishes the wicked. However, this truth is not adequate to explain suffering in every situation. There are times when bad things happen to good people; as well as times when good things happen to bad people. When things do not happen according to the principle, it does not mean that God is not just or God is not good. Rather God does preserve his own freedom in his will and acts. The fact that Job is suffering in this life and will eventually die does not prove that he is encountering God's wrathful face. Rather it is coincidental to the relationship between him and God. This literary reading, hence, is a competent reading that brings out the main message of the story and is able to lead the reader to see the development of the argument and the resolution of the argument at the end of the book.

Job in the Canon

The book of Job is not just an account of Job experience, but it is also within the canonical of the Old Testament. It serves the function within the canon as a corrective to a misapplication of the theology of the Deuteronomy. We cannot lose sight of the fact that the book of Job is canonical. It is not just the experience of one individual. Job's experience reflects something universal in the experience of God's people, and serves as a corrective to an oversimplistic application of an element that is in the mainstream of the Old Testament theology. The problem here is that people take what God says in Exodus and Deuteronomy about the nation and attempt to make it into a general principle for understanding for the experience of the individual. Job's experience serves as a counterbalance to the misapplication of this theology of Exodus and Deuteronomy.

The retribution principle is not discussed abstractly as a concept in the book, but is presented as the way people think that God works and relates to them. It is articulated in what Job's friends say, but it is not described as a philosophical principle. This way of thinking about the relationship between God and man is presented as: (a) false at the beginning of the book, (b) conceptually wrong in the dialogues of the story, and (c) is eventually and explicitly rejected at the end of the book. Along with this concept, the Joban author masterfully presents another true truth in the narrative framework of the book; that is, God is not bound by the retribution principle, but free and above all systems. Under the retribution principle, Job can only behold the judgmental face of God, but as he learns to reject this principle and to approach God in faith, he can now behold the gracious face of God and receives death as a peaceful end of his shalomic life, because he stands in faith toward God, the act should not have done in the retribution principle. In the retribution principle Job has to earn his place before God by being righteous or being condemned if he is unrighteous. There is no place for the grace of God in the retribution principle.

The truly divine truth is revealed at the end of the book. In order to understand and recognize the truly divine truth, Job has to endure the terrible suffering and anticipation of an ugly death which is inherent in it, and by the revelation of Yahweh at the end of the book. Both bring Job to understand the fallacy of the retribution principle and move him to transcend the retribution principle and learn to be at peace with possibility of death. In the end, Job not only passes his great suffering, but also has a greater faith in God. In the end the shift is from the understanding of one's relationship with God in terms of the retribution principle to the understanding of one's relationship with God in terms of faith. And at the same time, the shift is from the judgmental face of God (i.e. rewarding/punishing face) to the gracious face of God, and from seeing death as either the ultimate judgment or the surrender in this life to the punishment of God to death seen as a peaceful end of a shalomic life with and under God.

The basic harmony God reveals to Job at the end of the book does affirm that the apparently arbitrary and capricious God that Job has experienced is not how God ordinarily does things. Once the terrible testing is over, then God restores Job's fortunes by blessing him with children, property, and long life. This does not mean predictable, for these "blessings" are acts of God's grace not rewards for Job's righteousness.

Job and the Reference in James 5:10–11

Fundamental to Job's crisis is the question of meaning in life with God where he has no hope, no future, no justice, no relief, and no understanding as far as he can think of. Job is so alienated from God and his community. It is in this context that death is connected to the understanding of one's relationship with God. It is part of life with and under God. Though Job has no idea of committing a suicide, he wishes for death because it can end his life of oppression at the hands of an arbitrary and capricious God. With all its terror, death is still preferred and more appealing to the suffering life. Or-bach argues that according to current psychological criteria, Job would be considered a severe suicide risk.[26] Fortunately, though he had every reason to commit suicide, Job did not. This rejection of suicide as an escape from suffering that is what the apostle James refers to when he says:

> Brothers, as an example of patience in the face of suffering, take the prophets who spoke in the name of the Lord. As you know, we consider blessed those who have persevered. You have heard of Job's perseverance and have seen what the Lord finally brought about. The Lord is full of compassion and mercy. (James 5:10–11)

James speaks of the patient endurance of suffering as a characteristic of the life of faith. Compounding to the alienation from God is his faith which provokes Job to make a bold protest against God. Job is not silenced. He laments and relentlessly opposes to injustice and undeserved suffering. The conviction in his own integrity strengthens him the reason to keep struggling with God, a gracious God, even God may slay him (13:15). Job holds fast in his integrity and his life. He does not commit suicide. As James says, this is "Job's perseverance."

---

26. Israel Or-bach, "Job: A Biblical Message about Suicide," *Journal of Psychology and Judaism* 18 (1994): 241–247.

EPILOGUE

The Application in Thai Context

Thai Buddhists have a strong belief in *kamma*, the concept of rebirth, and *Nirvana*, which is a state of cessation of suffering and everything. They will look forward to achieving the state of *Nirvana*. They believe that *Nirvana* will destroy death. So sometimes they call *Nirvana* as "Deathlessness" or "immortality." Those who attain the state of *Nirvana*, after they die they will go beyond the cycle of rebirth and will not return to it again. The Buddha considered rebirth as misery; so the peace of *Nirvana* is the only good worth having. However, this is an irony: if we ask a Buddhist, "What do you do to release yourself from the law of *kamma*?" The answer is always, "to do good deeds," or "I don't know," or "to die." Never does one answer, "to reach the state of *Nirvana*."

Thai Buddhists place a strong emphasis on the funeral service because they see it as the most important rite of passage. It has an impact either directly or indirectly to the dead's next life. Thus, the Buddhist's perspective on death is totally different from that of the Old Testament, especially from the book of Job. Death is viewed as a negative matter and there is no hope, no rest, and no peace in it. So this book not only gives a correct understanding about the role and the concept of death in the book of Job, but also is useful in opening an evangelical dialogue with the Thai Buddhist people, for by faith in God in Christ even in death we can find peace and have hope in it. Death, for us, is in the hand of God. We do not fear death. It is not the punishment, nor the ultimate will of God. It is not God's evil will, nor intruding factor. It is inevitable, but not something that destroy our relationship with God.

There is always a tension in the Christian view of death. On the one hand, we understand death as judgment or punishment for sin, the "last enemy" that God has defeated in Christ. On the other hand, death is the shalomic end of a shalomic life before God. The key to reconciling these two views is the recognition that we are "in Christ." Because God has defeated death in Christ and by being baptized into Christ we are joined with him in his death and victory over death (Rom 6). Therefore, we can view death as a peaceful end to a shalomic life – but this is only true "in Christ." We, like Job, can embrace death as a shalomic end of a life lived before God.

Bibliography

Albertz, Rainer. "The Sage and Pious Wisdom in the Book of Job: The Friends' Perspective." In *The Sage in Israel and the Ancient Near East*, edited by John G. Gammie and Leo G. Perdue, 243–261. Winona Lake, IN: Eisenbrauns, 1990.

Allen, Ronald Barclay. "The Leviathan-Rahab-Dragon Motif in the Old Testament." ThM thesis, Dallas Theological Seminary, 1968.

Alter, Robert. *The Art of Biblical Narrative*. New York: Basic Books, 1981.

———. *The Art of Biblical Poetry*. New York: Basic Books, 1985.

Andersen, Francis I. *Job: An Introduction and Commentary*. Downers Grove, IL: InterVarsity, 1974.

———. "Yahweh, the Kind and Sensitive God." In *God Who Is Rich in Mercy*, edited by P. T. O'Brien and D. G. Peterson, 41–88. Australia: Lancer Books, 1986.

Anderson, B. W. *Creation versus Chaos: The Reinterpretation of Mythical Symbolism in the Bible*. New York: Association Press, 1967.

———. "The Earth Is the Lord's: An Essay on the Biblical Doctrine of Creation." *Interpretation* 9 (1955): 3–20.

———. "Water." In of *The Interpreter's Dictionary of the Bible*, vol. 4, edited by G. A. Buttrick, 806–810. Nashville: Abingdon, 1962.

Anderson, G. A. *A Time to Mourn, a Time to Dance: The Expression of Grief and Joy in Israelite Religion*. University Park, PA: Pennsylvania State University Press, 1991.

Archer, Gleason L., Jr. *The Book of Job: God's Answer to the Problem of Undeserved Suffering*. Grand Rapids, MI: Baker, 1982.

Ashmon, Scott. "The Wrath of God: A Biblical Overview." *Concordia Journal* 31 (2005): 348–358.

Baker, Wesley C. *More Than a Man Can Take: A Study of Job*. Philadelphia: Westminster, 1966.

Bakon, Shimon. "God and Man on Trial." *Jewish Bible Quarterly* 21 (1993): 226–235.

Bailey, Lloyd R. *Biblical Perspective on Death*. Overtures to Biblical Theology. Philadelphia: Fortress, 1983.

———. "Death as a Theological Problem in the Old Testament." *Pastoral Psychology* (1971): 20–33.

Balentine, Samuel E. "The Hidden God: The Hiding of the Face of God in the Old Testament." *Oxford Theological Monograph*. Oxford: Oxford University Press, 1979.

———. *Job*. Macon: Smyth & Helwys, 2006.

———. "My Servant Job Shall Pray for You." *Theology Today* 58 (2002): 502–518.

———. "Prayer in the Hebrew Bible: The Drama of Divine-Human Dialogue." *Overtures to Biblical Theology*. Minneapolis: Fortress, 1993.

———. "'What Are Human Beings, That You Make So Much of Them?' Divine Disclosure from the Whirlwind: 'Look at Behemoth.'" In *God in the Fray: A Tribute to Walter Brueggemann*, edited by Tod Linafelt and Timothy K. Beal, 259–278. Minneapolis: Fortress, 1998.

Baloian, Bruce E. *Anger in the Old Testament*. New York: Lang, 1992.

Barclay, John. "Mythology of Death in the Old Testament." *Scottish Journal of Theology* 26 (1973): 327–340.

Barnes, Albert. *Notes, Critical, Illustrative, and Practical on the Book of Job*. 2 volumes. New York: Leavitt, Trow & Co., 1846.

Barr, James. "The Meaning of Mythology in Relation to the Old Testament." *Vetus Testamentum* 9 (1959): 1–10.

———. "Philology and Exegesis." *Bibliotheca Ephemeridum Theologicarum Lovaniensium* 33 (1974): 39–61.

———. "Reading the Bible as Literature." *Bulletin of John Rylands Library* 56 (1973–1974): 10–33.

———. *The Semantics of Biblical Language*. Oxford: Oxford University Press, 1961.

———. "Why? in Biblical Hebrew." *Journal of Theological Studies* 36 (1985): 1–33.

Barré, Michael L. "Note on Job 19:25." *Vetus Testamentum* 29 (1979): 107–110.

Barton, George A. "Some Text-Critical Notes on Job." *Journal of Biblical Literature* 42 (1923): 29–32.

Beaucamp, Evode. *Man's Destiny in the Books of Wisdom*. Translated by John Clarke. Staten Island, NY: Alba House, 1970.

Beeby, H. D. "Elihu: Job's Mediator?" *Southeast Asia Journal of Theology* 7 (1965): 33–54.

Beet, W. Ernest. "The Message of the Book of Job." *The Expositor* 24 (1922): 111–120.

Blank, S. H. "Men Against God – The Promethean Element in Biblical Prayer." *Journal of Biblical Literature* 72 (1953): 1–14.

Boorer, Suzanne. "A Matter of Life and Death: A Comparison of Prov. 1–9 and Job." In *Prophets and Paradigms: Essays in Honor of Gene M. Tucker*, 187–204. Sheffield: Sheffield Academic Press, 1996.

Bottérro, Jean. *Religion in Ancient Mesopotamia*. Chicago: University of Chicago Press, 2001.

Botterweck, G. Johannes, Helmer Ringgren, and Heinz-Josef Fabry, eds. *Theological Dictionary of the Old Testament*. Translated by John T. Willis. 15 volumes. Grand Rapids, MI: Eerdmans, 1975–2003.

Brenner, Athalya. "God's Answer to Job." *Vetus Testamentum* 31 (1981): 129–137.

Brown, F., S. R. Driver, and C. A. Briggs. *A Hebrew and English Lexicon of the Old Testament*. Oxford: Clarendon, 1907.

Brown, William P. "Creatio Corporis and the Rhetoric of Defense in Job 10 and Ps 139." In *God Who Creates: Essays in Honor of W. Sibley Towner*, edited by William P. Brown, and S. Dean McBride Jr., 107–124. Grand Rapids, MI: Eerdmans, 2000.

———. *The Ethos of the Cosmos: The Genesis of Moral Imagination in the Bible*. Grand Rapids, MI: Eerdmans, 1999.

Brueggemann, Walter. "The Costly Loss of Lament." *Journal for the Study of the Old Testament* 36 (1986): 57–71.

———. "From Hurt to Joy, From Death to Life." *Interpretation* 28 (1974): 3–19.

———. "A Shape for the Old Testament Theology: II, Embrace of Pain." *Catholic Biblical Quarterly* 47 (1985): 28–46.

Burns, John Barclay. "The Mythology of Death and the Old Testament." *Scottish Journal of Theology* 26 (1973): 327–340.

Burrows, Millar. "The Voice from the Whirlwind." *Journal of Biblical Literature* 47 (1928): 117–132.

Buttrick, George Arthur, ed. *The Interpreter's Dictionary of the Bible*. 4 volumes. New York: Abingdon, 1962.

Child, Brevard S. *Introduction to the Old Testament as Scripture*. Philadelphia: Fortress, 1979.

Clifford, Richard. *Creation Accounts in the Ancient Near East and in the Bible*. Catholic Biblical Quarterly Monograph Series 26. Washington, DC: Catholic Biblical Association of America, 1995.

Clines, D. J. A. "The Argument of the Three Friends." In *Sitting with Job: Selected Studies on the Book of Job*, edited by Roy B. Zuck, 265–278. Grand Rapids: Baker, 1992.

———. *Dictionary of Classical Hebrew*. Sheffield: Sheffield Academic Press, 1995.

———. *Job 1–20*. Word Biblical Commentary 17. Dallas: Word, 1989.

———. "Job's Fifth Friend: An Ethical Critique of the Book of Job." *Biblical Interpretation* 12 (2000): 233–250.

———. "Job 5, 1–8: A New Exegesis." *Biblica* 62 (1981): 185–194.

———. "The Shape and Argument of the Book of Job." In *Sitting with Job: Selected Studies on the Book of Job*, edited by Roy B. Zuck, 125–39. Grand Rapids: Baker, 1992.

———. "Verb Modality and the Interpretation of Job IV 20–21." *Vetus Testamentum* 30 (1980): 354–357.

———. *What Does Eve Do to Help? And Other Readerly Questions to the Old Testament*. Journal for the Study of the Old Testament: Supplement Series 94. Sheffield: Sheffield Academic Press, 1990.

Coats, George W. "Death and Dying in OT Tradition." *Lexington Theological Quarterly* 11 (1976): 9–14.

Collins, John Joseph "The Root of Immortality: Death in the Context of Jewish Wisdom." *Harvard Theological Review* 71 (1978): 177–192.

Cox, Dermot. "The Desire for Oblivion in Job 3." *Liber Annus of Studii Biblici Franciscani* 23. Jerusalem: Franciscan Printing Press, 1973.

Cox, Samuel. *Commentary on the Book of Job*. 2 volumes. Translated by Francis Bolton. Grand Rapids: Eerdmans, 1949.

Crenshaw, James L. *Defending God: Biblical Responses to the Problem of Evil*. Oxford: Oxford University Press, 2005.

———. "The Influence of the Wise upon Amos: The 'Doxologies of Amos' and Job 5:9–16; 9:5–10." *Zeitschrift für die alttestamentliche Wissenschaft* 79 (1967): 42–52.

———. *Theodicy in the Old Testament*. Philadelphia: Fortress, 1983.

———. "When Form and Content Clash: The Theology of Job 38:1–40:5." In *Creation in the Biblical Traditions*, edited by Richard J. Clifford and John J. Collins, 70–84. Washington, DC: Catholic Biblical Association of America, 1992.

Curtis, John B. "On Job's Response to Yahweh." *Journal of Biblical Literature* 98 (1979): 497–511.

———. "Why Were the Elihu Speeches Added to the Book of Job?" *Proceedings, Eastern Great Lakes and Midwest Biblical Societies* 8 (1988): 93–99.

Dahood, Mitchell Joseph. "Chiasmus in Job: A Text-Critical and Philological Criterion." In *A Light to My Path: Old Testament Studies in Honor of Jacob M. Myers*, edited by Howard N. Bream, Ralph D. Heim, and Carey A. Moore, 119–130. Philadelphia: Temple University Press, 1974.

———. "*HDK* in Job 40,12." *Biblica* 49 (1968): 509–510.

———. "Hebrew-Ugaritic Lexicography 7." *Biblica* 50 (1969): 337–356.

———. "Northwest Semitic Philology and Job." In *The Bible in Current Catholic Thought*, edited by John L. McKenzie, 55–74. New York: Herder & Herder, 1962.

Danin, Avinoam. "Do You Know When the Ibexes Give Birth?" *Biblical Archaeology Review* 50 (1979): 50–51.

Davidson, Robert. *The Courage to Doubt: Exploring an Old Testament Theme*. Philadelphia: Trinity Press International, 1983.

Day, John. *God's Conflict with the Dragon and the Sea: Echoes of a Canaanite Myth in the Old Testament*. Cambridge: Cambridge University Press, 1985.

———. "Leviathan." *ABC* 4: 295–296.

———. "Yahweh and the Gods and Goddesses of Canaan." *Journal for the Study of the Old Testament*, Supplement Series 265. Sheffield: Sheffield Academic, 2000.

Delitzsch, Franz. *Biblical Commentary on the Book of Job*. 2 volumes. Translated by Francis Bolton. Grand Rapids: Eerdmans, 1949.

Dhorme, Edouard. *A Commentary on the Book of Job*. London: Thomas Nelson, 1967.

Dick, Michael B. "Job 31, the Oath of Innocence, and the Sage." *Zeitschrift für de altestamentliche Wissenschaft* 95 (1983): 31–53.

———. "The Legal Metaphor in Job 31." *Catholic Biblical Quarterly* 41 (1979): 37–50.

Diewert, David A. "Job 7:12: Yam, Tannin, and the Surveillance of Job." *Journal of Biblical Literature* 106 (1987): 203–215.

Driver, Godfrey Rolles. "Job 39:27–28: The *ky*-Bird (כי)." *Palestine Exploration Quarterly* 104 (1972): 64–66.

———. "Problems in the Hebrew Text of Job." In *Wisdom in Israel and the Ancient Near East*, edited by Martin Noth and David Winton Thomas, 72–93. *Vetus Testamentum Supplements 3*. Leiden: Brill, 1955.

———. "Problem in Job." *American Journal of Semitic Languages and Literature* 52 (1935–1936): 160–170.

———. "Two Astronomical Passages in the Old Testament." *Journal of Theological Studies* 7 (1956): 1–11.

Driver, S. R. and Gray, G. B. *A Critical and Exegetical Commentary on the Book of Job*. International Critical Commentary. Edinburgh: T&T Clark, 1921.

Delitzsch, Friedrich. *Babel und Bibel*. Leipzig: J. C. Hinrichs, 1902.

———. *Babel and Bible: Two Lectures*. New York: G. P. Putnam's Sons, 1903.

Eaton, J. H. *Job*. Old Testament Guides. Sheffield: JSOT Press, 1985.

Eichrodt, Walther. *Man in the Old Testament*. Translated by K. and R. Gregor Smith. London: SCM Press, 1961.

———. *Theology of the Old Testament*. Translated by J. A. Baker. 2 volumes. London: SCM Press, 1961.
Erlandsson, S. "The Wrath of YHWH." *Tyndale Bulletin* 23 (1972): 111–116.
Feinberg, Charles L. "The Book of Job." *Bibliotheca Sacra* 91 (1934): 78–86.
———. "The Poetic Structure of the Book of Job and the Ugaritic Literature." *Bibliotheca Sacra* 103 (1946): 283–292.
Fisher, L. R. "Creation at Ugarit and in the Old Testament." *Vetus Testamentum* 15 (1965): 313–324.
———. "From Chaos to Cosmos." *Encounter* 26 (1965): 183–197.
Fischer, S. "How God Pays Back: Retributive Concepts in the Book of Job." *Acta Theologica* 20 (2000): 26–41.
Fishbane, Michael A. *Biblical Interpretation in Ancient Israel*. Oxford: Clarendon, 1985.
———. "Jeremiah 4, 23–26 and Job 3, 3–13." *Vetus Testamentum* 21 (1971): 151–167.
———. "The Book of Job and Inner-Biblical Discourse." In *The Voice from the Whirlwind: Interpreting the Book of Job*, edited by Leo G. Perdue and W. Clark Gilpin, 86–98. Nashville: Abingdon, 1992.
Floysvik, Ingvar. *When God Becomes My Enemy: The Theology of the Complaint Psalms*. St Louis: Concordia Academic Press, 1997.
Fohrer, Georg. *Das Buch Hiob*. Gütersloh: Gerd Mohn, 1963.
———. "Das Hiobproblem und seine Losung." *Wissenschaftliche Zeitschrift der Martin Luther Universitat* 12 (1963): 249–258.
———. "The Righteous Man in Job 31." In *Essays in Old Testament Ethics*, edited by James L. Crenshaw and John T. Willis, 1–22. New York: KTAV, 1974.
Forrest, Robert W. Edward. "The Creation Motif in the Book of Job." PhD dissertation, McMaster University, 1975.
———. "The Two Faces of Job: Imagery and Integrity in the Prologue." In *Ascribe to the Lord: Biblical & Other Studies in Memory of Peter C. Craigie*, edited by Lyle Eslinger and Glen Taylor, 385–398. *Journal for the Study of the Old Testament*, Supplement Series 67. Sheffield: JSOT Press, 1988.
Fox, Michael V. "Job 38 and God's Rhetoric." *Semeia* 19 (1981): 53–61.
Freedman, David Noel. *Anchor Bible Dictionary*. 6 volumes. New York: Doubleday, 1992.
———. "Another Look at Biblical Hebrew Poetry." In *Directions in Biblical Hebrew Poetry*, edited by Elaine R. Follis, 11–28. Sheffield: JSOT Press, 1987.
———. "Notes and Observations: The Elihu Speeches in the Book of Job." *Harvard Theological Review* 61 (1968): 51–59.
———. "The Structure of Job 3." *Biblica* 49 (1968): 503–508.

Frietheim, Terence E. *God and the World in the Old Testament: A Relational Theology of Creation.* Nashville: Abingdon, 2005.

———. "God in the Book of Job." *Currents in Theology and Mission* 26 (1999): 87–91.

———. "The Repentance of God: A Key to Evaluation Old Testament God-Talk." *Horizons in Biblical Theology* 10 (1988): 47–70.

———. *The Suffering of God: An Old Testament Perspective.* Philadelphia: Fortress, 1984.

———. "To Say Something – About God, Evil, and Suffering." *Word & World* 19 (1999): 339–350.

Fullerton, Kemper. "Double Entendre in the First Speech of Eliphaz." *Journal of Biblical Literature* 49 (1930): 320–374.

———. "On the Text and Significance of Job 40:2." *American Journal of Semitic Languages and Literature* 49 (1932–1933): 197–211.

———. "The Original Conclusion to the Book of Job." *Zeitschrift für die alttestamentliche Wissenschaft* 42 (1924): 116–135.

Fyall, Robert S. *Now My Eyes Have Seen You: Images of Creation and Evil in the Book of Job.* Downers Grove: InterVarsity, 2002.

Gammie, John G. "Behemoth and Leviathan: On the Didactic and Theological Significance of Job 40:15–41:26." In *Israelite Wisdom: Theological and Literary Essays in Honor of Samuel Terrien*, edited by John G. Gammie, Walter A. Brueggemann, W. Lee Humphreys, and James M. Ward, 217–231. New York: Scholars Press, 1978.

Gaster, T. H. "Dead, Abode of the." In *The Interpreter's Dictionary of the Bible*, vol. 1, edited by George A. Buttrick, 787–788. Nashville: Abingdon, 1962.

———. "Leviathan." In *The Interpreter's Dictionary of the Bible*, vol. 3, edited by George A. Buttrick, 116. Nashville: Abingdon, 1962.

———. "Rahab (Dragon)." In *The Interpreter's Dictionary of the Bible*, vol. 4, edited by George A. Buttrick, 6. Nashville: Abingdon, 1962.

Gese, Hartmut. "Death in the Old Testament." In *Essays on Biblical Theology*. Translated by Keith Crim, 34–59. Minneapolis: Augsburg, 1981.

Gibson, John C. L. *Canaanite Myths and Legends.* Edinburgh: T&T Clark, 1977.

———. "On Evil in the Book of Job." In *Ascribe to the Lord: Biblical & Other Studies in Memory of Peter C. Craigie*, edited by Lyle M. Eslinger and J. Glen Taylor, 399–419. Journal for the Study of the Old Testament: Supplement Series 67. Sheffield: JSOT Press, 1988.

Ginsberg, R. L. "Interpreting Ugaritic Texts." *Journal of the American Oriental Society* 70 (1950): 156–160.

———. "Job the Patient and Job the Impatient." *Supplements to Vetus Testamentum* 17. Leiden: Brill, 1969.

———. "Ugaritic Myths, Epics, and Legends." In *Ancient Near Eastern Texts Relating to the Old Testament*, edited by James Pritchard. 3rd edition, 129–155. Princeton: Princeton University Press, 1969.

Glazov, Gregory Yuri. "The Significance of the 'Hand on the Mouth' Gesture in Job XL 4." *Vetus Testamentum* 52 (2002): 30–41.

Glenny, W. Edward. "How Well Do You Know God? The Dangers of 'Retribution Principle.'" *Searching Together* 23 (1995): 13–17.

Goitein, Shelomo Dov. "'ma'on' – A Reminder of Sin." *Journal of Semitic Studies* 10 (1965): 52–53.

Good, Edwin M. *In Turns of Tempest: A Reading of Job with a Translation*. Stanford: Stanford University Press, 1990.

———. *Irony in the Old Testament*. Philadelphia: Westminster, 1965.

Gordon, Cyrus H. "Leviathan: Symbol of Evil." In *Biblical Motifs: Origins and Transformations*, edited by Alexander Altmann, 1–9. Cambridge, MA: Harvard University Press, 1966.

Gordis, Robert. *The Book of God and Man: A Study of Job*. Chicago: University of Chicago Press, 1965.

———. *The Book of Job: Commentary, New Translation, and Special Studies*. New York City: Jewish Theological Seminary of America, 1978.

———. "Critical Notes: A Note on *Yad*." *Journal of Biblical Literature* 62 (1943): 341–346.

———. "Job XL, 29 – An Additional Note." *Vetus Testamentum* 14 (1964): 491–494.

———. "Job and Ecology (And the Significance of Job 40:15)." *Hebrew Annual Review* 9 (1985): 189–202.

———. "Virtual Quotations in Job, Sumer and Qumran." *Vetus Testamentum* 31 (1981): 410–427.

Gowan, Donald E. "God's Answer to Job: How Is It an Answer?" *Horizon in Biblical Theology* 8 (1986): 85–102.

Green, E. L. "Biblical Narratology." *Prooftexts* 1 (1981): 201–208.

Greenberg, Moshe. "Job." In *The Literary Guide to the Bible*, edited by Robert Alter and Frank Kermode, 283–303. Cambridge, MA: Belknap Press, 1987.

Greenspahn, Frederick E. "Hapax Legomena in Biblical Hebrew." *Society of Biblical Literature Dissertation Series* 74. Chico: Scholars Press, 1984.

Gros Louis, Kenneth R. R. "Isaiah: Chapter 40–55; The Book of Job; Ecclesiastes." In *Literary Interpretations of Biblical Narratives*, edited by Kenneth R. R. Gros Louis, 208–282. Nashville: Abingdon, 1974.

Gruber, Mayer I. *Aspects of Nonverbal Communication in the Ancient Near East*. 2 volumes. Rome: Biblical Institute Press, 1980.

———. "The Rhetoric of Familiarity and Contempt in Job 2:9–10." *Scriptura* 87 (2004): 261–266.

Gunn, David M., and Danna Nolan Fewell. *Narrative in the Hebrew Bible*. Oxford: Clarendon Press, 1993.

Gutmann, Joseph. "Leviathan, Behemoth and Ziz: Symbols in Art." *Hebrew Union College Annual* 39 (1968): 219–230.

Habel, Norman C. *The Book of Job: A Commentary*. Philadelphia: Westminster, 1985.

———. "He Who Stretches Out the Heavens." *Catholic Biblical Quarterly* 34 (1972): 417–430.

———. "In Defense of God the Sage." In *The Voice from the Whirlwind: Interpreting the Book of Job*, edited by Leo G. Perdue and W. Clark Gilpin, 21–38. Nashville: Abingdon, 1992.

———. "The Narrative Art of Job: Applying the Principles of Robert Alter." *Journal for the Study of the Old Testament* 27 (1983): 101–111.

———. "Of Things Beyond Me: Wisdom in the book of Job." *Currents in Theology and Mission* 10 (1983): 142–154.

———. "Only the Jackal Is My Friend: On Friends and Redeemer in Job." *Interpretation* 31 (1977): 227–236.

———. "The Role of Elihu in the Design of the Book of Job." In *In the Shelter of Elyon*, edited by W. Boyd Barrick and John R. Spencer, 3–33. Sheffield: JSOT Press, 1984.

———. "Yahweh Maker of Heaven and Earth: A Study in Tradition Criticism." *Journal of Biblical Literature* 91 (1972): 321–337.

Harris, R. Laird. "The Book of Job and Its Doctrine of God." *Grace Journal* 13 (1972): 3–33.

Hartley, John E. *The Book of Job*. The New International Biblical Commentary on the Old Testament. Grand Rapids: Eerdmans, 1988.

———. "The Genres and Message of the Book of Job." In *Sitting with Job: Selected Studies on the Book of Job*, edited by Roy B. Zuck, 65–78. Grand Rapids: Baker, 1992.

———. "Job." In of *The International Standard Bible Encyclopedia*, vol. 2, edited by Geoffrey W. Bromiley, 1064–1076. Grand Rapids: Eerdmans, 1979–1988.

Heidel, Alexander. *The Gilgamesh Epic and Old Testament Parallels*. Chicago: University of Chicago Press, 1963.

Hoffman, Yair. "Irony in the Book of Job." *Immanuel* 17 (1983/84): 7–12.

Holbert, John C. "The Function and Significance of the Klage in the Book of Job with Special Reference to the Incidence of Formal and Verbal Irony." PhD dissertation, Southern Methodist University, 1975.

———. "The Rehabilitation of the Sinner: The Function of Job 29–31." *Zeitschrift für die altestamentliche Wissenschaft* 95 (1983): 229–237.

Holladay, William L. *The Root Šûbh in the Old Testament*. Leiden: Brill, 1958.

Honsey, Rudolph E. "Exegetical Paper on Job 19:23–27." *Wisconsin Lutheran Quarterly* 67 (1970): 153–206.

Houtman, Cornelis. "Zu Hiob 2:12." *Zeitschrift für die alttestamentliche Wissenschaft* 90 (1978): 269–272.

Howe, George E. "Job and the Ostrich: A Case Study in Biblical Authority." *Journal of the American Scientific Affiliation* 15 (1963): 107–110.

Hummel, Horace D. "Enclitic *Mem* in Early Northwest Semitic, Especially Hebrew." *Journal of Biblical Literature* 76 (1957): 85–107.

———. *The Word Becoming Flesh*. St Louis: CPH, 1979.

Janzen, J. Gerald. "Another Look at God's Watch over Job (7:12)." *Journal of Biblical Literature* 108 (1989): 109–114.

———. "Critical Notes: Another Look at God's Watch over Job (7:12)." *Journal of Biblical Literature* 108 (1989): 109–116.

———. *Job*. Atlanta: John Knox, 1985.

———. "Job's Oath." *Review & Expositor* 99 (2000): 597–605.

———. "Lust for Life and the Bitterness of Job." *Theology Today* 55 (1998): 152–162.

———. "The Place of the Book of Job in the History of Israel's Religion." In *Ancient Israelite Religion: Essays in Honor of Frank Moore Cross*, edited by Patrick D. Miller, Jr., Paul D. Hanson, and S. Dean McBride, 523–538. Philadelphia: Fortress, 1987.

Jackson, J. J. "The Deep." In *The Interpreter's Dictionary of the Bible*, vol. 4, edited by G. A. Buttrick, 813–814. New York: Abingdon, 1962.

Jacob, E. "Death." In *The Interpreter's Dictionary of the Bible*, vol. 1, edited by George A. Buttrick, 802–807. New York: Abingdon, 1962.

Jastrow, Morris, Jr. *The Book of Job: Its Origin, Growth, and Interpretation*. Philadelphia: Lippincott, 1920.

Jenni, E., and C. Westermann. *Theological Lexicon of the Old Testament*. Translated by M. E. Biddle. 3 volumes. Peabody, MA: Hendrickson, 1997.

John, E. C. "The Old Testament Understanding of Death." *Indian Journal of Theology* 23 (1974): 123–128.

Johnston, Philip S. *Shades of Sheol*. Downers Grove: InterVarsity, 2002.

Jones, Edgar. *The Triumph of Job*. London: SCM Press, c. 1966.

Jordan, W. B. *The Book of Job: Its Substance and Spirit*. New York: Macmillan, 1929.

Joüon, P., and T. Muraoka. *A Grammar of Biblical Hebrew*. 2 volumes. Subsidia Biblica 14/1–2. Rome: Editrice Pontificio Istituto Biblico, 1991, corrected reprint 1993.

Kaddari, M. Z. "A Semantic Approach to Biblical Parallelism." *Journal of Jewish Studies* 24 (1973): 167–175.

Kautzsch, E. *Gesenius Hebrew Grammar*. Translated by A. E. Cowley. Oxford: Clarendon Press, 1910.

Kelly, Balmer H. "Truth in Contradiction: A Study of Job 20–21." *Interpretation* 15 (1961): 147–156.

Kessler, Martin. "Inclusio in the Hebrew Bible." *Semitics* 6 (1978): 44–49.

Kinet, Dirk. "The Ambiguity of the Concepts of God and Satan in the Book of Job." In *Job and the Silence of God*, edited by Christian Duquoc and Casiano Floristan, 30–35. New York: Seabury Press, 1983.

Kissane, Edward. J. *The Book of Job*. Dublin: Browne & Nolan, 1939.

Knight, Harold. "Job." *Scottish Journal of Theology* 9 (1956): 63–76.

Koehler, L., W. Baumgartner, and J. J. Stamm. *The Hebrew and Aramaic Lexicon of the Old Testmanet*. Translated and edited under the supervision of M. E. J. Richardson. 4 volumes. Leiden: Brill, 1994–1999.

Kosmala, Hans. "The term גֶּבֶר in the Old Testament and in the Scroll." *Supplements to Vetus Testamentum* 17 (1969): 159–169.

Kuntz, Kenneth. "The Form, Location, and Function of Rhetorical Questions in Deotero-Isaiah." In *Writing and Reading the Scroll of Isaiah: Studies of an Interpretive Tradition*, vol. 1, edited by Craig Broyles and Craig Evans, 12–41. Leiden: Brill, 1997.

Kuyper, Lester J. "The Repentance of Job." *Vetus Testamuntum* 9 (1959): 91–94.

Labuschagne, C. J. *The Incomparability of Yahweh in the Old Testament*. Leiden: Brill, 1966.

Laks, H. Joel. "The Enigma of Job: Maimonides and the Moderns." *Journal of Biblical Literature* 83 (1964): 345–364.

Laurin, Robert. "The Theological Structure of Job." *Zeitschrift für die Alttestamentliche Wissenchaft* 86 (1974): 86–89.

Levenson, Jon D. *Creation and the Persistence of Evil: The Jewish Drama of Divine Omnipotence*. San Francisco: Harper & Row, 1988.

Lillie, William. "The Religious Significance of the Theophany in the Book of Job." *Expository Times* 68 (1956–1957): 355–358.

Linafelt, Tod. "The Undecidability of בָּרַךְ in the Prologue to Job and Beyond." *Biblical Interpretation* 4 (1996): 154–172.

Littleton, Mark R. *When God Seems Far Away*. Wheaton: Harold Shaw, 1987.

Long, V. Philips. "Reading the Old Testament as Literature." In *Interpreting the Old Testament: A Guide for Exegesis*, edited by Craig C. Broyles, 85–123. Grand Rapids: Baker, 2001.

Longman, Tremper, III. *Literary Approaches to Biblical Interpretation*. Grand Rapids: Zondervan, 1987.

Longman, Tremper, III, and Peter Enns, ed. *Dictionary of the Old Testament*. 3 volumes. Downers Grove: InterVarsity, 2003–2008.

MacKenzie, Roderick A. F. "The Purpose of the Yahweh Speeches in the Book of Job." *Biblica* 40 (1959): 435–445.

Martin-Achard, Robert. *From Death to Life: A Study of the Development of the Doctrine of the Resurrection in the Old Testament.* Translated by John Penney Smith. Edinburgh: Oliver & Boyd, 1960.

May, Herbert G. "Some Cosmic Connotations of *Mayim Rabbim*, 'Many Waters.'" *Journal of Biblical Literature* 74 (1955): 9–21.

McCarthy, Dennis J. "'Creation' Motifs in Ancient Hebrew Poetry." *Catholic Biblical Quarterly* 29 (1967): 393–406.

McCurley, Foster R. *Ancient Myths and Biblical Faith: Scriptural Transformations.* Philadelphia: Fortress, 1983.

McFayden, John Edgar. *The Problem of Pain.* London: James Clarke, n.d.

McKeating, H. "The Central Issue of the Book of Job." *Expository Times* 82 (1971): 244–247.

McKenzie, John L. *Myths and Realities: Studies in Biblical Theology.* Milwaukee: Bruce Publishing, 1963.

McKenzie, R. A. F. "Job." In *The Jerome Bible Commentary*, vol. 1, edited by Raymond Edward Brown, Joseph A. Fitzmyer, and Roland E. Murphy, 511–533. Englewood Cliffs, NJ: Prentice-Hall, 1968.

Meek, Th. J. "Job 19:25–27." *Vetus Testamentum* 6 (1956): 100–103.

Melamed, E. Z. "The Breakup of Stereotype Phrases as an Artistic Device in Biblical Poetry." In *Scripta Hierosolymitana: Studies in the Bible*, vol. 8, edited by Chaim Rabin, 115–153. Jerusalem: Magnes Press, 1961.

Mettinger, Tryggve. "The God of Job: Avenger, Tyrant, or Victor?" In *The Voice from the Whirlwind: Interpreting the Book of Job*, edited by Leo G. Perdue and W. Clark Gilpin, 39–49. Nashville: Abingdon, 1992.

———. "God the Victor." In *The Voice from the Whirlwind: Interpreting the Book of Job*. Edited by Leo G. Perdue and W. Clark Gilpin, 45–46. Nashville: Abingdon, 1992.

Michel, Walter L. "Death in Job." *Dialog* 11 (1972): 183–189.

———. *Job: In the Light of Northwest Semitic: Prologue and First Cycle of Speeches, Job 1:1–14:22.* Vol. 1. Rome: Biblical Institute Press, 1987.

———. "Job's Real Friend: Elihu." *Criterion* 21 (1982): 29–32.

———. "SLMWT, 'Deep Darkness' or 'Shadow of Death'?" *Biblical Research* 29 (1984): 5–20.

———. "The Ugaritic Texts and the Mythological Expressions in the Book of Job." PhD dissertation, University of Wisconsin, 1970.

Miles J. *God: A Biography.* New York: Alfred A. Knopf, 1995.

Miller, Patrick D. "Prayer as Persuasion: The Rhetoric and Intention of Prayer." *Word & World* 13 (1993): 356–362.

Miller, Ward S. "The Structure and Meaning of Job." *Concordia Journal* 15 (1989): 103–119.

Mitchell, Christopher W. "Job and the Theology of the Cross." *Concordia Journal* 15 (1989): 156–180.

———. *The Meaning of BRK "To Bless" in the Old Testament*. SBL dissertation Series 95 Atlanta, GA: Scholars Press, 1987.

Moor, Johannes C. de. "El, the Creator." In *The Bible World: Essays in Honor of Cyrus H. Gordon*, edited by Gary A. Rendsburg, 171–187. New York: KTAV, 1980.

———. "Rapi'uma-Rephaim." *Zeitschrift für die alttestamentliche Wissenschaft* 88 (1976): 325–345.

Moore, Rick D. "The Integrity of Job." *Catholic Biblical Quarterly* 45 (1983): 17–31.

Morrow, William S. "Consolation, Rejection and Repentance in Job 42:6." *Journal of Biblical Literature* 105 (1986): 211–225.

Muenchow, Charles. "Dust and Dirt in Job 42:6." *Journal of Biblical Literature* 108 (1989): 597–611.

Muilenberg, J. "The Linguistic and Rhetorical Usage of the Particle *ki* in the Old Testament." *Hebrew Union College Annual* 32 (1961): 135–160.

———. "A Study in Hebrew Rhetoric: Repetition and Style." *Supplement to Vetus Testamentum* 1 (1953): 97–116.

Muraoka, Takamitsu. *Emphatic Words and Structures in Biblical Hebrew*. Jerusalem: Magnes Press, 1985.

Murphy, Roland E. *The Book of Job: A Short Reading*. New York: Paulist, 1999.

———. *Seven Books of Wisdom*. Milwaukee: Bruce, 1960.

Newell, B. Lynne. "Job: Repentant or Rebellious?" *Westminster Theological Journal* 46 (1984): 298–316.

Newsom, Carol A. *The Book of Job*. The New Interpreter's Bible, vol. 4. Nashville: Abingdon, 1994.

———. *The Book of Job: A Contest of Moral Imaginations*. New York: Oxford University Press, 2003.

———. "Considering Job." *Currents in Research* 1 (1993): 87–118.

O'Connor, Kathleen M. "Wild, Raging Creativity: The Scene in the Whirlwind." In *A God So Near: Essays on Old Testament Theology in Honor of Patrick D. Miller*, edited by Brent A. Strawn and Nancy R. Bowen, 171–179. Winona Lake, IN: Eisenbrauns, 2003.

Oldenburg, Ulf. *The Conflict between El and Baal in Canaanite Religion*. Leiden: Brill, 1969.

Ollenburger, Ben C. "If Mortals Die, Will They Live Again? The Old Testament and Resurrection." *Ex Auditu* 9 (1993): 29–44.

Olmo Lete, Gregorio del. "The 'Divine' Names of the Ugaritic Kings." *Ugarit-Forschungen* 18 (1986): 83–95.

Or-Bach, Israel. "Job: A Biblical Message about Suicide." *Journal of Psychology and Judaism* 18 (1994): 241–247.

Oden, Robert A., Jr. "Cosmogony, Cosmology." In *The Anchor Bible Dictionary*, vol. 1, edited by David Noel Freedman, 1162–1171. New York: Doubleday, 1992.

Oswalt, J. N. "The Myth of the Dragon and Old Testament Faith." *Evangelical Quarterly* 49 (1977): 163–172.

Ostborn, G. *Yahweh and Baal*. Lund: Gleerup, 1956.

Parker, Simon B., ed. *Ugaritic Narrative Poetry*. Translated by Mark S. Smith. Writings from the Ancient World Society of Biblical Literature 9. Chico, CA: Scholars Press, 1997.

Parsons, Gregory W. "Literary Features of the Book of Job." *Bibliotheca Sacra* 138 (1981): 213–229.

———. "The Structure and Purpose of the Book of Job." In *Sitting with Job: Selected Studies on the Book of Job*, edited by Roy B. Zuck, 17–33. Grand Rapids: Baker, 1992.

Patrick, Dale. "Short Notes: The Translation of Job 42:6." *Vetus Testamentum* 26 (1976): 369–371.

Patrick, O. "Job's Address of God." *Zeitschrift für die Alttestamentliche Wissenschaft* 91 (1979): 268–282.

Perdue, Leo G., and W. Clark Gilpin. "Introduction." In *The Voice from the Whirlwind: Interpreting the Book of Job*, edited by Leo G. Perdue and W. Clark Gilpin, 11–18. Nashville: Abingdon, 1992.

Perdue, Leo G. "Job's Assault on Creation." *Hebrew Annual Review* 10 (1986): 296–315.

Perlitt, L. "Ankalge und Freispruch Gottes." *Zeitschrift für Theologie und Kirche* 69 (1972): 290–302.

———. "Die Verborgenheit." In *Probleme biblischer Theologie: Gerhard von Rad zum 70 Geburtstag*, edited by Hans Walter Wolff, 367–382. Munich: Kaiser Verlag, 1971.

Pinker, Aron. "Job's Perspective on Death." *Jewish Bible Quarterly* 35 (2007): 73–84.

Polzin, Robert. "The Framework of the Book of Job." *Interpretation* 28 (1974): 182–200.

Pope, Marvin H. *Job*. Anchor Bible 15. Garden City: Doubleday, 1965.

———. "The Word *Sahat* in Job 9:31." *Journal of Biblical Literature* 83 (1964): 269–278.

Powell, M. A. *What Is Narrative Criticism?* Minneapolis: Fortress, 1990.

Pritchard, James B. ed. *Ancient Near Eastern Texts Relating to the Old Testament.* 3rd edition. Princeton, NJ: Princeton University Press, 1969.

Raabe, Paul R. "Human Suffering in Biblical Context." *Concordia Journal* 15 (1989): 139–155.

———. "The Two 'Faces' of Yahweh: Divine Wrath and Mercy in the Old Testament." In *And Every Tongue Confess: Essays in Honor of Norman Nagel,* edited by Gerald S. Krispin and Jon D. Vieker, 283–310. Dearborn, MI: Nagel Festschrift Committee, 1990.

Rein, R. C. *Cross and Affliction.* St Louis: CPH, 1944.

Riley, William, "The Book of Job and the Terrible Truth about God." *Scripture in Church* 18 (1988): 322–326.

Robinson, H. Wheeler. *The Christian Doctrine of Man.* Edinburgh: T&T Clark, 1924.

———. *The Cross in the Old Testament.* Philadelphia: Westminster, 1955.

Richards, Kent H. "Death." In *The Anchor Bible Dictionary*, vol. 2, edited by David Noel Freedman, 108–110. New York: Doubleday, 1992.

Riggans, Walter. "A Note on Job 6:8–10, Suicide and Death Wishes." *Dor le Dor* 15 (1986/87): 173–176.

Rowold, Henry L. "Life and Death, Death and Life: Echoes from the Book of Job." Unpublished paper presented at the 17th Symposium of Concordia Seminary. St Louis, MO, September 20, 2006.

———. "Mîhū'-lîhū': Leviathan and Job in Job 41:2–3." *Journal of Biblical Literature* 105 (1986): 104–109.

———. "The Theology of Creation in the Yahweh Speeches as a Solution to the Problem Posed by the Book of Job." ThD dissertation, Concordia Seminary in Exile, 1977.

———. "Yahweh's Challenge to Rival: The Form and Function of the Yahweh Speech in Job 38–39." *Catholic Biblical Quarterly* 47 (1985): 199–211.

Rowley, Harold Henry. "The Book of Job and Its Meaning." In *From Moses to Qumran: Studies in the Old Testament*, 141–183. London: Lutterworth, 1963.

———. *The Faith of Israel.* 2nd edition. London: SCM Press, 1956.

———. *Job.* The Century Bible: New Series, edited by Harold H. Rowley and Matthew Black. London: Thomas Nelson, c. 1970.

Sanders, Paul S. ed. *Twentieth Century Interpretation of the Book of Job: A Collection of Critical Essays.* Englewood Cliffs: Prentice-Hall, 1968.

Sarna, Nahum M. "Epic Substratum in the Prose of Job." *Journal of Biblical Literature* 76 (1957): 13–25.

Sauer, Alfred von Rohr. "Salvation by Grace: The Heart of Job's Theology." *Concordia Theological Monthly* 37 (1966): 259–270.

Schmidt, H. *Das Gebet der Angeklagten im Alten Testament*. Beiheft zur Zeitschrift für die alttestamentliche Wissenschaft 49. Giessen: Alfred Topelmann, 1928.

Scholnick, Sylvia Huberman. "Lawsuit Drama in the Book of Job." PhD dissertation, Brandeis University, 1975.

———. "The Meaning of *mišpāt* (*Justice*) in the Book of Job." In *Sitting with Job: Selected Studies on the Book of Job*, edited by Roy B. Zuck, 349–358. Grand Rapids: Baker, 1992.

———. "Poetry in the Courtroom: Job 38–41." In *Sitting with Job: Selected Studies on the Book of Job*, edited by Roy B. Zuck, 421–439. Grand Rapids: Baker, 1992.

Selms, A. van. "Job 31:38–40 in Ugaritic light." *Semitius* 8 (1982): 30–42.

Seybold, K. *Das Gebet des Kranken im Alten Testament*. Stuttgart: Verlag W. Kohlhammer, 1973.

Seitz, Christopher R. "Job: Full-Structure, Movement, and Interpretation." *Interpretation* 43 (1989): 5–17.

Shapiro, D. S. "The Book of Job and the Trial of Abraham." *Tradition* 4 (1961–1962): 210–220.

Skehan, P. W. "Job's Final Plea (Job 29–30) and the Lord's Reply (Job 38–41)." *Biblica* 45 (1964): 51–62.

Smick, Elmer B. "Another Look at the Mythological Elements in the Book of Job." In *Sitting with Job: Selected Studies on the Book of Job*, edited by Roy B. Zuck, 231–244. Grand Rapids: Baker, 1992.

———. "Job." In *The Expositor's Bible Commentary*, vol. 4, edited by Frank E. Gaebelein, 843–1060. Grand Rapids: Zondervan, 1979.

———. "Mythology and the Book of Job." In *Sitting with Job: Selected Studies on the Book of Job*, edited by Roy B. Zuck, 221–229. Grand Rapids: Baker, 1992.

Snaith, Norman H. *The Book of Job: Its Origin and Purpose*. Studies in Biblical Theology, Second Series 11. London: SCM, c. 1968.

Southwick, Jay S. "Job: An Exemplar for Every Age." *Encounter* 45 (1984): 373–391.

Sternberg, M. *The Poetic of Biblical Narrative: Ideological Literature and the Drama of Reading*. Bloomington: Indiana University Press, 1985.

Talmon, Shemaryahu, "Biblical rephā'îm and Ugaritic rpu/i(m)." *Hebrew Annual Review* 7 (1983): 235–249.

Thomas, David Winton. "צַלְמָוֶת in the Old Testament." *Journal of Semitic Studies* 7 (1962): 191–200.

Terrien, Samuel. "The Book of Job: Introduction and Exegesis." In *The Interpreter's Bible*, vol. 3, edited by George A. Buttrick, 875–1198. New York: Abingdon, 1954.

---. *The Elusive Presence: The Heart of Biblical Theology*. San Francisco: Harper & Row, 1978.

---. *Job*. Commentaire de l'Ancien Testament 13. Neuchâtel: Delauchaux et, 1963.

---. "Job as a Sage." In *The Sage in Israel and the Ancient Near East*, edited by John G. Gammie and Leo G. Perdue, 231–242. Winona Lake, IN: Eisenbrauns, 1990.

---. *Job: Poet of Existence*. Indianapolis: Bobbs-Merrill, 1957.

---. "The Yahweh Speeches and Job's Response." *The Review and Expositor* 68 (1971): 497–509.

Tromp, Nicholas J. *Primitive Conceptions of Death and the Nether World in the Old Testament*. Rome: Pontifical Biblical Institute, 1969.

Tsevat, Matitiahu. "The Canaanite God *Šälah*." *Vetus Testamentum* 4 (1954): 41–49.

---. "The Meaning of the Book of Job." In *The Meaning of the Book of Job and the Biblical Studies: Essays on the Literature and Religion of the Hebrew Bible*, 1–37. New York: KTAV, 1980. Repr. from Hebrew Union College Annual 37 (1966): 73–106.

---. "The Meaning of the Book of Job." In *Sitting with Job: Selected Studies on the Book of Job*, edited by Roy B. Zuck, 189–218. Grand Rapids: Baker, 1992.

Tur-Sinai, N. H. *The Book of Job: A New Commentary*. Jerusalem: Kiryath Sepher, 1957.

Urbock, W. J. "Blessings and Cursings." *ABD* 1: 755–761.

Vawter, Bruce. "Intimations of Immortality and the Old Testament." *Journal of Biblical Literature* 91 (1972): 158–171.

Vieth, Richard F. *Holy Power Human Pain*. Bloomington: Meyer-Stone Books, 1988.

Vischer, Wilhelm. "God's Truth and Man's Lie: A Study of the Message of the Book of Job." *Interpretation* 15 (1961): 131–146.

Wakeman, Mary K. *God's Battle with the Monster: A Study in Biblical Imagery*. Leiden: Brill, 1973.

Waltke, B. K., and M. O'Connor. *An Introduction to Biblical Hebrew Syntax*. Winona Lake, IN: Eisenbrauns, 1990.

Walton, John H. "Job 1: Book of." *Dictionary of the Old Testament: Wisdom, Poetry, and Writings*, 333–346. Downers Grove: InterVarsity, 2008.

Waterman, Leroy. "Note on Job 19:23–27: Job's Triumph of Faith." *Journal of Biblical Literature* 69 (1950): 379–380.

Webster, Edwin C. "Strophic Patterns in Job 3–28." *Journal for the Study of the Old Testament* 26 (1983): 33–60.

———. "Strophic Patterns in Job 29–42." *Journal for the Study of the Old Testament* 30 (1984): 95–109.

Weiss, Meir. *The Bible from Within: The Method of Total Interpretation*. Jerusalem: Magnes Press, 1984.

———. *The Story of Job's Beginning: Job 1–2: A Literary Analysis*. Jerusalem: Magnes Press, 1983.

Westermann, Claus. "The Literary Genre of the Book of Job." In *Sitting with Job: Selected Studies on the Book of Job*, edited by Roy B. Zuck, 51–63. Grand Rapids, MI: Baker, 1992

———. "The Role of the Lament in the Theology of the Old Testament." *Interpretation* 28 (1974): 20–38..

———. *The Structure of the Book of Job: A Form-Critical Analysis*. Translated by Charles A. Muenchow. Philadelphia: Fortress, 1977.

———. "The Two Faces of Job." In *Job and the Silence of God*, edited by Christian Duquoc and Casiano Floristan, 15–22. New York: Seabury, 1983.

———. *What Does the Old Testament Say about God*. Atlanta: John Knox, 1979.

Wevers, John W. *The Way of the Righteous: Psalms and the Books of Wisdom*. Philadelphia: Westminster, 1961.

Whedbee, J. William. "The Comedy of Job." *Semeia* 7 (1977): 1–39.

Whybray, Norman. *Job*. Sheffield: Sheffield Academic Press, 1998.

Wolters, A. "A Child of Dust and Ashes (Job 42:6)." *Zeitschrift für die alttestamentliche Wissenschaft* 102 (1990): 116–119.

Wolff, Hans Walter. *Anthropology of the Old Testament*. Philadelphia: Fortress, 1974.

Zimmerli, Walther. *Man and His Hope in the Old Testament*. Studies in Biblical Theology, Second Series 20. Bloomsbury: SCM Press, 1971.

———. "The Place and Limit of the Wisdom in the Framework of the OT Theology." *Scottish Journal of Theology* 17 (1964): 146–158.

Zuck, Roy B. "Job." In *The Bible Knowledge Commentary*, vol. 1, edited by John F. Walvoord and Roy B. Zuck, 715–777. Wheaton: Victor, 1983.

Zuckerman, Bruce. *Job the Silent: A Study in Historical Counterpoint*. New York: Oxford University Press, 1991.

Langham Literature and its imprints are a ministry of Langham Partnership.

Langham Partnership is a global fellowship working in pursuit of the vision God entrusted to its founder John Stott –

> *to facilitate the growth of the church in maturity and Christ-likeness through raising the standards of biblical preaching and teaching.*

Our vision is to see churches in the majority world equipped for mission and growing to maturity in Christ through the ministry of pastors and leaders who believe, teach and live by the Word of God.

Our mission is to strengthen the ministry of the Word of God through:
- nurturing national movements for biblical preaching
- fostering the creation and distribution of evangelical literature
- enhancing evangelical theological education

especially in countries where churches are under-resourced.

Our ministry

Langham Preaching partners with national leaders to nurture indigenous biblical preaching movements for pastors and lay preachers all around the world. With the support of a team of trainers from many countries, a multi-level programme of seminars provides practical training, and is followed by a programme for training local facilitators. Local preachers' groups and national and regional networks ensure continuity and ongoing development, seeking to build vigorous movements committed to Bible exposition.

Langham Literature provides majority world preachers, scholars and seminary libraries with evangelical books and electronic resources through publishing and distribution, grants and discounts. The programme also fosters the creation of indigenous evangelical books in many languages, through writer's grants, strengthening local evangelical publishing houses, and investment in major regional literature projects, such as one volume Bible commentaries like *The Africa Bible Commentary* and *The South Asia Bible Commentary*.

Langham Scholars provides financial support for evangelical doctoral students from the majority world so that, when they return home, they may train pastors and other Christian leaders with sound, biblical and theological teaching. This programme equips those who equip others. Langham Scholars also works in partnership with majority world seminaries in strengthening evangelical theological education. A growing number of Langham Scholars study in high quality doctoral programmes in the majority world itself. As well as teaching the next generation of pastors, graduated Langham Scholars exercise significant influence through their writing and leadership.

To learn more about Langham Partnership and the work we do visit **langham.org**

www.ingramcontent.com/pod-product-compliance
Lightning Source LLC
Chambersburg PA
CBHW051539230426
43669CB00015B/2662